D0002130

THEOLOGY AND MISSION

Papers and Responses Prepared for the
Consultation on Theology and Mission
Trinity Evangelical Divinity School
School of World Mission and Evangelism
March 22-25, 1976

David J. Hesselgrave, Editor

BAKER BOOK HOUSE
Grand Rapids, Michigan

THEOLOGY AND MISSION

FOREWORD

From time to time evangelical mission leaders have opportunity to consult together on issues affecting their world-wide task of evangelism and church development. However, a consultation of seminary professors, pastors and missionaries is unusual. The School of World Mission and Evangelism of Trinity Evangelical Divinity School is to be congratulated for sponsoring this study conference on theology and mission.

Further commendable service has been performed in compiling the materials of the conference into this volume, making it possible for the discussion to include many more participants. A big first step has been taken. The next step needs to be the utilization of the material. Each subject has wide implications affecting the global church, education for the ministry and the evangelization of the world. It is hoped that many evangelical pastors, professors, students and missionaries will seriously study this book. It can well be used as a primary resource tool for consultations, seminars, workshops, study groups and by individuals preparing their own responses to the important subjects presented.

Edwin L. Frizen, Jr.
Executive Director
Interdenominational Foreign
Mission Association

FOREWORD

The subject matter of this book is well chosen. It touches on very vital and crucial issues which are confronting the church in every country of the world. The book grew out of a conference which brought together the thinking and opinions of people from diverse backgrounds. Each one provides special insights from his own field of study.

The involvement of mission executives with the scholastic community brought a practical aspect to the consultation, and this is reflected in the book. This book is certainly not the final word on these subjects, but rather should be viewed as the beginning of discussions and the opening up of questions for further study and development over the coming years.

This consultation is a part of what seems to be a move toward having the academic community and the executive leaders of missions come closer together and contribute to each other. It is important for the practicing missionary and executive to delve into the philosophical and theological considerations related to current problems. It is also valuable, I believe, to have the academic community exposed to the pragmatic, day-to-day problems of the missionary and the executive. This consultation and the resulting book represent a real effort to bring these two streams together and to produce interaction that is profitable for everyone involved.

The problems singled out for this consultation are of vital concern to the missionary now and in the years immediately ahead. This volume is a valuable resource for the study of these crucial themes and perhaps will stimulate further writings which can add to our knowledge and understanding.

As the missionary serving on the field approaches these problems, he can perhaps contribute new insights about how they actually work out at the local level.

Wade T. Coggins, Executive Secretary
Evangelical Foreign Missions Association

7

PREFACE

Theology and mission go together. Without theology the mission of the church dissipates. Without mission the theology of the Bible stagnates. But it is one thing to believe that this is true, and quite another thing to keep the two conjoined and complementary. Pragmatism, professionalism, intellectualism and ecclesiastical and educational structures conspire to keep theologians and missiologists apart, and to keep sound theology and creative missiology in separate compartments.

At Trinity Evangelical Divinity School we are not really interested in a theology that does not missionize. Nor are we interested in a missiology that does not theologize. We attempt to keep the two together. For that reason the School of World Mission and Evangelism at Trinity is not independent of the larger school. Our students of mission and evangelism have the opportunity and obligation to take courses in other disciplines as well. And faculty from various divisions of the school are involved in our annual seminars for missionaries and mission administrators on furlough and are requested to contribute to the *Trinity World Forum* — the publication of our School of World Mission and Evangelism.

It was to be expected, then, that in the spring of 1975 when our mission faculty conferred as to a contribution that Trinity might make in this time of *unique* opportunity and challenge in the Christian world mission, we conceived of a consultation in which various members of our faculty might address themselves to some of the burning issues of missions today. Topics were chosen. Assignments to our colleagues were made. And personal invitations were sent out to a select group of mission administrators, professors of mission, and mission leaders in other capacities to gather for a Consultation on Theology and Mission to be held March 22-25, 1976.

The response exceeded our expectations. As Carl F. H. Henry subsequently reported in an article "Guidelines for Mission" in *Christianity Today* (April 23, 1976):

As the world population clock ticked to four billion inhabitants . . . some eighty evangelical leaders from thirty-four mission organizations and fifteen theological schools gathered last month in suburban Chicago to discuss worldwide Christian witness and biblical guidelines to undergird it. The occasion was a four-day Consultation on Theology and Mission sponsored by the School of World Mission and Evangelism at Trinity Evangelical Divinity School in Deerfield, Illinois.

Participants heard President Arnold T. Olson of the Evangelical Free Church of America give a keynote address on evangelicals and Israel. President Ingulf Diesen of the Mission Covenant Church of Norway spoke one evening on the missionary efforts of North Americans in Europe. Professor Arthur P. Johnston of Trinity gave a report on the 1975 meeting of the World Council of Churches in Nairobi.

At the heart of the consultation were the papers included in this volume. The major papers and the replies of designated respondents were summarized in plenary sessions. The writers of the major papers answered questions at that time (and later were asked to submit to their respondents the brief replies which are now included in this volume). Participants then divided into six study groups in which they discussed the issues put forth in the major papers. The findings of these study groups were then submitted to a committee composed of Dr. Vernon Mortenson, Mr. Robert Dillon, Dr. Terry C. Hulbert and Professor Howard Whaley. This committee collated the reports of the study groups and prepared them for inclusion in this volume. The reader will find the collation in Part Seven — "Summaries of the Reports of Six Study Groups."

It must be emphasized that these summaries do not constitute an official position on these issues on the part of Trinity Evangelical Divinity School or the participants in the consultation or any of the various organizations with which the participants are identified. They are included in this volume in order to enable readers to determine the direction of the group discussions.

My heartfelt gratitude is due President Kenneth Meyer, Dean Kenneth Kantzer, Mr. Joe Horness, Sr., Mr. Torrey Mosvold, and Mr. Milton Westlund for their encouragement and assistance toward the success of this consultation. Miss Louise Lazaro, Mrs. Michael McClure, and Mr. Bruce Fleming gave invaluable assistance in both the consultation and the final preparation of this manuscript. The contributions of authors, participants, committeemen, study group leaders, and student stewards have not gone unnoticed. And finally, as is ever the case in any successful venture of Trinity's School of World Mission and Evangelism, my colleagues Professor Arthur P. Johnston, who was program co-ordinator, Professor J. Herbert Kane and Professor James O. Buswell, III, merit commendation. May the Lord of the church be glorified and may His cause be furthered as a result of the dedicated stewardship of all of these heirs of the kingdom.

David J. Hesselgrave
Deerfield, Illinois
July 1, 1976

CONTRIBUTORS

Gleason L. Archer, Jr., Professor of Old Testament and Semitic Languages, Trinity Evangelical Divinity School

Philip E. Armstrong, General Director, Far Eastern Gospel Crusade

Harold O. J. Brown, Professor of Systematic Theology, Trinity Evangelical Divinity School

James O. Buswell, III, Visiting Professor of Missionary Anthropology, Trinity Evangelical Divinity School

Wade T. Coggins, Executive Secretary, Evangelical Foreign Missions Association

R. J. Davis, General Director Emeritus, Sudan Interior Mission

Wesley L. Duewel, President, O.M.S. International, Inc.

Norman R. Ericson, Professor of New Testament, Trinity Evangelical Divinity School

Paul D. Feinberg, Assistant Professor of Philosophy of Religion, Trinity Evangelical Divinity School

Horace L. Fenton, Jr., General Director, Latin American Mission

Walter Frank, General Director, Greater Europe Mission

Edwin L. Frizen, Jr., Executive Director, Interdenominational Foreign Mission Association

Norman L. Geisler, Professor and Chairman of the Division of Philosophy of Religion, Trinity Evangelical Divinity School

Vergil Gerber, Executive Director, Evangelical Missions Information Service, Inc.

Carl F. H. Henry, Visiting Professor of Systematic Theology, Trinity Evangelical Divinity School

David J. Hesselgrave, Professor of Mission and Director of the School of World Mission and Evangelism, Trinity Evangelical Divinity School

J. Herbert Kane, Professor of Mission and Chairman of the Division of World Mission and Evangelism, Trinity Evangelical Divinity School

Kenneth S. Kantzer, Vice President for Graduate Studies, Dean of the Divinity School and Professor of Biblical and Systematic Theology, Trinity Evangelical Divinity School

Walter L. Liefeld, Professor of New Testament, Trinity Evangelical Divinity School

Lloyd M. Perry, Professor and Chairman of the Division of Practical Theology, Trinity Evangelical Divinity School

Gilbert A. Peterson, Professor and Chairman of the Division of Christian Education and Director of the School of Christian Education, Trinity Evangelical Divinity School

Samuel Rowen, Coordinator of Curriculum Department, Missionary Internship

Charles M. Sell, Associate Professor of Christian Education, Trinity Evangelical Divinity School

Victor L. Walter, Assistant Professor of Pastoral Theology, Trinity Evangelical Divinity School

Warren Webster, General Director, Conservative Baptist Foreign Mission Society

David F. Wells, Professor of Church History, Trinity Evangelical Divinity School

Lester P. Westlund, Executive Secretary of Overseas Missions, Evangelical Free Church of America

E. Eugene Williams, Professor of Communications, Trinity Evangelical Divinity School

Richard M. Winchell, General Director, The Evangelical Alliance Mission

CONTENTS

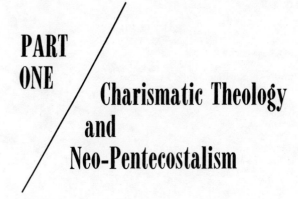

PART ONE

Charismatic Theology and Neo-Pentecostalism

Kenneth S. Kantzer

CHARISMATIC RENEWAL: THREAT OR PROMISE?

HISTORICAL BACKGROUND

Statistical Introduction

Time magazine describes the Pentecostal movement as "the fastest growing church in the [Western] hemisphere."[1] And well it might! In 1900 no Pentecostal church existed. Seventy-five years later the total world membership in Pentecostal bodies is estimated at well over ten million, and no one really knows how many more are scattered among churches not known as Pentecostal. The largest Pentecostal denomination in the United States is the Assemblies of God. It numbers over 785,000 in the homeland and has a foreign membership of 4,022,000. Only slightly smaller is the Church of God in Christ, a black Pentecostal church claiming half a million adherents, with most of its growth occurring since the Second World War. The third largest group in the United States is the Church of God with headquarters in Cleveland, Tennessee. This group numbers about 200,000 and claims a world membership of 400,000. The fourth largest, the United Pentecostal Church, was founded in 1945 and today numbers 175,000 members.[2]

South American Pentecostalism, however, provides the most impressive record of growth. Two-thirds of all Protestant groups throughout Latin America are Pentecostal groups; they have a total membership of over 2,000,000. In Chile, 90 percent of all Protestants are Pentecostal, and their total figure runs well over 1,000,000.[3]

Elsewhere in the world, recent Pentecostal gains are likewise astounding. In Italy Pentecostal groups claim a membership twice the size of all other Protestant bodies combined, including the post-Reformation church of the Waldensians. In South Africa the Pentecostal churches have grown to over half a million. The largest Protestant body in Russia, with a growth rate considerably higher than that of the Communist party, is the All Union Council of Evangelical Christians — a Baptist group which includes Pentecostals. The largest Free church in both Norway and Finland is the Pentecostal church.[4] It is second or third in size amongst the Free churches of Sweden. In Indonesia the Pentecostal church has grown with undiminishing vigor, now numbering well over 1,000,000. Even in Communist China the Pentecostal church has shown some evidence of growth.[5]

Although charismatic groups began to increase with amazing rapidity after the Second World War, the rest of the ecclesiastical world did not immediately become aware of the tremendous impact the Pentecostal movement was making here in the United States and elsewhere.[6] Beginning about 1960, however, the spread of the charismatic movement into the older, traditional branches of Christendom quickly brought world recognition.[7] Mr. David du Plessis, former Secretary of the Pentecostal World Conference, took upon himself a personal crusade to bring the Pentecostal movement to the World Council of Churches and to the older denominational groups.[8] The Full Gospel Businessmen's Fellowship International has appealed to men interested in the charismatic movement from whatever denomination they may come. It now has chapters in most of the large countries of the world.[9] Pentecostal churches were invited into the National Association of Evangelicals and now make up the largest block of churches in that conservative ecumenical body.[10]

Generally speaking, members within the older denominations have been won to the modern charismatic movement as the consequence of a determined missionary campaign on the part of the Pentecostals. These conversions have resulted from radical soul-searching and disillusionment with older, more liberally oriented denominations.[11] These "Neo-Pentecostalists," operating within the framework of the older denominations, tend to be less emotional and more orderly in the procedures of their meetings than are adherents of traditional Pentecostal groups.[12] Also they are more likely to stress the use of tongues as a personal gift to be exercised mainly in private devotions and in small groups.[13]

Doctrinal Commitments of the Charismatics

Characteristic of Pentecostal bodies, both in the United States and around the world, is a clear adherence to traditional Protestant orthodoxy.[14] Almost without exception this includes the doctrine of Holy Scripture as the verbally inspired and inerrant Word of God — the only rule of faith and practice.[15] With few exceptions, moreover, the basic doctrine of Pentecostalists is not Pentecostalism. The really fundamental conviction of any genuine Pentecostalist is the biblical gospel that sinners may find forgiveness of sin and full and everlasting life through personal faith in Jesus Christ, the Lord and Savior of men. Neither their theology nor their personal religion centers around speaking with tongues but around the person of Jesus Christ.[16]

The Pentecostal movement is divided over whether perfect holiness and freedom from sin are obtainable in this earthly life. The largest body, the Assemblies of God, does not adhere to the holiness doctrine. The connection between the holiness movements of the nineteenth century and the charismatic movement of the twentieth century, however, is very close. Both emphasize the need for a postconversion experience to raise the ordinary believer from "mere Christianity" to a high plane of spiritual victory and power. Although the line of cleavage between the two has always been preserved with a considerable degree of sharpness, the fact is, historically speaking, that the holiness groups prepared the way for the Pentecostal movement.[17] A considerable segment of the Pentecostal church merely added the supernatural charismatic gifts recorded in the Book of Acts to the doctrine of a postconversion work of the Holy Spirit necessary for a life of spiritual power.[18]

This postconversion experience, most frequently referred to as the baptism into or by the Holy Spirit, can take place simultaneously with the initial work of salvation, in which the individual is regenerated and justified. Logically, however, and in the actual experience of most believers, it occurs subsequent to the time of conversion — as soon as the believer has met the appropriate conditions for Spirit baptism. All who believe are saved and justified, but not all the saved and justified are baptized with the Holy Spirit.[19] The necessary prerequisites for receiving the baptism of the Holy Spirit are variously stated. These include, at the very least, a yielding of the will in obedience to the Savior.[20]

The significance of the charismatic or miraculous gifts, as seen by the Pentecostalist, is twofold. They are, first of all, supernatural signs to assure the believer (and others) that he has in truth received the baptism with the Holy Spirit.[21] They are also a gift to the church for its spiritual edification.

The normal effect of the baptism is to provide not only a new joy in the Christian life but also a new level of victory over sin (sinless perfection according to some, Christian maturity according to others) and a new power in Christian service and Christian witnessing.[22]

The exact nature of the language spoken by Pentecostalists is not a matter on which there is complete agreement of opinion. The general consensus certainly is that tongues are a miraculous ability to speak in an unlearned foreign earthly language which the speaker did not previously know. An infrequently held alternative view is that such tongues represent a speaking in the heavenly language (on the basis of I Cor. 13) spoken by the angels.[23]

An enduring theological problem of the modern Pentecostalist is why God allowed His church to carry on its work through eighteen centuries without the gift of tongues as employed in the New Testament.[24] The modern Pentecostalist is usually willing to grant that for almost two thousand years there were no significant *movements* emphasizing the gift of tongues in any way commensurate with what can be observed today, but for this phenomenon he has a ready explanation. Immediately after the days of the apostles, the church suffered a devastating decline of spiritual life and power. The charismatic gifts dwindled because the church did not meet the necessary conditions for God's fullest blessing.[25] The Old Testament, moreover, makes reference to the latter rains as exemplifying the final climactic outpouring of the Holy Spirit in the very last days before the return of the Messiah. So far from being an embarrassment to the Pentecostal, therefore, the long absence from the church of any special stress upon the charismatic gifts actually represents a fulfilment of biblical prophecy and portends the great and terrible day of the judgment of the Lord.[26]

WHAT DO THE SCRIPTURES SAY?

The phenomenal success of the Pentecostal movement in our time demands of the thoughtful Christian careful evaluation to see whether this movement is of God. At the same time the biblically oriented evangelical will insist that, in the final analysis, it is not a question of the success or lack of it by which the present-day charismatic movements must be evaluated. The question which really must be answered is, "What do the Scriptures say?" Very briefly we shall examine each of the biblical passages dealing with this phenomenon.

Mark 16:9-20

Very serious textual problems make it unwise to base any theological convictions on this passage. It is not found in the best texts. Critical scholars seeking to reconstruct the original are in general agreement that the passage is not genuine. It seems better, therefore, to take this passage not as a part of the inspired text, but rather as an attempt of a later editor to soften the otherwise rather abrupt ending of Mark 16:8.[27]

On the other hand, if this text were genuine, it would present as many problems for the Pentecostalist as for the non-Pentecostalist. Baptized believers are promised five signs.[28] Their purpose is not to provide assurance to a select few who have exercised some special faith that they have progressed to a higher spiritual level above mere salvation. The promise is to all who exercise saving faith, and the miracles are intended to confirm the truth of the gospel. It is possible to take this passage as Christ's promise to all who believe in Him that He will confirm their faith by these five miracle-signs. In fulfilment of this promise, He gave to the apostles power to work these miracles and thereby to confirm their witness both for their own and for future generations of believers.[29]

Acts 2: The First Reference to Tongues

Our Lord had commanded His disciples to wait in Jerusalem for the descent of the Holy Spirit. The promise was fulfilled on Pentecost when the disciples were baptized, were filled by the Spirit, and received the gift of speaking in tongues.[30]

The nature of the tongues spoken at Pentecost is without question a foreign earthly language not known by the apostles but recognized by others who were present as their own mother tongue. No interpreter was necessary. The speaking was immediately understood by the hearer without benefit of translator.

The miraculous nature of the speaking in tongues served as a supernatural and evidential sign that the promised Spirit had come and that the message of the apostles was true.[31]

Acts 10 and 11: The Second Reference to Tongues

Peter was given a miraculous sign so that he would be willing to go to the Gentiles and offer to them the gospel. When he did so, the Holy Spirit fell on all, just as at Pentecost; and the astounded Jews were thereby convinced that God had brought Gentiles also into the church. The apostles agreed that these Gentiles should be baptized and received into the church on the same "gospel basis" as Jews and half-Jews. The point, specifically, is not that something is needed in addition to salvation, but rather that a Gentile, without anything beyond personal faith in Christ, can be saved. The gift of the Holy Spirit was part of the experience of salvation. Exactly the same thing was happening to the Gentiles that had happened at Pentecost (11:17). The church summed up the whole experience in the words, "Well then, God has granted to the Gentiles also the repentance that leads to life" (11:18).[32]

The pointed reference made by Peter to the parallel between this event and the original Pentecost proves that what happened at Caesarea Philippi was not a usual occurrence. It would also suggest that the speaking in tongues here is precisely the same sort of speaking in an unlearned human language that it clearly was at Pentecost.[33]

Acts 19: The Third Reference to Tongues

Acts 19 tells of Paul's encounter with some uninstructed disciples — whether of Christ and John the Baptist or only the latter is not clear. Apparently the apostle had some doubts in his mind as to their spiritual state. He asked, "When you believed, did you receive the Holy Spirit?" On hearing their answer, Paul did not enter into a description of a postconversion experience. He raised, rather, the question as to whether they had ever believed and been baptized in the name of Christ. In short, he concluded that they had not experienced the first step into the New Testament church. The disciples then believed and were baptized in the name of Jesus, the Holy Spirit came on all twelve, and they all began speaking with tongues. The sign, as at Pentecost and at Caesarea, proved that the Holy Spirit was bringing them into the New Testament church. The sole condition mentioned for receiving the Holy Spirit and the supernatural sign thereof is that they should believe in Christ and be baptized. Nothing more!

In view of the analogous relationship which this scene bears to the experience of the household of Cornelius, the gift of tongues is evidently reckoned by the author to be precisely the same as on the two previous occasions. Presumably these new Christians spoke miraculously in a foreign tongue to validate the divine approval of what had taken place.[34]

Basic to the interpretation of all three passages in the Book of Acts is the hermeneutical principle that doctrine may be drawn only from what is specifically taught in the Scripture. For the contemporary Christian to draw his own conclusions as to the significance of events that are merely recorded in Scripture, without any direct or implied teaching by the biblical text as to the meaning of those events, is to introduce a subtle form of rationalism into the building of Christian theology.[35]

I Corinthians 12—14: The Only Didactic Passage

Speaking in tongues had become a disrupting influence in the Corinthian church. A pride in tongues, a seeking of the gift of tongues without love, and a disorderly and repulsive way of exercising the gift represented the source of the problem. In I Corinthians 12—14 the apostle provides instructions for the guidance of the church. Through the course of his discussion, the following matters are clarified:

A genuine gift. Speaking in tongues is a valid supernatural gift legitimately exercised by some Christians in the early church. It is not altogether clear whether Paul is simply saying that there is such a gift to the church and certain Christians have exercised it, or whether in addition he is also saying that what the *Corinthian* Christians were exercising, in spite of abuses, was in itself a genuine supernatural gift of speaking an unknown tongue. Perhaps Paul, either from ignorance or courtesy, did not wish to pass unequivocal judgment on this point. Since there is a possibility that any particular instance might be genuine, no one dare forbid speaking in tongues in any sort of universal condemnation.

Not a sign of higher experiences. The gift of tongues, as Paul discusses it in these chapters, has nothing to do with the level of spiritual experience in the faith. It serves, rather, as a miracle-sign to indicate whether certain groups, about which there was legitimate doubt, were really members of the New Testament church.[36]

Not intended for all. Speaking with tongues is a gift of the sovereign Holy Spirit intended only for some Christians. "Are all prophets?" Paul asks, "Are all teachers? Are all workers of miracles? Have all the gifts of tongues? Of prophecy? Do all speak in tongues?" And the answer expected is, "Of course not!" By contrast, all were baptized in one Spirit into one body in Christ (I Cor. 12:13).[37]

Must edify the church. The purpose of tongues, as of all spiritual gifts, is to edify the body of Christ, but more specifically, so Paul tells us, their purpose is to serve as a miracle-sign to convince the unbeliever of God's truth. This, of course, presented part of the problem. The way in which they exercised the gift, Paul warned the Corinthians, was such as to drive the unbeliever, in disgust, away from the church, rather than to convince him by the supernatural miracle that God was present and manifesting His power.

If no interpreter were present, then tongues would only serve for the private edification of the one who spoke. It is not altogether clear whether this is intended to be an approving statement or a disapproving statement. If we take it positively, Paul could mean that when someone exercised the gift in private, he secured a benefit of which Paul approved; if we take it negatively, he could mean that, when done in private, speaking in tongues served only the individual and, therefore, the selfish motives and purposes of the individual who exercised the gift. By contrast, the gift exercised in public with an interpreter brought an advantage to the whole church; and these special gifts were intended by God for the good of the church as a whole. Paul could, therefore, be administering a mild rebuke against the selfish nature of tongues spoken in private.[38]

Private tongues. Paul allows the possibility of exercising the gift of tongues privately outside the church even if it cannot be said that he encourages the Corinthians to do so. Such personal speaking in tongues, obviously, would not serve as a sign to unbelievers but would have as its purpose the edification of the individual speaker. So long as the gift is exercised privately in accord with appropriate Christian maturity, the church should neither foster it nor condemn it. In such matters each individual must answer to God for himself.

Not to be sought. The Corinthians placed a wrong value on the gift of speaking with tongues; and, as a result, they themselves were missing out on the blessing of God. Worse yet, they were bringing the church into disrepute amongst unbelievers. In the two lists of gifts mentioned in I Corinthians 12, the gift of tongues is put at the bottom to indicate its lower degree of value in the eyes of the apostle Paul. The gift, in fact, is worthless unless it is exercised in love. Though more profitable gifts may be sought, tongues must not be sought.[39]

Rules for speaking. Paul lays down explicit restrictions for the control of abuses of the gift of speaking in tongues. Not more than two, or at the most three, should ever speak in tongues at a single public meeting. The gift must be exercised in an orderly way by no more than one at a time. In a public meeting, moreover, an interpreter must be present so that the entire group may profit from the gift.[40] At Corinth women were not to speak publicly in tongues (though they might pray in public and lead in worship).[41]

Forms are varied. The form in which the speaking in tongues takes place can apparently vary. The apostle refers to a singing in the Spirit or in tongues, praying in tongues, the expression of praise to God for His mighty works, and exhortation in tongues that would edify the entire church. The tongues are probably understood by the apostle as unlearned foreign languages. This would fit exactly the description of tongues in Acts. It is impossible on exegetical grounds, however, to rule out the *possibility* of a language of heaven, but against this is the unambiguous nature of the "other tongues" in Acts and the reference to earthly languages in Corinthians.[42] It is also difficult to understand how speaking in tongues could be a miraculous sign if the language spoken was not known by the speaker, not known by any in the congregation, and not known to the interpreter who gave its meaning to the church.[43]

Some speaking in tongues is clearly demonic. The apostle also ascribes human motives to those who spoke in tongues in Corinth. Pride certainly caused some to produce the gift from their own resources or, at least, to exercise it in unloving ways not generated by the Spirit of God. Some Corinthians were simply misinstructed. They did not understand the real value of the gift of tongues but genuinely believed it to be one of the weightier graces.[44]

God dispenses sovereignly. The apostle contrasts temporary gifts for the church on earth with permanent gifts that will last for eternity. There will come a day, the apostle says, when all of these supernatural gifts will have accomplished their purposes, and then they will cease. By contrast love will endure forever.[45] The most powerful argument for the cessation of tongues and other supernatural gifts bestowed upon the New Testament church is the fact that their purpose was fulfilled in the confirmation of the apostles and in the completion of their New Testament witness to Christ.[46]

By the past tense of the verb "was confirmed," Hebrews 2:4 hints, at least, that the miraculous gifts for the apostolic age had largely stopped or were in the process of stopping. On the other hand, as with all biblical miracles, there is, in addition to their evidential value, a secondary purpose in the gracious will of God to provide for the needs of His people. Put quite simply, the lesser purpose remains; and if God wishes to bestow the gift today, He certainly can.[47]

WHAT ABOUT THE GIFT TODAY?
The Validity of Contemporary Speaking in Tongues

All Christians, Pentecostal or otherwise, recognize that some contemporary speaking in tongues is clearly the product of demonic influences. Speaking with tongues may also arise out of artificially induced human experiences. No truly committed charismatic would be willing to acknowledge this as a general rule, but he would be quite willing to recognize that some who have claimed the gift do not really have it.

Such humanly initiated speaking in tongues may originate from the noblest motives in the world. Believers genuinely desire to have God's very best. They read in Acts of the amazing results of the gift of the Holy Spirit and note the fact that, on three occasions at least, it is accompanied by speaking in an unlearned tongue. Sometimes unconsciously, they create the sign of God's gifts because they so desperately long to secure whatever it is that God has for them. In such cases it is necessary to distinguish between (1) the artificially induced or initiated human speaking with tongues and (2) the reality of the work of the Spirit.[48]

Why the Charismatic Movement Has Succeeded

Pentecostalists themselves are quick to point out that the first source of their strength is not their ability to speak in tongues. The real source, so they affirm, is the work of the Holy Spirit, who enables Pentecostalists to spread the good news with more than human power and blessing.

On biblical grounds, moreover, we must allow for the *possibility* of a contemporary miracle of speaking in genuine unlearned tongues. This justifies neither a charismatic movement nor a Pentecostal doctrine of the Holy Spirit, but it also does not permit us automatically to label everyone who claims such a miraculous gift as necessarily wrong.

Unfortunately, Pentecostal doctrine provides a false ground of spiritual security; still it is an attractive form of security that has tended to win many to the movement. A far more fruitful explanation for the widespread success of the movement, however, is to be found in the ecclesiastical background within which the Pentecostal works. The deadness of the nominal church of Christ in the twentieth century has proved a remarkably rewarding field of labor for charismatic missionaries. In spite of features which prove unattractive to many, they have offered to modern men who have lost hope the blessed reality of spiritual life in Christ. It must be confessed that sometimes a hungry and searching soul, without asking too many questions and without making adequate investigation of the Scripture, leaps before he looks and finds himself in an "exciting" spiritual adventure where experience, not Scripture, becomes his chart and compass.

Finally, an emphasis on lay participation in the spiritual ministry of the local church represents a key thrust of the charismatic movement around the world. Even the lowliest and most economically and socially bereft can find his place in a Pentecostal store-front church. He is seen as a person who has received the grace of God and who, if only he will meet the conditions for receiving the gift of tongues, can be equipped for important spiritual ministries in the church of Christ.

Lessons to Be Drawn from Pentecostalism

The amazing growth of Pentecostal bodies during the twentieth century is no accident of history. For the most part, it is due, rather, to adherence to spiritual principles which are taught in Scripture and the outworking of which can be observed in the pages of history.

(1) The greatest need of the world is life in Christ.

(2) The greatest need of the church today is practical biblical instruction.

(3) Key hermeneutical principles need to be taught as well as the factual content of Scripture.

(4) The focus of proper biblical instruction is upon theological and ethical teaching.

(5) The priesthood of every believer requires that laymen, not pastors, be called to do the work of the church; the pastor is the "coach."

(6) Every believer possesses gifts absolutely necessary for the well-being of the church and should be instructed to recognize and exercise them for the common good.

(7) The evangelical church of the suburb must learn to communicate the gospel transculturally to the inner city, to the black, to other racial minorities, and to the socially deprived.

Final Assessment: Threat or Promise?

Is the modern Pentecostal movement a threat or a promise? It is, in fact, *both*. It is a threat that the nominal churches have deserved because of failure to meet the need of men's hearts. It is a blessing in the sense that God through it has worked His work of grace within the hearts of many people.

The charismatic movement calls to evangelicals for a renewed dedication to Christ and to the work of His church in this world. As Kenneth Strachan has pointed out, "The law of sowing applies equally to all — he which soweth sparingly shall reap also sparingly; and he which soweth bountifully shall reap also bountifully."[49] This is a law of life, and it is true of the church — Pentecostal or non-Pentecostal. The charismatic movement, in spite of its unbiblical emphases and in spite of the handicap of its peculiar doctrines, has given itself unreservedly to the spread of the gospel; and God has honored its efforts by bringing much fruit. Let evangelicals learn, therefore, to sow in abundance that God in His grace may reap with abundance the harvest of redeemed.

FOOTNOTES

N. B. Bible quotations are from the New American Standard Version unless otherwise noted.

1. *Time,* November 2, 1962, p. 56. Two decades ago Henry P. VanDusen, president emeritus of Union Theological Seminary in New York City, hazarded the following prediction: "When historians of the future come to assess the most significant development in Christendom in the first half of the twentieth century, they will fasten on the ecumenical movement . . . but next to this they will decide that by all odds the most important fact in the Christian history of our time was a *New Reformation,* the emergence of a new, third major type and branch of Christendom, alongside of and not incommensurable with Roman Catholicism and historic Protestantism, in many respects startlingly analogous to the most vital and dynamic expressions of the 16th century Reformation . . . . These facts appear to me to present the most confounding and commanding problems for the years just ahead." "Caribbean Holiday," *Christian Century* 72 (Aug. 17, 1955), 947-48.

2. *Facts and Figures on the Assemblies of God* (Springfield, MO: Assemblies of God, 1975), p. 2. See also the now somewhat outdated but still authoritative nine-volume work by Walter J. Hollenweger, *Handbuch der Pfingstbewegung: Inaugural Dissertation zu Erlangung der Doctorwürde der Theologischen Fakultät der Universität Zürich, 1965* (Geneva: Privately photocopied and distributed, 1965). A digest of this definitive study is available in English — *The Pentecostals: The Charismatic Movement in the Churches* (Minneapolis: Augsburg Publishing House, 1972).

3. In view of the phenomenal growth of this movement within the Latin countries, the suggestion has been made that there is something in Pentecostalism especially appealing to the warm-blooded Latin temperament that would explain its success in terms of racial characteristics. The facts will not substantiate any such claim, however, as the success of the movement in northern Europe and elsewhere clearly proves. See the studies of L. M. Van Eeteldt Vivier, *Glossolalia* (unpublished doctoral dissertation from the University of Witwatersrand; Chicago: Microfilm Department, University of Chicago, 1960); and E. Mansell Pattison, "Behavioral Scientific Research in the Nature of Glossolalia," *Journal of the American Scientific Affiliation,* 20 (1968), 73-86. As to whether Pentecostalists are more subject to neurotic tendencies than the general populace, scientific studies have been adduced on both sides of the issue; and, at this point, the evidence is inconclusive. Scientific psychological testing, however, does seem to indicate a slight tendency for the gift of speaking with tongues to improve emotional health. For the charge that those who claim the gifts belong to a lower social and economic stratum of modern society, see Watson E. Mill, "Reassessing Glossolalia," *Christian Century,* 87 (Oct. 14, 1970), 121-27.

4. T. B. Barratt, a Norwegian pastor who came to the United States just after the turn of the century in order to raise funds for his missions program in Norway, is said to be the father of the charismatic movement both in Norway and in Europe. See Nils Block-Hoell, *The Pentecostal Movement: Its Origin, Development, and Distinctive Character* (Oslo: Universitets Forlaget, 1964), pp. 75-86.

5. Exact statistics on Pentecostal membership are exceedingly difficult to secure. This is true not only in Russia and in China, where the church endures persecution, but in the free world as well. Whereas Pentecostal statisticians might err a bit on the large side, other factors would seem to indicate that the figures generally given are much more likely to be erring on the small side than on the large. Grass roots Pentecostal churches are not greatly concerned about providing accurate and up-to-date data for church statisticians. The extremely rapid growth of the church in the last few years also tends to make accumulated reports out-of-date even before they are published. It is safe to say, therefore, that the actual figures probably run much higher than those that are listed. The most authoritative source for statistical studies of the spread of Pentecostalism around the world is Hollenweger, *The Pentecostals*.

6. Carl Brumback, *What Meaneth This? A Pentecostal Answer to a Pentecostal Question* (Springfield, MO: Gospel Publishing House, 1947), pp. 175-76.

7. For the penetration of Pentecostal cell groups into the major denominations, see Lee E. Arks, "Tongues and the Historic Churches," *The National Observer*, October 24, 1964; and John L. Sherrill, *They Speak with Other Tongues* (New York: McGraw Hill, 1964).

8. See Kilian McDonnell, "The Ecumenical Significance of the Pentecostal Movement," *Worship* 40 (Dec. 1966), 608-29.

9. This organization supports three publications: *Voice,* a monthly magazine; *Vision,* intended primarily for youth; and *View,* a quarterly dealing with various matters relating to the Pentecostal revival.

10. The role of Dr. Thomas Zimmerman, President of the Assemblies of God, in the National Association of Evangelicals and in the international "Key '73" evangelistic program was especially prominent.

11. Rev. Harold Bredesen, Reformed minister in New York State, indicates that before receiving the gift of tongues he had been liberally oriented in his theology, holding to quite critical and nonsupernaturalistic views of the Scripture, and was actually an employee for a time of the National Council of Churches. According to his own testimony, the baptism of the Holy Spirit and the speaking with tongues which resulted not only transformed his life and ministry but completely converted him from his liberal theological and unbiblical viewpoints to a position fully in line with traditional orthodoxy. See Sherrill, *They Speak with Other Tongues,* pp. 11-22.

12. This is difficult to establish because of the great divergences in such matters within the traditional Pentecostal bodies. The group is often judged on the basis of those who deviate most from the normal. See the testimony of Mrs. Stone, who notes that there is "less emotion in receiving the gift of tongues" among the Neo-Pentecostal advocates of the charismatic gifts — "What Is Happening Today in the Episcopal Church?" *Christian Life,* November 1961, pp. 38-41. See also her article, "A High Church Episcopalian Becomes Pentecostal," *Full Gospel Business Men's Voice,* October 1960, pp. 9-10.

13. Neo-Pentecostalists have a dilemma as to whether they should remain in their old denomination, as a witness in isolation from their fellow charismatics, or should join a Pentecostal denomination and lose the entree into their own denomination, towards which they often feel a heavy responsibility and within which they may carry on a Pentecostal mission.

14. "The only field of theology wherein Pentecostalism is distinctive is pneumatology, and that only in one particular phase of the work of the Holy Spirit . . . speaking with tongues . . . ." Harold A. Fischer, "Progress of the Various Pentecostal Movements Towards World Fellowship," unpublished master's thesis (Fort Worth: Texas Christian University, 1932), pp. 58-60. Most Pentecostal bodies

include in their formal statements of faith all the principle points of orthodox theology. Such items will include a statement on the doctrine of God and the Trinity together with a detailed presentation of Christology including the personal pre-existence of Christ, His incarnation and true human nature, His virgin birth, His sinless life, His supernatural miracles, His authoritative teaching, His vicarious death as an atoning sacrifice for the sin of man, His bodily resurrection, His present high priestly ministry in heaven, His personal and bodily return, the reality of heaven and hell, and salvation by grace through personal faith in Christ.

One of the very few exceptions to this rule is the United Pentecostal Church of the United States, which adheres to a Sabellian type of Christology. The Godhead exists, according to this group, as just one person; and Jesus Christ is this single personal God. On the basis of this doctrine the United Pentecostal Church is frequently referred to as the "Oneness Church" or the "Jesus Only Movement." It represents, however, a rare exception to the full and unequivocal presentation of a basically orthodox and Protestant theology set forth by most Pentecostal groups around the world. See Morton T. Kelsey, *Tongue Speaking: An Experiment in Spiritual Experience* (Garden City, NY: Doubleday and Co., 1964), pp. 85-86.

15. Exceptions to this exist in the faculties of some Pentecostal schools and among the so-called Neo-Evangelicals, as well as in individual private opinions of both lay and clerical leaders. Viewing Pentecostal denominations as a world movement, however, the statement in the text is overwhelmingly true.

16. See Brumback, *What Meaneth This?,* pp. 97ff.; note also the statement of Donald Gee made in 1955 at the opening of the Pentecostal World Conference in Stockholm: "The center of our message is Jesus." *Pentecost: A Quarterly Review of World-Wide Pentecostal Activity* 34 (Dec. 1955), 10.

17. See Harold Vinson Synan, *The Holiness-Pentecostal Movement in the United States* (Grand Rapids: Eerdmans, 1971). The Holiness churches appealed to the historical portions of the Book of Acts as setting forth a model for the contemporary church. A return to the doctrine and spiritual power of the original Christian church as described in Scripture is possible only if today's church reduplicates the experiences just as they are recorded in Acts. The events recorded in Acts become the paradigm for the theology and experience of all later churches. For a contrary view of the relationship between the Holiness and the Pentecostal movements, see Charles W. Carter, *The Person and Ministry of the Holy Spirit: A Wesleyan Perspective* (Grand Rapids: Baker, 1974).

18. It was out of just such searching for the biblical signs of the "Holy Ghost power" that the modern Pentecostal movement originated in Kansas City and in southern California at the turn of the century.

In typical fashion the constitution of the Pentecostal Fellowship of North America unites the two themes of holiness and the charismatic gifts: "We believe . . . that the full gospel includes holiness of heart and life, healing for the body, and the baptism of the Holy Spirit with the initial evidence of speaking in other tongues as the Spirit gives utterance" — cited by F. E. Mayer, *The Religious Bodies of North America,* Second Edition (St. Louis: Concordia Publishing House, 1956), p. 310. Similarly, the third largest Pentecostal body, the Church of God of Cleveland, Tennessee, teaches a doctrine of holiness of life and the attainment of moral perfection in this life as a divine work available for all Christians but actually experienced only by a minority on whom the Holy Spirit specially falls in the "baptism of the Holy Spirit."

Occasionally the experience of the Christian is set forth by Pentecostalists in three stages rather than just two. First comes the experience of salvation, then the experience of sanctification by the Spirit resulting in a life of sinless perfection, and finally the enduement with spiritual power; to this third experience is given the visible sign of speaking in tongues. The common position of the older Pentecostal groups, however, is to insist upon a twofold division. Logically baptism comes after conversion; it may or may not be separated from conversion by a period of time.

19. See Laurence Christenson, *Speaking in Tongues and Its Significance for the Church* (Minneapolis: Bethany Fellowship Publishers, c. 1968), p. 32.

20. F. R. Bruner summarizes these conditions as reflected in the Pentecostal literature:
   A. Conversion
   B. Obedience
      (i) Active Obedience.
         (a) Separation from Sin.
         (b) Heart Purification.
         (c) Prayer.
      (ii) Passive Obedience.
         (a) Yielding (Emptying).
         (b) Tarrying.
   C. Faith
      (i) The two kinds of faith —
            Faith in Christ for salvation.
            Faith toward the Holy Spirit for power and consecration.
         (a) Faith must be rightly directed.
         (b) Faith must be total.
      (ii) The free character of faith — faith is without merit.

A Theology of the Holy Spirit: The Pentecostal Experience and the New Testament Witness (Grand Rapids: Eerdmans, c. 1970), pp. 92-110. Every Pentecostal writer seems to set forth a different list of conditions for the baptism with the Holy Spirit. Although the vocabulary may vary, recurring items in all such writers are conversion, obedience, and faith.

21. "How did they *know* that the Holy Spirit had been poured out? . . . they heard them speak with tongues. Is speaking in tongues the only valid objective manifestation that a person has had this definite instantaneous experience of the baptism of the Holy Spirit? Scripture does not say that it is the only one. But in showing us the pattern, Scripture gives us no consistent suggestion of any other" (Christenson, *Speaking in Tongues and Its Significance,* pp. 53–54). For a statement more clearly tied to the traditional Pentecostal movement, see Brumback, *What Meaneth This?,* p. 187.

22. See Articles 7 and 8 of *The Statement of Fundamental Truths,* the official listing of doctrines by the Assemblies of God.

Article Seven: All believers are entitled to and should ardently expect and earnestly seek the promise of the Father, the baptism in the Holy Ghost and fire, according to the command of our Lord Jesus Christ. This was the normal experience of all in the early Christian Church. With it comes the enduement of power for life and service, the bestowment of the gifts and their uses in the work of the ministry (Luke 24:49; Acts 1:4, 8; I Cor. 12:1-31). This experience is distinct from and subsequent to the experience of the new birth (Acts 8:12-17; 10:44-46; 11:14-16; 15:7-9). With the baptism in the Holy Ghost come such experiences as an overflowing fullness of the Spirit (John 7:37-39; Acts 4:8), a deepened reverence for God (Acts 2:43; Heb. 12:28), an intensified consecration to God and dedication to His work (Acts 2:42), and a more active love for Christ, for His Word and for the lost (Mark 16:20).

Article Eight: The Baptism of believers in the Holy Ghost is witnessed by the initial physical sign of speaking with other tongues as the Spirit of God gives them utterance (Acts 2:4). The speaking in tongues in this instance is the same in essence as the gift of tongues (I Cor. 12:4-10, 28), but different in purpose and use.

The same position is outlined in the personal testimony of Carl Brumback, *What Meaneth This?,* p. 248: "ONE experience must be received by all who would enter the kingdom — the new birth . . . . In like manner, all believers are commanded to receive ONE experience — the baptism or filling with the Spirit. Again, physical, emotional and intellectual reactions are as varied as the recipients, but again ONE evidence uniformly accompanies the experience — *The witness of the Spirit through us in other tongues."*
See also Wade H. Horton, *The Glossolalia Phenomenon* (Cleveland, TN: Pathway Press, 1966), p. 52.

23. Robert Glenn Gromacki, "The Language of Speaking in Tongues," *The Modern Tongues Movement* (Philadelphia: Presbyterian and Reformed Publishing Co., c. 1967), pp. 53-68.

24. The Pentecostalist will usually insist that a careful reading of history proves that the gift of tongues never really died out, that a line of godly charismatic Christians can be traced through the centuries.

For those who hold that the gift of tongues is merely one sign among others, the proportions of the problem are greatly reduced. It can then be admitted that many of the saintly fathers of the church were baptized with the Holy Ghost and power, but were uninstructed and, therefore, did not secure the added blessing of the sign.

25. It is claimed that charismatic demonstrations have existed inside the church, on the edge of the church, and outside the church ever since its earliest days. As a matter of fact, the gift of tongues appeared before the church existed. It is probably not worth our while in this short paper to trace the history of tongues outside of the Scripture. The data are obscure and highly contested. Much depends on precisely what one defines as the gift of tongues. References to the gift have been found in Plato, in Virgil, in the mystery religions among the Moslems and in certain modern sects like the Mormons and the Irvingites. In the ancient church, Justin Martyr, the Montanists, Tertullian, Irenaeus, Origen, Pachomius, Augustine — all have been claimed for the Pentecostal experience. During the medieval period, likewise, occasional outcroppings of the miraculous gift of speaking in tongues are observable on the edge of the church. Luther, Wesley, Edward Irving, Finney, the Holiness movement in general, and various representatives on the modern mission field are cited in support of the gift of tongues.

Many of these claims rest upon extremely doubtful evidence. For our purposes the important thing is to note that throughout the long centuries of the history of Christendom there have been no significant movements (as opposed to particular individuals or isolated groups) that have exercised the gift of tongues except the Montanist group of the early church. The Montanists strove to revive the early church with supernatural gifts and to maintain the supernatural prophetic authority of the apostles as an enduring part of the second-century church. Within this structure, the gift of tongues was exercised by Montanists in support of their claims to the continuation of the miraculous gifts of New Testament Christianity.

26. See Deut. 11:14; Jeremiah 5:24; Joel 2:23, 28, 29; and Acts 2:17-21.

27. See the critical texts of Nestle, et al. The common version was probably an interpolation based on the description of the activities of the early church found in the Book of Acts, the supposition being that this is most likely what our Lord would have said.

28. The five specific miraculous signs are: (1) exorcism; (2) speaking in tongues; (3) freedom from danger from poisonous serpents; (4) the capacity to drink any poisons without being harmed; and (5) the healing of the sick by the laying on of hands.

29. A fair interpretation of Mark 16:15-20 would permit the possibility that miracle power is promised to all believers. Modern proponents of speaking with tongues, of

course, do not usually claim that all five of these signs are to be performed by every believer. The Book of Acts records instances of four of these miraculous signs occurring in the early church. It never suggests, however, that *every* believer in Christ has *all* these prerogatives as a *continuing* ability. In the same way the rest of the New Testament seems to exclude the possibility that all believers were to receive all of these gifts. Neither in Acts nor in the remainder of the New Testament, for example, is there any suggestion that all believers shall be free from danger from poisonous potions or that all believers were to be able to cast out demons or to handle poisonous snakes without fear of harm. The fact is, if this passage is genuine and if it is to be interpreted in harmony with the rest of Scripture, then it must be understood to teach that some believers (but not all) will be able to perform these various supernatural acts. The question remains then: "Who are to perform them?" The passage does not answer this question precisely, but it tells us that the original *apostles did perform* them; other passages make plain that *not all believers performed* them, and, finally, irrespective of who it was who performed them, they were done for the good of all believers.

This would place the apostles on the same footing as the prophets of the Old Testament. See the Book of Deuteronomy, chapters 13 and 18, with its supernatural tests for a genuine prophet of God. In a similar way, these miraculous signs attested the new message of the gospel so that faith would not need to be a blind faith but rather a resting of the mind upon the sufficiency of evidence. This seems also to be the point of Hebrews 2:3, 4: "How shall we escape if we neglect so great a salvation? After it was at the first spoken through the Lord, it was confirmed to us by those who heard, God also bearing witness with them, both by signs and wonders, and by various miracles and by gifts of the Holy Spirit according to His own will." Miracles and (supernatural) gifts of the Holy Spirit confirmed (aorist tense, completed action) the message of the apostles. This was their primary purpose. If the apostolate ceased (and most Pentecostalists affirm that it has), the miraculous gifts likewise were no longer needed for the *primary* purpose for which they were originally given.

30. Whether the reference is to the entire 120 or only to the twelve apostles is not certain. Note, however, that the promise of our Lord was directed specifically to the apostles (see Luke 24:49 and Acts 1:2-8).

The nearest reference for the pronoun "they" of verse 2 is the twelve apostles who are especially singled out of the 120. The statement by the crowd that all who participated in the speaking with tongues were specifically Galileans and the further references to the twelve apostles and not to the 120 seem to designate the smaller group.

There is no justification in the passage for the Pentecostal claim, "We believe the baptism of the Holy Spirit according to Acts 2:4 is given to believers who ask for it." The baptism was promised to the disciples, and the Spirit fell on all who were present. The passage is very explicit in pointing out that *each* of the believers present was involved. This, incidentally, is true in every passage in Acts which makes reference to the baptism of the Holy Spirit. Through the entire Book of Acts there is no hint whatsoever that the baptism of the Spirit is a second, postconversion experience, intended only for those believers who meet the special additional conditions required for this further work of grace.

31. Although Acts 5:32 refers to the gift of the Holy Spirit, it does not mention tongues or any of the charismatic gifts and, therefore, is not directly pertinent to our topic. It is perhaps important to note again that the Holy Spirit is not given to some believers only, namely those who have met the condition of obedience. Obedience is not an additional consideration by which the already saved believer may receive the Holy Spirit, but rather obedience is the result of the receiving of the Holy Spirit. The tenses are extremely important. God gave (past tense) His Holy Spirit to those who now are obeying (present tense) Him in the sense here of accepting Him as the

Messiah. The obedience of the disciples, who accepted Jesus, is contrasted with the disobedience of the Sanhedrin, who rejected God's Messiah.

32. Presumably the apostles and the Jews might have argued that if the supernatural evidence indicated that Cornelius had the second gift of the Spirit, he must also have had the first gift of salvation. As far as the teaching of Acts is concerned, however, the point is that Cornelius will be saved if he responds to the message of the gospel brought to him by Peter. The message came and Cornelius received the gifts of the Holy Spirit and spoke with tongues; and thus the Jews, according to the passage, knew that the Gentiles could be saved and, therefore, must be baptized and received into the church.

33. In Acts 2 the phrase *"other* tongues" is included, but in Acts 10 and 11 reference simply is made to speaking in tongues.

34. See Victor Bartling, "Notes on 'Spirit Baptism' and 'Prophetic Utterance,' " *Concordia Theological Monthly* 34 (1968), 708-14.

Peter states that what happened to Cornelius was like that which formerly happened *at the beginning.* He thereby implies that this was not the usual procedure every day of the week when the gospel was preached and men were brought into the church and united with Christ by the baptism with the Holy Spirit.

Naturally we cannot say that the Bible did record every instance in which the gift of tongues was actually experienced. We certainly can say, however, that the Book of Acts gives no doctrinal teaching whatsoever to indicate that speaking with tongues is the invariable accompaniment of the baptism or infilling of the Spirit. In the only three cases where the gift of tongues is recorded, it serves as a miraculous sign in a very special situation which the author of Acts set forth as presenting a need for an indication of divine approval.

35. Christenson, for example, concludes that the Book of Acts contains not a single theological statement or precept in reference to tongues. It merely records the occurrence of the phenomenon. As a result, though he is a devout defender of the charismatic gifts for this day, he is wary of drawing doctrinal conclusions from the Book of Acts, but rather draws his conclusions from teaching in I Corinthians 12-14 (see his *Speaking in Tongues,* p. 32). Watchman Nee, on the other hand, in the introduction to *The Normal Christian Life* (Fort Washington, PA: Christian Literature Crusade, 1961) writes: "Christianity is built not only upon precepts but also upon examples. God has revealed His will . . . by having certain things done in His church so that in the ages to come others might simply look at the pattern and know His will . . . . One of his chief methods of instruction is through history." Du Plessis agrees: "Fundamental to Pentecostal persuasion is the conviction that, in one Pentecostalist's words, 'The N. T. is not a record of what happened in one generation, but it is a blueprint of what should happen in every generation until Jesus comes' " *Pentecost,* p. 6.

36. As we have tried to show, there is in the New Testament church no special postconversion baptism experience which is then evidenced by speaking in tongues. According to I Cor. 12:13, all believers possess the Holy Spirit and form one body in Christ. Love is the primary test of the presence of the Holy Spirit in the believer. We accept God's word that, if we believe in Jesus Christ, we thereby also are baptized by Christ into the New Testament church. Our ground for this conviction is not the gift of tongues but the promise of God received by faith and tested by the fruit of the Spirit.

37. Most Pentecostalists distinguish between the sign of tongues, generally the experience referred to in Acts, and the gift of tongues as outlined in I Cor. 12 and 14. The sign is given once and certifies that the believer has been baptized with the Holy Spirit. This sign may never be repeated. The gift is the continued exercise of tongues for personal edification or for the edification of the church. This latter is desirable

for all, but it is not necessarily promised for all or available for all. The sign, however, is available for all who meet God's conditions to receive the Holy Spirit.

Minor differences between the tongues of Acts and Corinthians cannot be overlooked, but they are not such as to warrant our describing two kinds of "tongues," each with a clearly distinguished purpose. Note the following differences:

(1) In every occurrence in Acts the gift comes on all believers in the group. In I Corinthians speaking in tongues is more of an individual affair.

(2) On three occasions in Acts, the gift seems to represent a once-and-for-all exercise of the gift — a sort of threefold extension of Pentecost. Peter's reference to the coming of the Holy Spirit and the speaking in tongues at Caesarea specially harks back to the Pentecostal gift. The implication is that the gift of tongues was a special miracle to signify divine approval of certain unique events in the early formation of the church, but that it definitely was not a continually exercised gift within the church. In Corinthians, however, just the reverse is true. There the gift is exercised by individuals and appears again and again in the worship services of the Corinthians. Perhaps it would be fair to add that it is exercised far more than the apostle feels is warranted by the true work of the Spirit.

(3) Finally, in the Book of Acts no notice is taken of the rules of order laid down by the apostle in I Corinthians. In Acts the Spirit falls on all. There is no clear indication that everyone speaks in order rather than all at once; no limit of three is adhered to; and, finally, no reference is made to an interpreter. On the other hand, the biblical data are so limited (we have just the bare statement that they spoke in tongues in all the passages except Acts 2) that it is unwise to draw any precise conclusion as to the form in which the speaking with tongues took place. In the case of Acts 2 it is clear, of course, that the apostles (presumably all of them) spoke in foreign earthly languages which they had not learned. And each foreigner, apparently, interpreted his own language as he heard it from the lips of the apostle. In I Corinthians, by contrast, the local church is gathered together, and the gift is exercised within the framework of regular congregational worship. Here an interpreter is necessary so that all, not just some who happen to recognize the language being spoken, will profit from the exercise of the gift.

Paul is not so much adding new instructions where previously no instruction existed as he is providing instructions as to how the gifts should be exercised in a different situation — as a recurring experience in actual church worship by contrast with what was appropriate in the initial formation of a local church when men were first being introduced to the gospel.

Only if one takes the Book of Acts to be teaching that every believer who has met the specific prerequisites is to receive the gift of tongues as the initial sign of the Spirit's baptism or filling do we find any real conflict with I Corinthians. It is precisely this doctrine, of course, that is *not* taught by the Book of Acts. Rather, in Acts, speaking in tongues is a miraculous sign to show that certain problem groups, whose acceptance into the New Testament church was seriously questioned or opposed, were really a part of the church. Tongues, therefore, in Acts and in I Corinthians are in essence the same — spiritually edifying gifts to serve as divinely authenticating *signs.*

38. Philip Schaff writes: "Glossolalia was, as in all cases where it is mentioned, an act of worship and adoration, not an act of teaching and instruction." *History of the Christian Church,* 8 vols. (Grand Rapids: Eerdmans, 1952), vol. 1, pp. 230-31. Schaff could support this from some biblical passages. It is certainly true of all private speaking in tongues. It is doubtful if he could clearly substantiate this with respect to what the Bible says about the gift of tongues at Pentecost or when exercised with an interpreter present in the church, in which case Paul compares it with prophecy.

39. Pentecostalists themselves are among the harshest critics of such abuses of the

Spirit's gifts. See, for example, Horton, *The Glossolalia Phenomenon,* pp. 279-80. Naturally, if tongues are a supernatural gift from God dispensed in accordance with His good pleasure, man is never to seek to induce the gift by human means. Note, by contrast, the instructions given by Harald Bredesen to assist Yale students in learning to speak with tongues: "Repeat certain elementary sounds . . . such as bah-bah-bah or something similar," cited by Stanley D. Walters, "Speaking in Tongues," *Youth in Action,* May 1964, p. 11. See also similar instructions of Christenson as cited by John Miles, "Tongues," *Voice,* 44 (Feb. 1965), 6.

40. The point of the apostle seems to be that *one* interpreter must be present — meaning, probably, one interpreter for each speaking in tongues. The statement could also be understood to mean that one single interpreter alone must provide the interpretation for however many (up to three) exercise the gift of tongues.

41. The apostle's injunction against women participating in the speaking in tongues and the statement that they should be silent in the church may be regarded as either the biblical view of the nature of women or the ancient world's view that it was disgraceful for a woman to show her face in a public meeting. The choice of alternatives becomes important for our application of this passage to the church of today. Whatever may be decided at this point, it is clear that 'one of the rules for the Corinthian church, as laid down by the apostle Paul, is that no woman should participate in the speaking in tongues. It is the conviction of the writer that the apostle is addressing himself to a problem rising partly out of a cultural context and, therefore, that the specific prohibition for women cannot be applied directly and without qualifications to the American church scene of today. See Russell C. Prohl, *Women in the Church* (Grand Rapids: Eerdmans, 1957).

42. Certainly this was not the case in Acts 2 and from the statements of the apostle Peter it seems quite clear that the tongues referred to in Acts 10 and 11 as well as Acts 19 are to be reckoned likewise as unknown foreign languages, not learned by the speaker but derived from a supernatural enablement. I Corinthians 14:10, 11 also suggests a bona fide language *in this world.*

43. Note that there is a distinction between an interpreter who understands a foreign language and translates it and an "interpreter" who simply gives by divine revelation the meaning of a language completely unknown to him. The latter, of course, is what most Pentecostalists claim on the ground that "interpretation" is also a supernatural gift. It is still very difficult to see how this could serve as an evidential miracle to the unbeliever (I Cor. 14:22) unless someone is present who knows and verifies the unknown tongue. And it is certainly not what Luke understood tongues to be in Acts 2.

The suggestion that the apostle Paul spoke in more languages in the sense that he knew more earthly languages than those at Corinth to whom he was writing was probably true, but it does not fit the data. In I Cor. 14:14, for example, Paul tells us that in his own speaking in tongues his spirit prays; but his mind is unfruitful. This seems to indicate that Paul is not speaking of his own ability to converse in foreign languages, but that he himself, when he exercised the (supernatural) gift of tongues, spoke in a language that he had not learned.

44. Note that Paul has not really settled the question as to whether the Corinthians, in some cases at least, were exercising a truly supernatural gift in ways not intended by God or were creating for themselves a human work with only the illusion of the divine.

45. The attempts by Gromacki and others (see Stanley Toussaint, "I Corinthians and the Tongue Question," *Bibliotheca Sacra,* 102 (1963), pp. 311-15) to argue on the basis of I Cor. 13:10 ("when that which is perfect is come, then that which is in part shall be done away," KJV) that tongues will cease with the "perfect" or completed revelation of the New Testament do not appear warranted by careful exegesis

of the text. While agreeing generally with their conclusion, this writer takes verse 10 to be an axiomatic truth which Paul is enunciating. When the finished product arrives, you don't need halfway measures. By the end of time, at the latest, all these gifts will have perfectly fulfilled their purposes. It is possible that the gift of speaking in tongues fulfilled its whole purpose by the time of the completion of the New Testament, but evidence must be forthcoming from passages other than I Cor. 13:10. On this point Pentecostalist Donald Gee has the better of the argument. See his discussion in *Concerning Spiritual Gifts* (Springfield, MO: Gospel Publishing House, n.d.), pp. 51-52.

46. No one has stated this argument more cogently than did Benjamin B. Warfield in *Miracles: Yesterday and Today—True and False* (Grand Rapids: Eerdmans, 1953). See page 21: "They [miracles] were part of the credentials of the apostles as the authoritative agents of God in founding the church. Their function thus confined them to distinctively the Apostolic Church, and they necessarily passed away with it."

47. Geoffrey W. Bromiley states the case with appropriate caution: "Scripture does not explicitly restrict these gifts to the apostles or to their day, and hence we have no ground on which to limit the sovereign disposing of the Spirit . . . . Though we may not command or claim the charismata or any specific charisma, the Spirit's donation may still be looked for as and when He himself decides." *The Fundamentals of the Faith,* ed. Carl Henry (Grand Rapids: Zondervan, 1969), p. 159.

48. Many non-Pentecostalists, as well as some Neo-Pentecostalists, have sought to explain the gift of tongues in terms of modern psychology. Stuart Bergmise judges the contemporary exercising of glossolalia to be reflections of distorted memories ("Speaking with Tongues," *Torch and Trumpet,* Nov. 1964, p. 16).

More charitable judgments are provided by others, such as Tournier and Christenson (see above, the discussion as to the nature of the language spoken). For them the biblical tongues and contemporary speaking in tongues represent a quasi-language from the depths of the soul reflected in a verbal release of internal emotional feelings.

At the end of his life C. G. Jung suggested in a tentative way that these verbal expressions are the human response to supreme being pressing upon man's unconscious in a way that goes beyond the possibility of consciously directed activity or any merely human language. Cf. *Memories, Dreams, and Reflections,* ed. Aniela Jaffe (New York: Random House, 1963), pp. 351ff. See Kelsey's psychological defense of speaking in tongues today in *Tongue Speaking,* pp. 169-217.

Naturally, such explanations must not be employed to interpret the genuine speaking in tongues recorded in Acts and experienced by the apostle Paul and by others in the early church. An interesting, but probably unanswerable, question is: How much of the actual speaking in tongues by the Corinthians was of this sort? Fortunately we have Paul's teaching and example to guide us. We do not need to pass final judgment upon present-day claims to speaking with tongues. As long as certain rights of the church are safely guarded and the individual who speaks in tongues privately is protected from certain dangerous tendencies, each Christian must answer to God for himself.

49. "The Missionary Movement of the Non-Historical Groups in Latin America," Part III of *The Study Conference on the Message of the Evangelical Church in Latin America,* Buck Hill Falls, Pa., November 10-12, 1957 (New York: Commission on Cooperation in Latin America of the Division of Foreign Missions of the National Council of Churches of Christ in the U.S.A.), p. 10.

Paul D.
Feinberg

CHARISMATIC THEOLOGY AND NEO-PENTECOSTALISM: THE BAPTISM IN THE HOLY SPIRIT

INTRODUCTION

While the debate between charismatic and noncharismatic theologians has centered on the matter of the spectacular gifts of the Spirit like tongues and healing, the Pentecostal teaching concerning the baptism in the Holy Spirit is in many ways more important and certainly more fundamental. This teaching is so central to charismatic theology that if it were taken away, the remainder would no longer be Pentecostalism or Neo-Pentecostalism. As one studies charismatic pneumatology, one soon discovers that the emphasis is not so much upon the doctrine of the Holy Spirit as it is upon the doctrine or, as Pentecostals would prefer, upon the experience of the *baptism* in the Holy Spirit. Harold A. Fischer writes that the charismatic movement is in agreement with other conservative evangelical Christians on the doctrine of the Holy Spirit except at this one point:

> The only field of theology wherein Pentecostalism is distinctive is pneumatology, and that only in one particular phase of the work of the Holy Spirit . . . . Their distinctive trait is speaking with tongues as a manifestation of the Spirit. Pentecostals contend that subsequent to conversion (but can on occasion be simultaneous) there is an "enduement with power" the evidence of which is speaking with other tongues "as the Spirit gives utterance" (Acts 2:4).[1]

Though Neo-Pentecostals come from such widely diverse religious backgrounds as the Assemblies of God, Roman Catholicism, Presbyterianism and Methodism, they do have one point of convergence — the baptism in the Holy Spirit. For them no other doctrine or experience has such cohesive power. Donald Gee says:

> Let me remind you that it is this unique testimony that has gathered this great World Conference together. It is good that we should realize that fact. We say, quite truly, that the centre of our message is *Jesus*. But we shall gladly acknowledge that other Christians say that just as truly. That testimony would make a Christian Conference, but not a "Pentecostal" Conference, and this is a World *Pentecostal* Conference . . . . What is the unique thing that makes

the Pentecostal Movement a definitely separate entity? It is the Baptism in the Holy Spirit with the initial evidence of speaking with other tongues as the Spirit gives us utterance. And on this point the Pentecostal Movement speaks with an impressive unanimity.[2]

Because of the centrality of this teaching to the charismatic movement, this paper will attempt to examine critically the scriptural support offered for it. While the conclusion reached concerning the Pentecostal and Neo-Pentecostal doctrine is essentially negative, it will be argued that the doctrine of the baptism in the Holy Spirit as presented in Scripture is central to the direction and equipping of the church for the task of world-wide evangelism.

THE CHARISMATIC AND NEO-PENTECOSTAL DOCTRINE ON SPIRIT BAPTISM

Definition

The experience which the charismatic theologians call being "baptized" in the Spirit is designated in Scripture in a number of different ways. It is being "filled" with the Spirit (Acts 2:4), "receiving" the Spirit (Acts 2:38), being "sealed" by the Spirit (Eph. 1:13) or being "anointed" with the Spirit (II Cor. 1:21). Ralph M. Riggs says, "It must not be considered that these different terms refer to different experiences."[3] When the New Testament speaks of a "full" or "fuller" experience of the Holy Spirit, it is the Pentecostal contention that a distinct work subsequent to that of the Spirit in the life of the believer at conversion is intended. All Christians in some measure receive the Holy Spirit at conversion. But there is more! The New Testament Christians and all *advanced* Christians today will sooner or later receive this further work of the Spirit. They will experience a *full* reception of the Holy Spirit.[4]

The term *baptism* is peculiarly appropriate for this experience because it carries with it the idea of being overcome by an element greater than oneself. It means, in Werner Skibstedt's words, that "a person is supernaturally, experientially, and in full consciousness immersed in or submerged by the power of the Holy Spirit."[5]

Furthermore, it is not uncommon for charismatics to distinguish between the "baptism *of*" (or *by*) the Spirit and "baptism *in,*"(or *with*) the Spirit. Every Christian upon conversion has been baptized of or by the Spirit, where the Spirit is the *agent* of the work. However, not every Christian has been baptized by Christ, where Christ is the agent, in or with the Spirit, where the Spirit is the *element*. To put it another way, all Christians have been baptized by the Spirit into Christ (conversion), but Christ has not yet baptized all believers in the Spirit (an enduement with power for witness and service).[6]

In sum, the most important characteristics which are discernible from the above definition are: (1) this is an experience which is usually, although not necessarily, distinct from and subsequent to conversion; (2) Spirit baptism is a *full* reception of the Holy Spirit who in some sense is the possession of all believers; (3) it has as its purpose the enduement or enablement of the believer for service. What has not been said above, and is of no small importance, is that baptism in the Holy Spirit is witnessed to by the physical sign of speaking with other tongues.

Defense

Pentecostals, Neo-Pentecostals and charismatics offer three lines of argument in support of their views.

The first line of argument is found in the life and experience of our Lord Jesus Christ. The events in the life of Jesus at the Jordan are of peculiar importance to Neo-Pentecostals for they establish an invaluable example for later Christian doctrine and experience. If Jesus was baptized in the Spirit for the carrying out of His mission some thirty years after His supernatural conception and birth, then Christians should not be surprised that they receive the baptism in the Spirit after conversion to equip them for service. Pentecostals contend Christ Himself passed through two great experiences with the Spirit. He was conceived by the Spirit, and then at the Jordan He was endued with power to carry out His messianic mission (Matt. 1:18, 20; Luke 1:27, 31; cf. Matt. 3:13-17; Mark 1:9-11; Luke 3:21, 22). Thus, our Lord serves as a perfect model for those who wish a full Christian life. It is Christ's experience that lends final credibility to this charismatic teaching.[7]

The second line of argument is derived from the life and experience of the church. The major source of this argument is to be found in the Book of Acts, but an appeal is also made to the contemporary phenomenon in charismatic circles.

The Old Testament and the gospels only prophesy a future baptism in the Spirit. The epistles, while they discuss the Spirit, do not expound in any detail this teaching of a subsequent baptizing. Thus, the burden of the argument is borne by the history of the early church as it is recorded in the Book of Acts. For instance, Glen Reed teaches, "In the Book of Acts are found all instances of persons receiving the baptism in the Spirit which are to be found in the Bible."[8] Therefore, the prerequisite for understanding the Neo-Pentecostal view of the Spirit rests with a proper exegesis of the passages in Acts which deal with the Spirit.

The experience of the disciples on the Day of Pentecost (Acts 2:1-4) is the most important instance of the subsequent operation of the Holy Spirit in the lives of believers. Prior to the events that transpired on the Day of Pentecost the disciples were Christians. There is abundant evidence to show that they had some initial experience with the Holy Spirit. Christ had said that they were not of this world (John 17:14), their names had been written in heaven (Luke 10:20), they were spiritually clean (John 15:3) and united to Jesus as a branch is to a vine (John 15:4, 5). Moreover, in John 20:22 ("Receive the Holy Spirit") the disciples had experienced partial and initiatory reception of the Holy Spirit. Nevertheless, they had not as yet been baptized in the Spirit.

Thus, as the Day of Pentecost approached, the fearful, timid disciples tarried with the express purpose of waiting for the promise of the Father (Acts 1:4, 5). When the Day of Pentecost was fully come, the Holy Spirit fell upon them (Acts 2:4). Having experienced the promise of the Father, the disciples were filled with the Spirit, and began to speak in tongues (Acts 2:4). Their fear was replaced with boldness. Their ineffectiveness was ended, and some three thousand souls believed (Acts 2:41). Herein lies, Neo-Pentecostals believe, the weakness of the contemporary church. The church is not usually taught to wait for an enduement with power before it seeks to perform its mission in the world (cf. Acts 1:8). This neglected truth is the key to the church's renewal and mission.

A second event which occurred on the Day of Pentecost and is deserving of attention is Peter's charge to his listeners (Acts 2:38). The order contained in Peter's statement to his hearers was to be the pattern for the lives of Christians subsequent to the Day of Pentecost. They were to (1) repent, (2) be baptized for the forgiveness of their sins, and (3) then receive the gift of the Holy Spirit. Baptism for the forgiveness of their sins put them into the body of Christ. This occurred at conversion. It is only following this that they were to receive the gift of the Holy Spirit. In the view of most charismatics, most Christians never receive more than a portion of the promise. If they desire to be all that Christ intended for them, they should press on in the sequence proclaimed in Acts 2:38.

The Samaritan converts (Acts 8:4-25) are also seen as illustrations of the teaching concerning Spirit baptism. The believers at Samaria had believed and been baptized, but they did not receive the Holy Spirit until Peter and John came down and prayed with them (Acts 8:14-17). As the two apostles laid their hands upon them, they received the Spirit. This passage is of no small importance to those of the charismatic persuasion. This was a post-Pentecost occurrence. It involved believers who had been baptized, but who had not been baptized in the Spirit. Thus, spiritual baptism is not merely water baptism. Being baptized in the Spirit is subsequent to conversion, and is necessary if the Christian is to be spiritually complete.

The apostle Paul also had a further experience of the Holy Spirit (Acts 9:19). On the road to Damascus he met the Lord, but he received the Spirit only after he had arrived in Damascus (Acts 9:17). This full experience of the Spirit came three days after his conversion en route to Damascus. If the greatest missionary the church has ever produced was not satisfied with only being a Christian, why should those who follow him accept or expect less?[9] Paul sought to be a Spirit-filled man. His whole ministry is eloquent testimony to the need for this second experience.

It is somewhat more difficult to sustain the Neo-Pentecostal or charismatic teaching on the matter of Spirit baptism from the sequence of events surrounding the experience of Cornelius' household (Acts 10–11). The text does state that those who believed were converted, were baptized in the Spirit, and spoke in tongues; but all these phenomena occurred apparently at once (Acts 10:43-48; cf. Acts 11:1-18; 15:7-9). There does not appear to have been an interval between conversion and baptism in the Spirit. Thus, it is normally insisted that the experience of Cornelius' household is the ideal to which all believers should aspire. The new Christian should receive the baptism in the Holy Spirit *immediately* upon the reception of Christ as Savior. However, the experience of most believers is not like that of Cornelius and his household. Their faith is too weak or their knowledge of this doctrine too imperfect to enable them to be endued with power at once.

It should be noted, however, that even in this special or ideal case there was a sequence involved in salvation and empowerment for service. Riggs writes: "Could we not even consider that this visitation was God's ideal? His perfect pattern: believe Christ, receive the Holy Spirit in immediate *succession.*"[10]

Finally, Paul and the disciples at Ephesus (Acts 19:1-7) are cited as proof for the charismatic case. It seems that upon coming to Ephesus Paul found some disciples who had believed but had *not* received the Holy Spirit. Paul's question, "Did you receive the Holy Spirit when you believed?" implies that there is the possibility that one may believe and yet not receive the fulness of the Holy Spirit.[11] It is possible for the disciples of Christ not only to be without the experience of the Holy Spirit, but also to be ignorant that it even exists.

The experience of these early Christians is being repeated today. J. Rodman Williams says:

> This then brings us to the crucial point, namely, that many people today in the so-called "charismatic movement" are experiencing a similar input of divine energy. Prof. Berkhof, as we noted, wrote in the past tense, of those who "experienc*ed* still another blessing . . . the 'filling by the Holy Spirit' or 'baptism by the Holy Spirit.' " We may now shift into the present and say, "*are* experiencing." It is happening across the world, and bids fair to the greatest renewal movement of our time.[12]

The third line of argument offered in support of the Neo-Pentecostal or charismatic teaching on the baptism in the Spirit is drawn from the teaching of the epistles. The primary passage for consideration is I Corinthians 12:13. Since this is a difficult passage for the charismatic position, there is no unanimity in the way in which it is interpreted. One interpretation attempts to maintain a distinction between being baptized *by* the Spirit (I Cor. 12:13) and being baptized *in* or *with* the Spirit (the gospels and Acts). Baptism by the Spirit into Christ is experienced by all Christians at the time of conversion, and it is this work of God that places us in the body of Christ. This is Paul's teaching in the Corinthian letter. Paul's teaching, however, is to be distinguished from that of the Gospels and Acts. As has been argued above, these portions of Scripture teach a postconversion experience of the Spirit for empowerment.

A second treatment of this passage is to be found in a recent work by Neo-Pentecostal writer Howard M. Ervin.[13] It is his contention that the usual charismatic distinction can be found within I Corinthians 12:13. The first part of the verse (13a) describes what takes place in the experience of all Christians at conversion, while the second half (13b) has reference to the enduement for service. "And we were all made to drink of one Spirit" is the apostle's way of describing the placing of the Spirit's fulness within the believer.

By way of summary, it has been shown that charismatic or Neo-Pentecostal theology distinguishes between merely receiving the Holy Spirit at the time of conversion and His full reception and empowerment for witness and service. It is argued that this is supported by the life of Christ and the practice of the church, and is capable of being harmonized with the teachings of the epistles.

A CRITICAL APPRAISAL
OF THE CHARISMATIC OR NEO-PENTECOSTAL
DOCTRINE OF SPIRIT BAPTISM

Scripture References Using the Phrase, "To Baptize in the Holy Spirit"

Is the view just presented defensible from Scripture? What do the Scriptures say about baptism in the Holy Spirit? It should be noted that the expression "baptism in the Spirit" does not occur in the New Testament. What does occur in the New Testament in a number of instances is the verb "to be baptized" in conjunction with the Holy Spirit. "To be baptized in the Holy Spirit" is found seven times in the New Testament. Four of these occurrences are in the gospels, two are in Acts, and one is in I Corinthians. Though various English translations use different prepositions connecting "to be baptized" and "the Holy Spirit," the Greek text uses the same preposition *en* (in) in each instance (there are a few manuscripts which omit the *en* in Mark 1:8 and have only the dative, but the weight of evidence is in favor of its inclusion).

What do the New Testament writers say about being baptized in the Spirit? In five of the instances these words refer to the event that took place on the Day of Pentecost. In Matthew 3:11, Mark 1:8, Luke 3:16, John 1:33, and Acts 1:5 the expression predicts the outpouring of the Spirit on the Day of Pentecost. In the gospels the prophecy is uttered by John the Baptist, while the passage in Acts records the words of Jesus. Jesus refers to John the Baptist's words, and makes it clear that they will be fulfilled "not many days hence." Thus, it should be clear that all the passages in the gospels and the reference in Acts 1:5 definitely deal with the historical events that occurred on the Day of Pentecost.

Should some regular pattern of conversion-baptism in the Spirit be drawn from these occurrences? Hardly. There was something unique and unusual about the happenings on the Day of Pentecost. Anthony Hoekema puts it well:

> From this moment on the Spirit was to dwell in the church as His temple, and to take up His permanent residence in every member of that church. This outpouring of the Spirit on Pentecost Day, therefore, was a historical event of the greatest importance —

unique, unrepeatable, once-for-all. It may be thought of as an event comparable in magnitude to the resurrection of Jesus Christ.[14]

No, these passages do not lay down some normative teaching which is binding on believers today. Could the disciples have received this baptism before the Day of Pentecost if their faith had been strong? Certainly not. The descent of the Spirit is intimately tied to the ascension of Christ (John 16:7; Acts 1:5). Hoekema is right; there was something very special about what transpired on the Day of Pentecost.

The second occurrence of "to be baptized in the Spirit" in Acts is found in connection with Peter's report to the Christians at Jerusalem about the conversion of Cornelius' household in Caesarea a few days earlier. He reported that as he began to speak to them, the Holy Spirit fell upon them as He had on the disciples on the Day of Pentecost (Acts 11:15, 16). What Peter described was indeed a Spirit baptism like that which the disciples had received. However, it was quite different from the Spirit baptism of charismatic or Neo-Pentecostal theology. It was not an experience distinct from and subsequent to conversion. It was *simultaneous with* conversion. This should be clearly seen from the fact that Cornelius was not baptized with water until after he had received his baptism in the Spirit (Acts 10:47, 48). Thus, the baptism was not a step of faith *beyond* that involved in conversion, but an integral part of it. The point which has just been made has been a matter of concern to Neo-Pentecostals. It has been claimed that this baptism is an example of the ideal — conversion followed *immediately* by baptism in the Spirit. One cannot escape the distinct impression that this is an *ad hoc* move to save a theological doctrine that is not supported by the exegesis of the text.

Furthermore, there is an important difference between what occurred on the Day of Pentecost and what transpired at the conversion of Cornelius' household. In the former case the Holy Spirit was poured out on 120 *disciples* in fulfilment of the Father's promise. This marked the birthday of the church. It initiated a new relationship of the Spirit to God's people. Accordingly, it can never be repeated. On the other hand, when Cornelius and his household received their baptism in the Spirit, there was a significant difference in that those who received this baptism had *not* previously been believers. The baptism in the Spirit is now related to those who had *not* been Christians. It is an integral part of conversion.

Why should there be something special about the conversion of Cornelius and his household? Why should this baptism be accompanied with speaking in tongues? The answer is to be found in Acts 11:18. Peter (who had been sent by God from Joppa) says, "Well then, God has granted to the Gentiles also the repentance that leads to life." While Gentiles had been saved under the Old Testament economy, it is only after Pentecost that they become *fellow heirs,* a part of the same body and partakers in the Jews' promises in Christ (Eph. 3:6). This was not easy for a Jew steeped in the Old Testament to accept. Peter is a good case in point. Therefore, there are signs similar to those which occurred on the Day of Pentecost to attest the legitimacy of what was happening. In any case, what transpired in Acts 10 and 11 is a far cry from what is taught in Neo-Pentecostal theology.

The final use of the expression "to be baptized in the Spirit" is found in I Corinthians 12:13. As mentioned above, there is not a consensus among charismatics as to how this passage should be understood. If one claims that the baptism spoken of in the gospels and Acts is to be distinguished from that of the Corinthian letter, then this verse has no bearing upon the Neo-Pentecostal teaching about a subsequent work of the Holy Spirit. This passage deals with a baptism at the time of conversion which places one into the body of Christ.

However, if one accepts Ervin's interpretation, then I Corinthians 12:13 again becomes germane. The first part of the verse describes what happens at conversion, while the second part teaches a further work in the life of the believer. This interpretation, however, cannot be supported by careful exegesis of the text. The first clause and second clause are clearly parallel. The scope of the first clause is coincidental with that of the second clause. This can be seen in the fact that both use the word *all* to show that what is said refers to every Christian. The oneness of believers is being stressed. This is pictured through two figures — baptism in the Spirit and drinking of the Spirit. If, as some charismatics contend, the second clause is intended to exclude some who are included in the first clause, the point of Paul's argument is lost. The unity or oneness being stressed is lost. There is only one way in which this disastrous result can be avoided. One could claim that all the Christians at Corinth had received this special baptism in the Spirit for empowerment. This baptism had been received subsequent to conversion. They were now enjoying the fulness of the Spirit. Such a view is doubly dubious. It rests on pure speculation. Furthermore, it would appear to contradict Paul's evaluation of the Corinthians as being carnal or babes in Christ (I Cor. 3:1).

Our findings to this point may be summarized as follows. The expression "to be baptized in the Holy Spirit" is found seven times in the New Testament. Five of these seven occurrences have reference to the Day of Pentecost. Because of its unique nature, it has been argued that this event is not normative for Christian experience. The conversion of Cornelius' household does not support the Neo-Pentecostal view of baptism in the Spirit since the baptism was not subsequent to but simultaneous with conversion. The experience was an integral part of conversion, not a further work in the life of a believer. Finally, the passage in I Corinthians is either irrelevant to the discussion at hand or a refutation of the charismatic view. Therefore, in those passages that speak of "being baptized in the Spirit," there is no evidence of a baptism in the Spirit which is subsequent to the work of the Spirit at conversion.

Passages Other Than Those Using the Phrase,
"To Baptize in the Holy Spirit"

At this point it might be argued that the Neo-Pentecostal use of the term "to be baptized in the Spirit" is different from the way in which the biblical writers use it. But, could it not be possible that support for the Neo-Pentecostal position is to be found in texts other than the seven mentioned above? Indeed, some other passages have been cited in support of the doctrine. Attention must be given to these texts.

It has been argued that Jesus' life and experience serve as an example of the veracity of the doctrine. He was conceived by the Spirit and some thirty years later was baptized in the Spirit to carry out His mission. The question that needs to be raised directly here is: *Was Christ's baptism a baptism in the Spirit* in the Neo-Pentecostal sense? Enough questions can and should be raised that make such a contention seem highly unlikely. Why is Christ's baptism nowhere called a Spirit baptism? He came to John to be baptized. He experienced John's baptism. In the immediate context John's baptism is distinguished from the baptism in the Spirit.

Did Christ only partially receive the Holy Spirit for the first thirty or so years of His life? Is it not clear that the one thing Christ's baptism can not be is a full reception of the Holy Spirit? While it is true that little is known about the time between Christ's infancy and His baptism, the little information that is available would seem to contradict any position that holds that Jesus' experience of the Spirit was only partial. For instance, Luke records that Jesus astonished the rabbis when He entered into disputation with them. Furthermore, Jesus told Mary that He had to be about His Father's business (Luke 2:41-52). Would not this presuppose the full experience of the Holy Spirit? The descent of the Spirit upon Him at the time of the baptism was not to take up residency. It was to *identify* Jesus as the one who would baptize in the Spirit (John 1:33).

Was the purpose of Christ's baptism empowerment for service? One should not rule this out entirely, but surely this was not the primary purpose of this experience. At first John did not want to baptize Jesus. Jesus answered him that it was necessary to fulfill all righteousness (Matt. 3:15). In what sense? Christ's baptism was His *induction* into the mediatorial offices of prophet, priest and king (cf. Exod. 29:4-7) and His *identification* with His people (cf. Isa. 53:12; II Cor. 5:21).

If this is the Neo-Pentecostal baptism in the Spirit, why is it not attended with the physical sign of speaking in tongues? This is an important part of charismatic doctrine, but nowhere is it recorded that Jesus spoke in tongues.

Finally, why are Christians nowhere commanded to seek an experience similar to that of Christ? There are numerous commands to follow Christ's example in particular acts (e.g., the Christian is to bear his cross as Christ bore His), but one could look long and far without finding a command to be baptized in the Spirit as Jesus was. Could this not be because Christ's baptism was uniquely related to His messiahship? This point has been argued previously.

It is now appropriate to return to a consideration of Acts 2:38, 39. Can one find justification here for the Neo-Pentecostal view on the baptism in the Spirit? Is the sequence so central to this teaching supportable from this text? The answer again is no. There is no evidence of a *process* which only a *portion* of the body of Christ experiences. After Peter preaches his great sermon on the Day of Pentecost, a number who hear are under conviction. They ask what they must do. Peter does say, "Repent, and . . . be baptized . . . and you shall receive the gift of the Holy Spirit." However, note these important differences from standard Neo-Pentecostal doctrine. (1) Whatever occurred to those who believed transpired at the time of conversion (Acts 2:41). (2) There is no indication that the "gift" or "baptism" in the Spirit (2:33, 38) is to *some* Christians and not to *all*. Peter says the promise is "to you, to your children and to *all* who are afar off, *even as many* as the Lord calls." The promise of God is co-extensive with the call of God (2:39). (3) If Acts 2:38 speaks of a charismatic baptism in the Spirit and verses 39-41 are the actual record of that experience, then some important omissions must be noted. Those three thousand souls who responded to Peter's preaching did not experience the miraculous manifestations that the disciples had had earlier on that day. There was no rushing mighty wind, no flaming tongues and no speaking in tongues (the physical sign of being baptized in the Spirit)![15]

Finally, something must be said about Paul and the disciples at Ephesus (Acts 19:1-7). Admittedly, this is the most difficult passage to understand. There is good reason to think that the twelve men whom Paul met at Ephesus were not Christians at all. One might be misled by the fact that they are called disciples, but it should not escape notice that they were in fact disciples of John the Baptist. While it is true that Paul may have at first thought they were believers, their reply to his question and subsequent events indicate otherwise. John R. W. Stott notes these points:

> They have never even heard of the Holy Spirit (verse 2); they had to be told that the "one who was to come," in whom John had told them to believe, was in fact Jesus (verse 4); and Paul not only laid hands on them but had first to baptize them into "the name of the Lord Jesus" (verse 5). Can those who have never heard of the Holy Spirit, nor been baptized into Christ, nor even apparently believed in him, be called Christians? I think not. These disciples of John certainly cannot be made typical of the average Christian believer today.[16]

If there is support in Scripture for the charismatic doctrine of baptism in the Spirit, this would have to be it. The central or distinguishing doctrine of Pentecostalism and Neo-Pentecostalism rests at best on one passage where the expression is not used, a passage which *prima facie* appears to describe an unusual rather than normative event and which is found in a historical narrative rather than a didactic portion of Scripture.

SOME FINAL CONCLUSIONS AND PRACTICAL CONSIDERATIONS

The argument of this paper so far has been that the baptism in the Spirit is not scripturally sound. There is value, however, in asking how such a doctrine happened to develop.

First, the Neo-Pentecostal doctrine of Spirit baptism rests upon a distinction which is not in the original text. In all seven passages where one finds the expression "to be baptized in the Spirit" the

Greek preposition is *en* (in) followed by the Greek noun *pneuma* (Spirit). Thus, a teaching which distinguishes between baptism of or by and baptism with or in the Spirit and which talks of a baptism with the Spirit as agent as well as a baptism with Christ as agent though the Greek words and order are the same in each case is making a distinction where Scripture has none. At the very least such a doctrine totters for lack of exegetical support.

Stott has argued that every baptism has four aspects: a subject, an object, an element and a purpose. These are all present when one harmonizes the seven passages which deal with the baptism in the Spirit. Christ is the baptizer. Believers — *all* believers — are the baptized. The element in which they are baptized is the Spirit,[17] while the purpose is the inclusion of all Christians into one body — the church.[18]

Second, there is a failure to distinguish where Scripture does in fact make a distinction. While the indwelling, sealing, baptizing, and filling of the Spirit all occur at the time of conversion, they are *not* the same. These expressions have to do with different aspects of the Holy Spirit's work on behalf of the believer. The indwelling, sealing, and baptizing works of the Spirit are once for all, while the filling of the Spirit is a continuing necessity.

Failure to distinguish what is in fact distinguished in Scripture leads inevitably to confusion and error. The charismatic teaching on the baptism in the Spirit is a good case in point. The indwelling, sealing, baptizing, and filling works of the Spirit are taken by Neo-Pentecostals as different means of expressing the same truth. One can only conjecture why this should be so. The fact that the prophecies of a baptism in the Spirit in the gospels and Acts 1:5 were fulfilled on the Day of Pentecost when the disciples were filled with the Holy Spirit (Acts 2:4) might explain why some would come to this erroneous conclusion. However, such a conclusion can be shown to be false on Neo-Pentecostal grounds. If the aforementioned argument proves an identification, then it proves too much. Even charismatics teach that the baptism in the Spirit is a once-for-all experience. However, the filling of the Spirit is clearly a continuing experience (Eph. 5:18). Thus, if the baptism in the Spirit and the filling of the Spirit were the same, the Christian should be baptized continually. One can show the inconsistency in the Neo-Pentecostal doctrine by noting that it is common to claim that Acts 2:1-3, 5-12 deals with a once-for-all experience, but Acts 2:4 deals with a continuing experience. If the proposed distinction for these

experiences in Acts 2 is correct, then the Neo-Pentecostal identification of these various expressions is shown to be false.

Third, the charismatic doctrine of the baptism in the Spirit rests
upon a questionable, if not downright false, hermeneutical principle. The *practice* of the church, particularly as it is recorded in
Acts, is played off against the *teachings* given to the church in the
epistles. Admittedly, the task of the theologian is to harmonize
Scripture.[19] But the question is this: Should that which *might be
implicit* in some recorded practice be allowed to control one's interpretation of what is *explicitly* taught in Scripture? It seems that
common sense demands that the answer to that question be no.
Nevertheless, one observes that the trend today is to allow practice
or experience to determine doctrine!

Before closing the paper, some practical considerations are in
order. In the history of the church, errors in doctrine have often
arisen because of the neglect of, or confusion about, an important
area of truth. Such is the case here. An understanding of the baptism in the Spirit is of great importance to the program of mission
and evangelism, and yet one seldom hears of the doctrine except in
charismatic and Pentecostal circles. As alluded to above, the baptism in the Spirit is that act of Christ whereby the Christian is
placed into the body of Christ — the church (I Cor. 12:13). While it
has been duly noted that the baptism in the Spirit is a positional
truth (i.e., not something that we seek in experience),[20] nevertheless it is not wise to draw too sharp a dichotomy between
position and practice. The New Testament does not. What the
Christian *is* affects what he or she *does*. Sound theology is intensely
practical.

The first practical implication to be drawn from the baptizing
work of the Spirit is that there is *unity* in the body of Christ (I Cor.
12:13, 20; Eph. 4:1-6). While the church has members from every
nation, tongue, and kindred, there is a unity that transcends these
natural distinctions. Thus, Paul can assert that it is impossible for a
part of the body to say that it has no need of the other members
(I Cor. 12:14-25). There is a beauty to all this. The weaker, less
spectacular members are indispensable! The missionary is no better
than the theologian and vice versa. Each needs the other. Each
should help the other.

But there is more to be drawn from the unity of the body of
Christ. All members of the body participate in both the suffering
and victory of individual members (I Cor. 12:26). The church can
not be nationalistic; it must have a concern for the needs of

brothers and sisters in Christ everywhere.

A second practical implication has to do with the relation of the body to its head (Eph. 4:15, 16; Col. 1:18). It is the head that gives direction to the body. Without a head the body is dead. A two-headed body is a monstrosity. So it is in the church. Her direction must come from her Head — Christ. It was He who said, "Go" (Matt. 28:19) and "you shall be My witnesses" (Acts 1:8). Can the church call a moratorium on world evangelism? No! Not if she is to follow the directions of her Head. She must go with urgency for it is yet day, but the night cometh when no man shall work.

Finally, because the believer has been baptized in the Spirit and is related to the Head, he has been equipped for service. The Head of the church gave gifts to His body upon His ascension (Eph. 4:7-13). These gifts have as their purpose "the equipping of the saints for the work of service, to the building up of the body of Christ" (4:12). There is no need to wait for or earnestly seek some further experience of the Spirit. The enablement and empowerment for the task *have* already been provided for the Christian. All that is required is that the believer act on this glorious provision. There is no divine command for which there is not corresponding divine enablement. The task of evangelism in the ultimate sense is not the church's task; it is God's task and He has provided for it. May the church do her part.

FOOTNOTES

1. Harold A. Fischer, "Progress of the Various Modern Pentecostal Movements Toward World Fellowship," unpublished master's thesis (Fort Worth: Texas Christian University, 1932), pp. 58, 60.

2. Donald Gee, *Pentecost,* 34 (Dec. 1955), 10.

3. Ralph M. Riggs, *The Spirit Himself* (Springfield, MO: Gospel Publishing House, 1949), p. 63. Riggs suggests two further terms: "fell" (Acts 10:44) and "earnest" (II Cor. 1:21, 22).

4. This teaching is found in almost every Neo-Pentecostal work. A few that teach a second work of grace are: Lawrence Christenson, *Speaking in Tongues and Its Significance for the Church* (Minneapolis: Bethany Fellowship, 1968), p. 40; Robert Frost, *Aglow with the Spirit* (Northridge, CA: Voice Christian Publications, 1965), pp. 14ff.; John Sherrill, *They Speak with Other Tongues* (New York: McGraw-Hill, 1964), p. 153; J. Rodman Williams, *The Era of the Spirit* (Plainfield, NJ: Logos International, 1971), pp. 42ff.

5. Werner Skibstedt, *Die Geistestaufe im Licht der Bibel,* tr. and ed. Otto Witt (Reisach, Württemberg: Karl Fix, Berlag Deutsche Volksmission Entschiedener Christen, 1946), p. 59.

6. Frederick Dale Bruner, *A Theology of the Holy Spirit* (Grand Rapids: Eerdmans, 1970), p. 60.

7. See, e.g., Christenson, *Speaking in Tongues,* pp. 36ff.

8. Glen A. Reed, "Pentecostal Truths 322" (mimeographed notes for a course taught at Central Bible Institute, Springfield, Mo., 1952-54), p. 3.

9. A. W. Kortkamp, "What the Bible Says About the Baptism of the Spirit," Tract No. 4285 (Springfield, MO: Gospel Publishing House, n.d.).

10. Riggs, *The Spirit Himself,* p. 53.

11. Ibid. See also Frost, *Aglow with the Spirit,* pp. 17-18.

12. J. Rodman Williams, "Theological Perspectives of the Person and Work of the Holy Spirit" (an unpublished paper given at the Conference on the Person and Work of the Holy Spirit, Princeton Theological Seminary, April 3-5, 1974), p. 6.

13. Howard M. Ervin, "These Are Not Drunken, As Ye Suppose" (Plainfield, NJ: Logos International, 1968), pp. 46-47.

14. Anthony A. Hoekema, *Holy Spirit Baptism* (Grand Rapids: Eerdmans, 1972), pp. 16-17.

15. James D. G. Dunn, *Baptism in the Holy Spirit* (Naperville, IL: Alec R. Allenson, Inc., 1970), pp. 52-54.

16. John R. W. Stott, *The Baptism and Fullness of the Holy Spirit* (Downers Grove, IL: Inter-Varsity Press, 1964), p. 19.

17. There is another possibility suggested by John F. Walvoord, *The Holy Spirit* (Grand Rapids: Dunham Publishing House, 1958), p. 147. He suggests that *en* (in) does not introduce a dative, but an instrumental locative. If this be so, then the Holy Spirit would be the instrument of the baptism rather than the element. Either view is syntactically possible.

18. For Stott's full treatment see *The Baptism and Fullness of the Holy Spirit,* pp. 24-29.

19. Hendrikus Berkhof, *The Doctrine of the Holy Spirit* (Richmond: John Knox Press, 1964), p. 87. Berkhof raises the problem of harmonization. Two considerations should be noted. First, is it not the case that the problem arises here because certain conclusions are drawn from the historical portions which appear to conflict with the didactic sections? Second, which material should control any attempt to harmonize: the historical or the didactic? Both Stott *(The Baptism and Fullness of the Holy Spirit,* pp. 8-9) and Hoekema (*Holy Spirit Baptism,* p. 15) claim that the didactic portions are fundamental.

20. Walvoord, *The Holy Spirit,* p. 146. See also Charles C. Ryrie, *The Holy Spirit* (Chicago: Moody Press, 1965), p. 77.

RESPONSE / Edwin L. Frizen, Jr.

To discuss theology and missions without considering the current charismatic movement would be a serious omission. Dr. Kantzer has given a concise historical survey of Pentecostalism, a helpful evaluation of the biblical passages important to the Pentecostal and charismatic movements, and his assessment that the charismatic movement contains both a threat and a promise.

In this study, it is necessary to differentiate the three movements — Holiness, Pentecostal, and Neo-Pentecostal (charismatic). The holiness revival of the late nineteenth century prepared the way for Pentecostalism.[1] The beginning of the modern Pentecostal movement is sometimes associated with the outbreak of glossolalia at the Azusa Street Methodist Mission in Los Angeles in April 1906.[2] It has been noted that the writings on the baptism of the Holy Spirit by some well-known evangelicals, such as A. J. Gordon and R. A. Torrey, have had much influence on the Pentecostal and Holiness movements.[3]

The position that the gift of tongues is not for this age was strengthened by the teaching of the Plymouth Brethren, as well as by the writings of C. I. Scofield and the notes of the Scofield Reference Bible.

World-wide expansion of the Pentecostal and charismatic movements is certainly a fact of the 1970s. This has become increasingly evident in studies of church growth.[4] It has been further documented in reports published by Evangelical Missions Information Service following workshops in Africa, Asia, and Latin America.[5]

The development of Neo-Pentecostalism among Christians of almost all denominations and church groups seems to have been as surprising to classical Pentecostals as it has to non-Pentecostals. Dr. Russell T. Hitt says that the charismatic revival "has proved to be one of the major phenomena of Christendom in the U.S. and around the World."[6]

Popular usage of the term *charismatic* for the Neo-Pentecostal movement is really misleading. The New Testament use of *charismata,* or gift manifestations of the Holy Spirit, is not limited to the spectacular gifts, such as tongues and healing.[7]

It is not difficult for a non-Pentecostal, noncharismatic evangelical to identify with the position so clearly presented by Dr. Kantzer.

It is somewhat surprising that speaking in tongues has been given such prominence among so many Christians when there is so little teaching on the subject in the New Testament. J. Sidlow Baxter wrote:

> If we would know what the Holy Spirit's permanent "gifts" to the church are, we must consult the New Testament Epistles . . . . When we do so, we find that from beginning to end of the twenty-one epistles in our New Testament, "speaking in tongues" appears in only one passage — I Corinthians 12 to 14; and even there it is assigned a subordinate place.[8]

THE VALIDITY OF
CONTEMPORARY SPEAKING IN TONGUES

Some conservative evangelicals leave no room for a valid expression of glossolalia today.[9] On the other hand, John R. Rice, well known for his conservative views, does allow for a possible expression of tongues.[10] And many noncharismatic conservatives appear to hold a position similar to that of A. B. Simpson's "seek not, forbid not."[11] Christians need to heed the injunction, "Try the spirits whether they are of God" (I John 4:1).

William Fitch quotes a statement prepared by the Latin America Mission giving guidelines for facing the charismatic movement. A part of the statement reads:

> We do not believe that every outward manifestation of a so-called gift is necessarily from the Spirit of God. On the contrary, the Bible teaches that the opposite is true . . . (Matt. 7:22-23 . . . Matt. 24:24). Thus the devil may counterfeit the gifts of the Spirit, and this requires constant vigilance on our part, warning and instructing our brethren against such errors.[12]

A missionary of the Overseas Missionary Fellowship, Raymond W. Frame, related two cases of speaking in tongues in China which proved to be by demonic powers.[13]

LESSONS TO BE DRAWN FROM PENTECOSTALISM

Noncharismatics should seriously consider lessons to be learned from this movement which is often found at the growing edge of the church. In addition to the lessons suggested by Dr. Kantzer, several others which relate more specifically to overseas situations have been delineated by C. Peter Wagner,[14] Donald C. Palmer[15] and the 1970 Consultation on Latin America at Elburn, Illinois.[16]

Prejudice must not keep us from learning methods of effective evangelism and church growth from our Pentecostal brethren.

FINAL ASSESSMENT:
THREAT OR PROMISE?

I concur with Dr. Kantzer's conclusions; however, I must underscore the threat of the charismatic movement. Through its experiential syncretism, the charismatic movement is a great aid to the ecumenical movement.[17] The charismatic movement is also a threat to the stability of the church because of its emphasis on experience. It is divisive.[18] The charismatic movement tends to focus on the prominence of human leadership.[19] It is noted for its proponents who "treat the body as if it were all tongue."[20]

Yet conservative evangelicals must recognize the danger of reacting to these and other threats of the charismatic movement to the extent that the Holy Spirit will be grieved and quenched.

FOOTNOTES

1. Michael P. Hamilton, ed., *The Charismatic Movement* (Grand Rapids: Eerdmans, 1975), pp. 61-113.

2. Roger C. Hedlund, "Why Pentecostal Churches Are Growing Faster in Italy," *Evangelical Missions Quarterly,* 8 (Spring 1972), 129.

3. Hamilton, *The Charismatic Movement,* p. 92.

4. One of the major church growth studies which should not be neglected by non-Pentecostal mission personnel is William A. Read, Victor M. Monterroso, and Harmon A. Johnson, *Latin American Church Growth* (Grand Rapids: Eerdmans, 1969).

5. Africa, Asia and Latin America *Pulse,* 1973-1975.

6. A forthcoming book by Russell T. Hitt, *The New Wave of Pentecostalism: A Second Look,* quoted in a promotional brochure of *Eternity* magazine, February, 1976.

7. Merrill F. Unger, *The Baptism and Gifts of the Holy Spirit* (Chicago: Moody Press, 1974), p. 13.

8. J. Sidlow Baxter, *Rethinking Our Priorities* (Grand Rapids: Zondervan, 1974), p. 111.

9. Leslie Madison, "Calvary and the Charismatic Movement," *Calvary Review* XIV (Winter 1975), 6-7.

10. John R. Rice, "The Power of Pentecost," *Sword of the Lord* XLI (Oct. 17, 1975), 1.

11. A. B. Simpson, "Seek Not — Forbid Not" pamphlet (Nyack, NY: Christian and Missionary Alliance n.d.).

12. William Fitch, *The Ministry of the Holy Spirit* (Grand Rapids: Zondervan, 1974), pp. 60-62.

13. Ibid., p. 62.

14. C. Peter Wagner, *Look Out! The Pentecostals Are Coming* (Carol Stream, IL: Creation House, 1973), pp. 41-171.

15. Donald C. Palmer, *Explosion of People Evangelism* (Chicago: Moody Press, 1974), p. 136.

16. "Summary Report," Latin America *Pulse,* October 1970, pp. 1-10.

17. W. A. Criswell, *What to Do Until Jesus Comes Back* (Nashville: Broadman, 1975), p. 100.

18. W. Elwyn Davies, "The Russia I Saw," *Progress* (Oct.-Nov. 1975), pp. 8-9.

19. "The Deepening Rift in the Charismatic Movement," *Christianity Today* (Oct. 10, 1975), p. 52.

20. Edward F. Murphy, *Spiritual Gifts and the Great Commission* (South Pasadena, CA: Mandate, 1975), p. 55.

RESPONSE / Lester P. Westlund

INTRODUCTION

Few subjects have generated as much discussion and debate in recent years as the charismatic movement, especially that part relating to the speaking in tongues. It is not the purpose of this response to argue the biblical interpretations involved on both sides of this subject. Others have done that in this consultation. It is my purpose to study the subject as it relates to the local church and to the mission overseas.

OBSERVATIONS

I shall begin by making several observations. Some of you will disagree with me from the beginning. However, in my denomination and in several that are similar to it, I have observed through many years that certain characteristics have attached themselves to the charismatic movements. Perhaps these are less evident to people from other backgrounds or in other evangelical movements.

Tendency Toward Division

In the denomination in which I serve, and others similar to it, the tongues movement has been extremely divisive. In fact, I do not know of a single instance where inroads by the tongues movement into the local church has not brought about a split in the membership. Some have responded by suggesting that if our churches practiced speaking in tongues regularly in public services we would have no division. I presume that is true. However, that would deny our understanding of the biblical teaching concerning tongues. The Bible does not indicate that so much emphasis should be given to one of the lesser gifts.

Tendency Toward a Lack of
Consistent Bible Teaching

The charismatic movement, including tongues, does not seem to grow out of a consistent, systematic and deep study of the Bible. There is a great deal of emphasis on experience but not so much on Bible study. Of course, this is not true of every individual nor of every church. Experience is important. However, experience must be grounded in the clear teaching of the Word of God.

Tendency Toward Relying on Emotions

The tongues movement seems to be oriented toward feelings. There does not seem to be an emphasis on the well-grounded life that expresses its joy in the reality of faith in Christ. Rather, the important matter seems to be *how I feel*. I need the kind of faith that holds when I do not feel well, and the kind of biblical assurance that tells me Christ is there.

CONCLUSIONS

It is my strong conviction that non-Pentecostal churches and missions must provide their people with well-thought-out written statements that express the attitude of the organization toward the charismatic movement. This is an absolute essential regardless of what the persuasion of the organization might be. In keeping with my personal opinion such a statement ought to include the following items:

Private freedom. How individuals conduct devotions in their private homes or prayer closets is a personal matter. There should be no attempt to regulate the private lives of missionaries or local church people.

Public limitation. Speaking in tongues should not be permitted in public. I am aware that some will respond that this is limiting a spiritual gift. My answer would be that the church places limits on a number of things that are biblical. For instance, holy communion is one of the sacraments. Yet, we limit the number of times it takes place. Some say every Sunday, others say once a month. Baptism is also a sacrament, yet some churches have baptismal services every Lord's Day and others only once or twice a year. It seems to me the Scriptures give the church considerable authority in regulating affairs to best carry out the responsibilities that are hers.

Alternative. I believe the church ought so to state its position that none can misunderstand. If there is unwillingness to live in keeping with these regulations the persons involved ought to be invited to worship elsewhere where the practices are more in keeping with their position.

In conclusion let me urge upon our churches and missions the teaching of the Word of God. No rules or regulations will ever replace the clear authority of God's Word. This is always the very best deterrent against extremes and against false teaching.

RESPONSE / Lloyd M. Perry

The two papers by Dean Kantzer and Dr. Feinberg have presented a careful analysis of the historical, philosophical and scriptural backgrounds of the charismatic movement. They dealt both with the gifts which are stressed by the movement and with the basic doctrine of Spirit baptism.

Dean Kantzer quoted *Time* magazine as stating that the Pentecostal movement is the fastest growing church in the (Western) hemisphere. This fastest growing church has had far-reaching effects upon local church congregations throughout the world. In addition to several pastorates, I have taught practical theology for twenty-eight years and served as consultant to a number of congregations. This has given me an opportunity to see the influence of this movement on local church situations. The one congregation to which I make reference in this paper is characteristic of many throughout the world.

A series of events seemed to blend together in this congregation to precipitate what might be referred to as a charismatic crisis. The crisis became so serious that a consultant was asked to assist the church.

In 1973 faith healing began to be taught in some of the adult Sunday school classes. During that same year, an unstructured Bible school class was formed so that the presentation could be made without formal preparation, thus giving the Holy Spirit complete freedom to control the class without human obstruction. A number of the church members started attending neighborhood meetings held in private homes. These meetings were led by visitors from other cities. In these meetings healing, prophecy, the gift of tongues and exorcism were promoted. (Dean Kantzer wisely pointed out the fact that dissatisfaction with the local church has prompted many to leap into exciting spiritual adventure without investigating the scriptural foundations.) The singing was warm, the fellowship was supportive, and individual and group Bible study was encouraged. Those attending found in these meetings that which the established local church had failed to provide. The surface manifestations seemed to be of greater importance than the source from which those manifestations came. Spirit baptism, which Dr. Feinberg emphasizes as the unifying emphasis of the various charismatic groups, was not a subject of special study by this group. The outward manifestation of the gifts was the important thing.

A general unrest developed in the church. The pastor, after serving the church for sixteen years, tendered his resignation. He had been theologically conservative in his doctrine but was a topical preacher. That type of preaching did not provide the congregation with a systematic biblical doctrinal foundation which would steady them in times of theological stress.

When the pastor resigned, the center of control was removed. He had been in complete charge of the church and had not trained his elders in administrative procedures nor developed them doctrinally. As Dean Kantzer pointed out, the willingness of the charismatic groups to give the lay people a chance to participate appeared very attractive to those who had been denied participation in their local church.

Those emphasizing the need for outward evidence of the spiritual gifts infiltrated the ministry of music and the adult Sunday school class discussions and became very energetic in promoting the house meetings. So much disruption was being caused that the board of elders could think of no way to correct the situation short of excommunicating about twenty-five members. At that point, they called for advice from a church consultant.

What steps were taken under the guidance of the Holy Spirit to try to bring order out of chaos? These are not given in chronological order since in a period of crisis, time is a very important factor and many steps must be taken at once.

(1) The pulpit supply committee insisted that the guest preachers present expository messages and give the congregation an opportunity to follow the messages in their Bibles.

(2) The prayer meetings were devoted to prayer and Bible study. An organized Bible study was conducted by the associate pastor and the elders took charge of the prayer time.

(3) The board of elders were given private instruction in church administration and biblical doctrine. This was done through direct instruction and literature.

(4) The church consultant and a representative of the board of

elders met with the charismatic group and solicited their suggestions for improving the ministry of the church.

(5) The worship services were changed so that both the formal and less formal elements were included.

(6) Lines of communication were established between the boards of the church and the congregation. Reports of activities and decisions were made to the church body.

(7) Steps were taken to promote friendliness within the church family. A welcoming committee was established and church social events were encouraged.

(8) The church was urged to raise money to help fellow members.

(9) The church membership voted to adopt a clarification of the article of faith relating to the doctrine of the Holy Spirit. This document was signed by the teachers in the Christian education program, all church officers, and all missionaries supported by the church.

(10) The church began emphasizing a ministry of reconciliation in accordance with II Corinthians 5:20. Instead of hoping their problems would go away, the church took steps to reach out and teach the people. Measures to solve the conflict creatively were adopted.

. I agree with Dean Kantzer that one of the greatest needs of the church today is practical biblical instruction. Our churches must provide biblical solutions to the problems of our people. The biblical illiteracy of many of our congregations, the refusal to allow lay members to share in the worship services, the failure to recognize our mutual responsibilities as members of the body of Christ, and our hesitancy to admit that there are doctrinal distinctives have made the present-day church a fertile field for doctrinal deviations. We must shoulder some of the responsibility ourselves and take steps to set our churches in order.

REPLY / Kenneth S. Kantzer

As a result of the papers, responses, and discussions at this conference, several matters relating to Pentecostal doctrine have become clearer or, perhaps, solidified and intensified for me.

(1) *All* of evangelicalism has become too much experience-oriented — to the point that its precious doctrine of the complete and final authority of Holy Scripture has been jeopardized. If the Pentecostal or charismatic movement is to maintain an honored place in the kingdom of God, it must sink its roots deeper into Scripture. Experience can only be the fruit, not the root, of enduring biblical Christianity. Pentecostalists must learn not to pick out of Scripture isolated phrases and historical records which mirror their Pentecostal experience; they must be willing to till earnestly the relevant passages of Scripture and prepare adequately and faithfully their exegetical homework.

Likewise non-Pentecostalists must cease preaching against the excesses of Pentecostalism, which are, no doubt, in most cases real enough. They must refrain from poring through scriptural passages to discover what will be useful to put down their charismatic brothers and sisters. Rather, they must work at exegesis of the whole of Scripture and preach effective expository (instead of topical) sermons. Otherwise, hungry people will turn to whoever promises the most with the most enthusiasm, and who can exceed a convinced Pentecostal in sheer enthusiasm?

(2) Again and again I have been amazed at the tolerant attitude of the apostle Paul. He was distinctly unsympathetic with what the Corinthian church was doing. He was not simply concerned lest they speak in tongues the wrong way, but he was disturbed by tongues spoken even in the right way. Speaking in tongues simply should not have a large place in Christian life and worship. He feared greatly that the whole body was viewed as a tongue. Still he did not forbid speaking in tongues. He encouraged the Christians to seek all the true gifts of the Spirit.

The non-Pentecostal who seeks to be guided wholly by the biblical principles, therefore, may be convinced that modern speaking in tongues is gibberish; that it is a learned technique; that it derives from conscious imitation; that it represents rampant emotionalism; that it is a natural skill; that it is a dangerous drug which makes one feel good at cost to the soul; that it substitutes a lazy prayerful mood for the hard, but proper, work of thinking through prayer requests and strenuous wrestling in prayer; that it is all this and much worse — *but* he must learn to put up with it for Christ's sake because his Lord does. The non-Pentecostal puts up with it even more readily because he knows his Lord tolerates him in spite of his sin. Evangelicals must recognize that God uses mysterious methods to bring about His kingdom. They must not forbid speaking in tongues.

(3) Pentecostalism introduces all too often a dangerous divisiveness into any church where it is present. When Pentecostalism is accompanied by the unbiblical doctrine that tongues is the initial sign of the Spirit-filled life, the cause of division is obvious. But even when the charismatic believer maintains sound doctrine, he must learn not to set up parachurch structures, such as prayer meetings centered around speaking in tongues; he must learn not to create a church within a church. If the charismatic really is specially gifted of the Spirit, the church needs his gift. Also he must learn to be silent. The spirit of true prophecy is subject to the prophet. He can be silent without being condemned by his Lord for disobedience and without damage to his own spiritual life. He can exercise the gift only in private so as to enable him to bring good to the body as the body is willing to receive the good. There in private he can pray that the church will be more open to the Spirit of God; but the biblically guided charismatic must not insist that he exercise this particular gift in public, and he must not in sectarian fashion withdraw himself over this issue from the body that needs him and his personal Christian ministry.

(4) Finally, other groups of Christians without exercising the gift of tongues experience the same tremendous feeling of joy and peace as do the Pentecostals and charismatics. It is not the tongue that brings joy and peace but the work of the Spirit of God. The reason the charismatic associates joy with the speaking in tongues is that he is convinced speaking in tongues is the sign of a great and good work of God in his heart. He himself, however, when pressed, confesses that it is the divine Spirit and His work which is crucial; and it is this conviction which brings all evangelicals into a deep

unity within the body of Christ where each may allow room for the other and find in the other a needed source of spiritual instruction and growth.

REPLY / Paul D. Feinberg

The respondents to the papers on the charismatic movement point to difficulties that arise between those committed to the movement and those opposed to it. The conflict at times has been severe. Are there some guidelines that one can lay down to govern a Christian's actions? Let me suggest three:

Christian love to all men. Scripture is clear in teaching that Christians are to be the channels through whom the love of God flows to all men (Rom. 13:8-10), even those who are not believers (Matt. 5:44). It should be remembered that failure to exhibit this love does not demonstrate anything about those with whom we disagree; it does show a great deal about the quality of our obedience to Christ.

Fellowship within the body of Christ. Our responsibility to those who have been redeemed by the blood of Christ and who are a part of His body, the church, is even greater. Not only should we love them, but we should promote fellowship that will strengthen and preserve the unity of the body (Eph. 4:3-13). The debate between charismatic and noncharismatic is a debate between brethren in Christ. All too often the conduct of both sides has not measured up to the standard required of Christians toward unbelievers.

Cooperation with those of like mind. That love is due all men and that fellowship should not be broken with believing brethren ought not obscure the fact that for the efficient and harmonious pursuit of certain goals it will probably be necessary that close cooperation be limited to those of like mind. A mission board should have the right to exclude those who differ on charismatic gifts so that harmony may prevail. Public worship will most likely be enhanced if those who do not believe in the public expression of tongues worship apart from those who do.

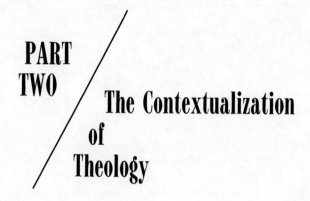

PART TWO

The Contextualization of Theology

Norman R.
Ericson

IMPLICATIONS FROM THE
NEW TESTAMENT
FOR CONTEXTUALIZATION

INTRODUCTION

The dynamic of the New Testament literature consists of its life orientation. Rather than being an abstraction of principles, ideas or dogmatics, it is a treasury of the experiences of the early church. It includes material from the preaching of the apostles, directions from traveling evangelists, and samples of the homilies of the early church ministers. In addition to this there are special types of literature which reflect the ideological and literary customs of the day.

For the purposes of this paper, it is most important to recognize that the New Testament literature arises out of a context. The authors did not so much intend to be transhistorical as historical; they did not so much intend to be transcultural as culturally relevant; and they did not intend for their message to be antisocial or asocial, but directly instructive as to the proper expression of the Christian faith.

In other words, the New Testament is a prime example of contextualization, and the thesis of this paper is that there are patterns in the New Testament which give us direction as to the nature of acceptable contextualization, indicating both imperatives as well as limitations.

It seems that little attention has been given to this matter within evangelical studies, and several reasons for this may be suggested. First is the characteristic emphasis on the unity of Scripture. On the one hand I have no reluctance in accepting the important principle that God is never self-contradictory, and therefore neither is His inscripturated Word. But on the other hand, if this is emphasized to an extreme, the distinctive features of the individual units of literature can be lost. Indeed, I assert that the unique theological emphasis of a writer often has been lost. This I think is also true with regard to the context out of which the individual units of the literature have arisen. The distinctive features of each synoptic gospel give us indication that the nature of the audience has a great effect on the structure, verbalization and emphases applied to the various pericopae out of the life of Jesus Christ. We may cite as examples Matthew's anti-Jewish polemic as contrasted with Luke's cosmopolitan appeal.

A second reason for the fact that contextual studies of the New Testament have been minimal is the single-minded way in which we view and use the canonical literature. Too often we hear the phrase, "The Bible is all you need." Without denying a degree of truth in the statement, the errant implications must be emphasized. Such a statement fails to recognize the many factors which create distance between the modern reader and this ancient literature. Among these factors are historical setting, socio-cultural setting, ideological environment, geography and demography. While we appropriately emphasize the timelessness of God's message through His Son and the apostles, we must also recognize that it was delivered into an environment, a context. And it cannot be fully understood or transmitted into another context or environment without a full comprehension of the original context. Unfortunately we neither study nor teach enough of the original situation of the New Testament. As a result we presume that there is a one-to-one relationship between the ideology, vocabulary, society, culture and politics of the first century and the twentieth century. We fail to take account of factors which qualify the words and sentences which have been transmitted to us outside of the original human context.

Related to this is the third reason for the fact that contextual studies of the New Testament have been minimal. This is the tendency to think of the biblical literature as a programmed manual of operations. In fact this tendency is known to issue in three-ring notebooks with all of the Christian life neatly sorted out into categories and steps. Such systems use a mechanistic form of eclectic hermeneutic, making little (if any) allowance for the dynamic of the original context or the variables of the contemporary context. Maybe we can learn classical Greek in a programmed primer, but there is no indication in Paul, for example, that he intended to design a manual of operations. Rather he deals in the dynamic of the situations, working under the spontaneous influence of the gracious Spirit of God. If ever there is success in the "programmed Christian life" it is because the persons involved have agreed to accept this as their context of operation! That is, the programmed manual *creates* a context.

There is another factor which impedes contextual studies of the New Testament or the Bible in its entirety. This is the effort to extract and absolutize the teachings of the Bible. While we admit that there are propositional statements of truth in the Bible, it must also be recognized that the systematizing of Christian truth has two ever-active dangers. The first is the mold which the systematizer brings to the biblical propositions. Be they philosophical, cultural or tagmatic, the walls of the mold shape the nature of the statements; the statements are made outside the context of the Bible or the original life situation. Secondly, the abstracted statements tend to be sterile. That is, they are largely divorced from real-life situations. The biblical record indicates to us that truth is understood in history, not in abstraction; in life, not in absolutely accurate statements; and in community, not in isolated intellectual experience.

Simplistic implementation of evangelism also retards contextualization studies. When the ideology of a person or a community conforms to that of the biblical contents, the simple appeals to believe and be baptized are appropriate. Too often, however, these words are technical terms far removed from the mental context of the hearer and thus in his view are "weird," superstitious, or astrological. It is not true that all we need to do is get them saved, for headnodding and headcounting are contextualized expressions of evangelistic systems. What is needed, however, is the expression of the good news in the context of the hearer. Eternal truth must be stated in ways in which it can be comprehended, and applied in ways that can be acted out in his environment.

Finally, indifference to contextualization has been brought about by too little emphasis upon hermeneutics. On the one hand we agree to the general principle of the historical-grammatical method, but we quickly veer from this to a creed which itself is a contextualized expression of an ecclesiastical tradition. And the creeds are subject to the failings of other forms of systemization. Rather than merely assenting to our commonly held method, or resorting dogmatically to our creeds, we must more often raise the question of hermeneutic principle. The Bible is our firm foundation, but our hermeneutical methods must always be scrutinized for the elimination of the blind spots. And this is especially true in evaluating the effect of the original context and the contemporary context on the distribution of God's Word to mankind and their comprehension of it.

EXAMPLES OF CONTEXTUALIZATION
WITHIN THE NEW TESTAMENT
Acts 15:1-29

The prominent example of contextualization in the Christian church centers around the council at Jerusalem. Conflict had arisen because of the many Gentiles who gladly received the gospel of Jesus Christ. Certain persons at Antioch insisted that in order to be saved the brothers had first to be circumcised according to the custom of Moses (Acts 15:1). On the other hand certain believing Pharisees insisted that *after* believing it was necessary for the Gentile believers to be circumcised and to keep the law of Moses (Acts 15:5). There are two issues at hand in this discussion. The first regards the method of salvation for Gentiles: Is circumcision compulsory? The second question follows on a negative answer to the first: What are the conditions for table fellowship between Christian Jews and Christian Gentiles?

The incident at Antioch, as reported in Galatians 2:11-14, clarifies the second question. Peter, most likely in response to his vision and the Spirit baptism of Cornelius (Acts 10), was willing to have fellowship at table with Gentiles. But when he heard of the offense this gave to Jewish Christians in Jerusalem, he separated himself in deference, not to the Gentile Christians, but to the Jewish Christians who were complaining. Paul, from the perspective of the believing Gentiles, insisted that Peter (and Barnabas) were play-acting by doing for approval what they knew to be nonessential.

The result of the conference at Jerusalem is a declaration, not that Gentiles must be circumcised or keep the Mosaic law to be authentic Christians, but rather of the minimal courtesies which would allow fellowship between believing Jews and believing Gentiles. F. F. Bruce writes:

> Centuries of devotion to the laws governing food and purity had bred in [many Jewish Christians] an instinctive revulsion from eating with Gentiles which could not be immediately overcome. Gentiles quite happily ate certain kinds of food which Jews had been taught to abominate, and the laxity of Gentile morals, especially where relations between the sexes were concerned, made the idea of reciprocal hospitality between them and Jewish Christians distasteful.[1]

There are three observations to be made here: (1) the Gentiles were not compelled to observe circumcision or other "customs" of Moses; (2) the Jewish Christians were not compelled to *stop* circumcising, nor to stop observing the Mosaic customs; (3) the context for the declaration by letter is one of deference to the Gentile

Christians and was established for the purpose of table fellowship between Gentile Christians and Jewish Christians.

This significant decision by the early Jerusalem church gave recognition to two different contexts. The first is the context of Jewish Christians who continued to observe the customs of Moses. The second context is the mixed community, comprised of Jewish Christians and Gentile Christians in fellowship on compromise terms. The latter context is a new contribution made by the progress of Christianity. Previously there was a clear distinction between the Jews and proselytes on the one hand and the Gentiles on the other. The category of "God-fearers" as indicated by Luke (Acts 13:16ff., etc.) only heightened the distinction. By the decision of the Jerusalem council it was possible for the God-fearers to be of equal status and in full fellowship with Jewish Christians. The partitioning wall and the cultural barriers were crossed.

I Corinthians 8:1 — 10:22

But there is a third context which is not presented in the accounts of Acts 15 and Galatians 2. This is the community of Gentile Christians. It is our second example of contextualization from the New Testament. The fact that it deals with one of the very items forbidden in Acts 15:29 for the sake of fellowship between Jewish and Gentile Christians places a special focus upon the context. The issue concerns "food offered to idols." In the context of a mixed community of Jews and Gentiles the Gentiles were directed not to partake of foods offered to idols, but in his letter to the Corinthians Paul deals with the issue in the context of Gentile Christians without reference to Jewish Christians. Because of this difference in context he makes no appeal to the Jerusalem letter, nor does he require abstinence from food offered to idols as the Jerusalem letter did. Because the situation is different he deals with the issue from the perspective of absolute truth and as it relates to the Christian welfare of the Corinthians themselves.

Inasmuch as Paul is here dealing with Gentiles, he uses no proof texts from the Jewish canon, but rather makes appeal to truths which are coordinate with the gospel tradition and no doubt immediately acceptable to the Corinthian Christians. His appeal is based upon two pairs of truths. The first pair is that an idol has no real existence in the world (8:4) and that food has no intrinsic religious value (8:8). The second pair is that the table of the Lord is authentically what the idol banquets purport to be (10:16) and that worshiping anything but God Himself is in effect worshiping demons. As the logical consequence to these four truths, Paul makes two direct statements of prohibition. A Christian may not eat in the temple of an idol; a Christian is to deliberately run from idolatry.

But if truth forms the basis for evaluating a cultural phenomenon, meaning and effect comprise the criteria for participation. Eating in an idol temple *means* worshiping the idol. Paul accepts this as being absolutely true in Corinth, and therefore prohibits *all* eating in a temple in order to avoid the impression that Christians also worship the idols of Corinth. But outside of the temple, eating meat may or may not connote worship of the idol. This depends, first of all, upon the Christian himself. Does it stir thoughts of the idol? If so, it is wrong and must be avoided. But if not, the meat is merely nourishment, one of the good gifts of God. Secondly, it depends upon the observers: if it means idol worship to them, it must be avoided by the Christian in the presence of the observers.

Now rather than being a matter of inconsistency, which it superficially is, Paul's tactic gives us a clear indication of how to deal with contextual behavior. It is *meaning* which determines the acceptability or nonacceptability of cultural forms. If the *meaning* is intrinsically contrary to Christian truth, no Christian may participate. If, however, the practice is wrong only in the view of *some* people, then the Christian must abstain *only* in their presence.[2]

The pinnacle of Paul's enculturation is expressed in I Corinthians 9:19-23. He accepts — for the sake of evangelization — the life-style (enslaved), ideological mold (Judaistic or lawless), and personal deficiencies (weak conscience) of the people to whom he ministers. Thus we have a third context indicating ways in which Paul adapted his ministry among Gentiles to their culture.

I Corinthians 5:1-8

In this same letter to Corinth Paul again makes use of the particular cultural context with which he is dealing. Here a young man is reported to have absconded with his stepmother. The shame of the event lies in two matters. First, it is wrong for a Christian to do this; second, it is wrong that the Corinthian church has not acted or shown any concern in this affair. It is such a shameful act that it is condemned even by the contemporary ideology. There is no question here of the society's being the standard for right and wrong, but when the society agrees with Christian standards that agreement can be used as a persuasive argument. Thus Paul evaluates the culture and uses what parts of it are compatible with Christianity and, as in the matter of idol worship, rejects what is incompatible. Paul does not indicate that contemporary ethical systems are useless, nor does he indicate that Christians must have more intense ethical systems. Rather, correspondences between Christian standards and societal standards may be fully utilized.

Colossians 3:18 — 4:1

There is one more major indication of Paul's contextualization of the gospel message. Each of his letters is patterned in such a way as to end with a generalized exhortation. Many of them are situational, that is, they address particular problems in the local church. On the other hand, there is a frequent occurrence of a *haustafel* — a direct reflection of the Greco-Roman society. In such passages members of the household are addressed according to category: wives, husbands, children, fathers, slaves and masters. Here Paul addresses a social structure that was characteristic of the Roman world. Particularly because of the categories of slave and master there is a variance from the Jewish societal culture to which Paul was accustomed. It seems significant that in these lists Paul usually has more to say to the slaves than to any other family category. The reason for this is the effect of the new freedom realized by the slaves within their Christian experience. Because they found Paul's message of equality before God valuable (Gal. 3:28) they began to respond in aggressive manners. Paul's exhortation, then, is that they are to recognize the lordship of Jesus Christ as being superior to that of their masters and that abusive masters will receive just return for their unjust treatment (Col. 3:25).

But that is only one side of the problem. Paul's letter to Philemon, the slave owner, is an indication of the way Paul dealt with the issue from the side of the master. In that letter he emphasized that a Christian slave is no longer a slave but a brother (v. 16), and that this should be true in the social relationship as well as in the Christian experience.

There is one more passage which deals with this issue significantly. Paul directed each Christian to live where he was called. In I Corinthians 7:21 he refers explicitly to slaves: "Were you a slave when you were called? Don't let it bother you; but if you are even able to become a freedman, rather utilize [the opportunity]."

This personal translation indicates the ambiguity of the specifics, but the principle is clear. Society and culture are the tools and locus of Christian operations. Whether a person is a slave (and a freedman of the Lord) or freeborn (and enslaved to the Lord) the propagation of the gospel is the primary goal. Inside of the social institutions there is among Christians the kind of understanding that both ameliorates any humiliation and heightens the believer's sense that he must serve the Lord in society.

Now there are several points to be made here. First, Paul addresses the society as it is, without pressing for external change. This is an indication at the first of an enculturated message; that is, he speaks to the people within the societal context, and tells them how to interpret and understand their roles from a Christian perspective. Paul's lack of pressure for external change must be seen within the context of his major mission in life.

Paul could not be involved in matters that pertain to society or cultural change because of his intense commitment to the gospel. We must understand his very narrowly defined life mission before we draw conclusions about the social relevance of his message. Recall two examples. From I Corinthians 7 and 9 we learn that Paul gave up the normal marital relationship for the sake of the gospel. Or, if that is not narrow enough, in the first chapter of the same letter he indicates that he would not even administer the rite of baptism because he was called to evangelize. If then Paul has so finely limited his mission to evangelization, we cannot expect him either to be personally involved in social action, or to prescribe a plan for remodeling Roman society.

He did, however, lay the very seed principles that would bring about the most honorable results. These principles are implicit in the *haustafel* and somewhat more explicit in the directions to slaves and masters: (1) the primary human relationship is to God Almighty; (2) interpersonal relationships are equal before God; and (3) societal responsibilities are to be performed sincerely with the realization that ultimate evaluation comes from God. These principles are to be extended and used for the evaluation of societal structure, as the basis for judging interpersonal relationships, and for affirmative action on the part of Christians to enhance the living of all mankind and especially of fellow Christians.

There are other examples of contextualization. Patterns of discipline, for example, vary with the general context. Matthew 18 is set within the strong Judaic context of that gospel and therefore emphasizes the Mosaic pattern of two witnesses. I Corinthians 5:3-

5 is set within the Greek context and here the authority is the church; it is to take aggressive action against a sinning member. Even the very nature of the condemnation varies in these two contexts: in Matthew the unrepentant offender is to be considered a "foreigner," while in Corinth he is to be turned over to Satan! Another situation of discipline appears in III John, where the elder declares that he is going to personally confront the arrogant Diotrophes. This is quite in keeping with the hierarchical structure in the Asian churches at the end of the first century. Or, finally, there is the discipline of reconciliation which is requested of Euodia and Syntyche in Philippians 4. Here a third party is directed to lead these Christian women into a restored relationship. The point of all this is that there is no single pattern of church discipline presented in the New Testament. The method is appropriate to the socio-cultural environment and to the nature of the local church; it is, in addition, directly related to the nature of the offense.

Finally, allusion may be made to the general contextualization brought about by the switch in language from Aramaic to Greek and the many ideological implications of this. In place of Aramaic phrases, such as "Son of Man," there is the appearance of "Lord" and "eternal life" as part of the idiom intelligible to the Greek world. F. F. Bruce says:

> We recognize in [Paul's] writing the concepts and phrases, especially from a Stoic background, which were in the air at the time and which he was quite ready to use in a Christian context; but Paul's gospel, while it was pre-eminently the gospel for the Hellenists, was no Hellenized gospel.[3]

And it ought also to be mentioned that the literary forms of the New Testament arise from their context. The use of letters is one example: first as genuine letters to congregations, then as treatises with some epistolary form, and finally as the amalgam of letters and apocalyptic. In addition there are the poems in Greek structural patterns (Phil. 2:5-11; I Tim. 3:16). These forms of contextualization are a far cry from the contemporary extraction of Western hymnody or choruses for use in the Third World.

CRITERIA FOR CONTEXTUALIZATION

Several observations can be made about these instances of New Testament contextualization. It seems that there are three categories in which to consider and evaluate contextualization.

Truth

As indicated in the previous examples, there is a body of truth which is assumed and occasionally declared. This truth, whether implicit or explicit, forms the absolute standard by which everything must be evaluated. The core of this truth is that God Almighty has spoken definitively through Jesus Christ and has effected eternal salvation through His life, death and resurrection. This truth is formulated in various ways in the New Testament, whether it be the "gospel" of I Corinthians 15:3-11 or the apologetic of Peter on Pentecost (Acts 2:14-36) or the preaching material which was later to become our canonical gospels. It is by this truth and the logical extensions of this truth that all of society, culture and ideology are to be evaluated.

Meaning

Cultural events and objects often have no intrinsic worth, but rather have the value and significance attributed to them by the common mind of the society. It is not so much the object or the action, in many cases, as it is the meaning of the object or the action. This is true even in regard to words. Words denote and connote. The Christian in society must so contextualize that the right meanings are delivered through the cultural forms and ideology. We must be continually aware that the meanings of actions or objects in Western society will not regularly have the same meanings in the Third World. The Christian must then be careful not to deliver the wrong meaning by his mode of behavior or cultural participation. The question must always be asked: What does this *mean* to the people? This is what Paul did with regard to the food offered to idols at Corinth.

Communication

At the verbal-ideological level consistent attention must be given to effectiveness. How is our gospel communicated? On the one hand this is verbal, notional, literary and traditional, as the evangelizers attempt to transmit the gospel in ways that are intelligible to the members of the recipient culture. On the other hand it is behavioral. How are the people to know that God is love if there is no activity which in culturally meaningful ways demonstrates the love of God in the lives of the evangelizers?

These three criteria form the basis for the evaluation of a contextualized gospel. It honors the Word of God, it respects culture as the natural product of God's creation, and it emphasizes the goal of the Word who came and lived among us — effective communication. All three of these are both positive and negative determinants.

STAGES IN CONTEXTUALIZATION

But it also remains to be said that the communication of the gospel must occur in progressive stages. Five stages may be posited in an effort to observe the graduated presentation of the gospel to people in a different culture.

Translation of the Scripture

There are two crucial factors here. First is the effectiveness of the translation — there must be a dynamic equivalence of the original message. But just as crucial is the selection of the passages which are to be translated first for communication to fresh recipients. These decisions should be patterned after early messages by the apostles as reflected in the New Testament.

Informational Presentation

Whereas translation reflects the original patterns of the biblical literature, the informational presentation must be adapted to both the gospel content and the mind-set of the hearers. This will initially be believer to unbeliever (evangelistic); later it will be believer to believer (instructional). But in both cases the presentation must be adapted to the sentence structure and to the notional and ideological patterns of the community. It may reflect less of the Hebraic or Greek sentence structure and mental patterns than does translation. The goal is the comprehensibility of the message in the minds of the hearers. Most incorrect at this stage would be precise translation of selected verses out of the New Testament. Rather, the truths contained in such verses must be removed, not only from their literary context, but also from their linguistic and ideological context.

A contemporary example of failure to develop an informational presentation is the quoting of proof texts to prospective converts. The impropriety of this is evident in the linking conjunctions of so many of these verses, and in the very foreign nature of the sentence structure and logic. The informational presentation must be designed with the hearer in mind. It must be the basic truths of the gospel contextualized into the language and thought patterns of the recipients.

Didactic Presentation

While the informational presentation is selective, and contains merely the basic elements of Christian truth, the didactic presentation works toward two more advanced goals. First is increased comprehensiveness. Effort is given to include a larger portion of New Testament teaching, and to introduce niceties of thought that are characteristic of the gospel, but may not be natural to the recipients. Second, the presentation is structured according to the logical system which is natural to the recipients. It does not have to be in structural patterns that are characteristically Western, nor in conformity with our philosophical patterns. Again, the intelligibility and organizational pattern must be natural to the ideological context.

Hortatory Presentation

The primary goal of the hortatory presentation is persuasion. On the basis of given truth, or previously learned truth, the hearers are urged to respond in a particular manner. It is crucial here that the persuasive techniques be contextualized. This requires a familiarity with the systems of persuasion available both in the language and in the ideological patterns of the people.

Extensional Presentation

This is perhaps where the greatest amount of omission occurs, at least in the American context. There comes a time in the believing community when the members must speak to the society in which they live. There will be times when there must be censure of accepted behavior patterns, when the political system must be evaluated, and when the economic structure must come under criticism. This is to be done by extension of the explicit truths of Scripture in ways that relate to the context in which the believers live. There must be a clear distinction between extensional presentation and the other four types of presentation. The first four are like preaching; they contain and deliver the very Word of God, and thus must be very responsible, authoritative presentations. The extensional presentation, on the other hand, by its very nature must be somewhat tentative and experimental, and must be subject to the judgment of those Christians who hear it. It is not to be confused with the canonical Word of God, but it must issue from the truths of God's Word. It must be understood as a human application of divine truth to context, and it must be done with serious accountability to the Lord. Perhaps it should not even be associated with the reading of Scripture, but it must issue from a mind that is fully saturated with the Word of God.

The extensional presentation is the ultimate determinant as to whether or not the church will have an effect upon society and the life situation of the people. Beginning within the church, according to the pattern of Paul, instructions must be given to members of households and to members of the economic (II Thess. 3:12) and political community (Rom. 13:1-7). In each case the directive must be reflective of God's truth, meaningful in the culture, and communicative. By implication then, what is directly appropriate to the members of the Christian church must be extended by them into the community in which they live. By extension Christians must ever press to put biblical values into action within the society, to enhance the communication of the gospel, and to demonstrate the redemption and release that are offered in the gospel (Luke 4:18). In the tradition of the prophets, Christians must speak against injustice, exploitation, and pseudo-religiosity.

The question must then be raised: What is the range or degree of variation allowed to contextualization? Four categories may be used to indicate the degrees of contextualization which are acceptable and what the limits are.

(1) The core: revelation and salvation effected in Jesus Christ.

(2) The substance: the gospel tradition in apostolic transmission.

(3) The application: exhortations addressed to particular people.

(4) The expression: quality of life in a cultural setting.

The amount of contextualization allowable is least in number one, and greatest in number four. The core and substance of the gospel are to be constant; only the linguistic and conceptual patterns may vary from one language to another. The application will be universal in those exhortations which deal with personal qualities and Christian virtues, but will be entirely contextualized when dealing with matters of social custom or economic arrangements. Similarly the quality of life must exhibit universal Christian virtues, but in contextualized manners which deliver the message in meaningful cultural behavior.

There may be some fear in accepting the possibility of contextualization, even in limited degrees. But we should not be overwhelmed by the negative possibilities and bypass gains available to the Christian mission. It should be remembered that the first-century Christian church was able to move from the Hebraic context into the Greco-Roman context with great success. Not only that, it was in this Western context that the majority of our New Testament literature found its origin. We should also remember that our Protestant, fundamentalist, evangelical Christian churches are a manifestation of contextualization. And we have not (all) lost the faith.

CONTROLS FOR CONTEXTUALIZATION

In addition, Paul gave controls by which a member of another culture may maintain Christian authenticity. The first standard by which he evaluated the behavior of the Corinthians is the commandments of the Lord (I Cor. 7:10; cf. 7:25). Of course by "the commandments of the Lord" he alluded to what has become our canonical gospels. This standard is the first appeal for all contextual decisions. Second is the mind of the faithful Christian who is instructed by the Spirit of God (I Cor. 7:25; cf. 7:40). In matters which extend beyond the explicit directives of the apostolic tradition, the mature mind in Christ must be the dynamic standard by which decisions and determinations are made. Of course the value of the decisions are only as good as the quality of the person's spiritual life. But this is nothing new; it has always been true that the effectiveness of a person is determined by his relationship to God.

There is a third factor which must certainly have implications by extension, though Paul mentions it only once. In I Corinthians 7:14 he indicates that a believer who is married to one who remains an unbeliever has a sanctifying effect both upon the unbelieving mate (so that the marriage may be perpetuated) and upon the children (so that they are not reprobate). This is a very important principle which must extend into all of a Christian's participation in a cultural context. The individual Christian is a sanctifying power. By membership in a family or a community organization, by participation in a cultural event or a political body, the Christian is exerting a sanctifying influence. The cultural phenomenon is no longer neutral; to some extent it has been Christianized by the believer's participation. If, or when, that effect is no longer present the believer must no longer be a participant. As salt of the earth, believers must exert sanctifying influences upon culture and society.

In addition to this, the author of the Epistle to the Hebrews describes the dynamic corrective force of God. He exhorts his readers that the living Word of God is penetrating, perceptive, and revealing. When disobedience occurs, the Word of God is active and quick to discern (Heb. 4:12, 13). For the person who in sincere obedience to the will of God attempts to contextualize the expression of the gospel, there is the comfort that the divine Word is a power for correction where there is error. Basically then, the minister to another society must live in the very presence of God so that the mind of Christ and the dynamic of the divine Word will be the controlling force in his life and understanding.

CONCLUSION

Contextualization has been at all points a concomitant of the divine communication to man. This is singularly expressed in the incarnation, elaborated in the apostolic mission to the Roman world, and has continued throughout the Western progress of Christianity. The New Testament gives patterns which indicate that there is an amount of contextualization which is necessary, but also that there are limits. The gospel tradition cannot be changed, but the situational expression of the Christian life — at the other end of the spectrum — must be fully contextualized as compatible with Christian truth. There are also standards by which contextualization can be measured and evaluated — Scripture, the mature Christian mind, and the corrective force of the divine Word.

FOOTNOTES

N. B. Bible quotations are in the author's translation unless otherwise noted.

1. F. F. Bruce, *New Testament History* (Garden City, NY: Doubleday & Co., Inc., 1971), p. 286.

2. Observe that Paul presumes that a person will speak his opinion. This itself is a socio-cultural phenomenon and must not be interpreted mechanistically. Also Paul presumes that there is good communication between the Christian and the objector, and does not require that we always, at all times, abstain from everything against which anyone at anytime might object! It is strictly situational.

3. Bruce, *History,* pp. 245-46.

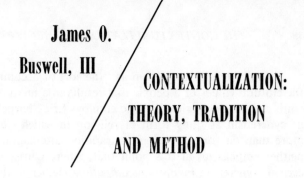

James O. Buswell, III

CONTEXTUALIZATION: THEORY, TRADITION AND METHOD

DEFINITIONS AND USAGES

At the International Congress on World Evangelization in Lausanne, Switzerland in 1974, the term *contextualization* was introduced by Byang Kato as "a new term imported into theology to express a deeper concept than indigenization ever does."[1] He explained, "We understand the term to mean making concepts or ideals relevant in a given situation . . . . Since the Gospel message is inspired but the mode of its expression is not, contextualization of the modes of expression is not only right but necessary."[2]

Bruce Nicholls "touches up" at the same base, saying that contextualization "includes all that is implied in indigenization" and more.[3] He calls contextualization "the current ecumenical catchword" and goes on to cite the definition of Gadiel Isidro of Manila as "the attempt [in relation to the task of communication in Asia] to analyze the situation and then from an absolute perspective of the Gospel make this absolute unchanging Gospel speak with relevance to the needs of Asia."[4] Nicholls provides his own comprehensive definition as he continues:

> Communication includes research into the problem of language and translation, analyzing the changing patterns of culture and religion, and entering into the pain of human suffering caused by political, social, and economic oppression. Communication means personal involvement, discerning areas of spiritual need as points of contact, areas of agreement as bridges of communication and clarifying biblical thought forms to insure transference of meaning. It recognizes that the Holy Spirit is the real agent of communication.[5]

Both Kato and Nicholls thus focus upon the communication aspect of contextualization, limiting their perspective to that of the outsider approaching from another culture. However, recognizing the danger that syncretism might result from an uncontrolled projection of contextualization, they retreat somewhat from their initial definitions. As a result of their inadequate definitions of "syncretism" they fail to appreciate the full meaning of contextualization.

Nicholls defines syncretism as "the sort of accommodation to the cultural values of a people that results in a mixture of biblical truth and ethnic religion."[6] Kato employs Eric Sharpe's definition of syncretism as "any form of religion in which elements from more than one original religious tradition are combined."[7] Since neither emphasizes at this point that, where Christianity is concerned, syncretism involves *incompatible* elements, they each appear to misunderstand the nature of cultural accommodation inherent in legitimate contextualization. Thus Nicholls in his presentation limits contextualization to "the translation of the unchanging content of the Gospel of the kingdom into verbal form meaningful to the peoples in their separate cultures and within their particular existential situations,"[8] Reducing contextualization to an essentially linguistic task, he concludes:

> The more one reflects on the task of contextualization the more conscious one becomes of the *larger task,* of seeking to structure theological thought within each separate culture in such a way that the total corpus of biblical truth is more faithfully communicated to every man in his own culture.[9]

Kato, on his part, appears to misunderstand Joachim Getonga's references to early ethnocentric evangelism as a result of which he was forced to "abandon almost all the culture which he had acquired from his own African society."[10] Kato questions him on this, seeming to assume that "the beliefs of his parents" included only "elements that are incompatible with the Word of God."[11]

Fortunately in the discussion which followed, the definition of syncretism was clarified. Syncretism occurs "when critical and *basic elements* of the Gospel are lost in the process of contextualization . . . ."[12] But although contextualization was further elaborated, the main focus of application was upon textual meanings refined and clarified for the receiving society in terms of their own culture.

Other dimensions of the concept seem to have been in the minds of those who introduced the term in ecumenical circles. Daniel von Allmen, also suggesting a contrast with the earlier concept of "indigenization," attributes the "new terminology" to "specialists in theological teaching in the Third World."[13] In their view, contextualization "is an attempt to express the fact that the situation of theology in a process of self-adaptation to a new or changing context is the same in Europe as in Asia or in Africa."[14] Whereas the emphasis at Lausanne seems to have been on the problems of cross-cultural communication, the emphasis of von Allmen and those he cites is on the preparation of theologies by non-Western Christians. "There is no short cut to be found," he insists, "by simply adapting an existing theology to contemporary or local taste."[15] He summarizes at one point: "No true 'indigenization or contextualization' can take place [merely] because foreigners, the 'missionaries,' suggest it; on the contrary, true indigenization takes place only because the 'indigenous' church has itself become truly missionary, with or without the blessing of the 'missionaries.' "[16]

A third perspective on contextualization closely related to the Lausanne emphasis, but the "other side of the coin," was suggested by the section on "Culture and Identity" of the Bangkok Conference of 1972. Repeatedly quoted in the literature before and after the conference was the motto, "Culture shapes the human voice that answers the voice of Christ."[17] Here the focus is neither on the missionary communicator, nor the indigenous theologian, but on the target population which is receiving, not a contextualized gospel, but rather, one dressed in unfamiliar cultural context. Ignorant of the vital role of the Holy Spirit as communicator, the non-Western recipient responds to the motto with the question:

> "Is it really I who answer Christ? Is it not another person instead of me?" This points to the problem of so-called missionary alienation . . . . However, the problem is: how can we ourselves be fully responsible when receiving Salvation from Christ? How can we responsibly answer the voice of Christ instead of copying foreign models of conversion — imposed, not truly accepted?[18]

Here we have one result of failure to contextualize the message. (Further reference to the problem of alienation, its causes and consequences, will be treated below.)

It appears from these and other usages that the concept of contextualization may be broken down into different kinds, and that many of them, despite the comparative novelty of the term *contextualization* in this regard, have already had a respectable history, both in missiology and in field applications. Furthermore, it also appears that the proliferation of labels for the conditions, processes, and methods in question might have been avoided had those coining the terms been acquainted with established anthropological terminology covering the dynamics of culture contact and change. It is hoped that some degree of standardization may yield a more widespread familiarity with and application of the crucial methods involved. I propose to break down the term into the following three categories: contextualization of the witness, contextualization of the church and its leadership, and contextualization of the Word.

Contextualization of the Witness: Inculturation

For cross-cultural witness a major problem is to make the gospel message intelligible in the idiom of the language and culture of the receivers. The witness is handling a message that is supracultural (i.e., noncultural) in two different cultural media — his own and that of the receiver. The process of disengaging the supracultural elements of the gospel from one culture and contextualizing them within the cultural forms and social institutions of another, with at least some degree of transformation of those forms and institutions, we shall call "inculturation." For the missionary there is always a twofold dependency in this process: dependency upon the counsel and wisdom of adult converts, and dependency upon the leading and insights given by the Holy Spirit.

Professor G. Linwood Barney of the Nyack Alliance School of Theology and Mission originated the term *inculturation*. "The crucial question," he writes, "would seem to be: 'Can the supracultural find adequate and meaningful forms of expression in any culture?' "[19] The answer being in the affirmative, Barney introduces the term by saying, "The essential nature of these supracultural components should neither be lost nor distorted but rather secured and interpreted clearly through the guidance of the Holy Spirit in 'inculturating' them into this new culture."[20] He then makes a threefold distinction vital to the thesis and method of contextualization as he employs a middle category between the supracultural absolutes and the cultural relativities:

> God is absolute, underived and unchanging. But consider the following implications. The Gospel is given of God. Therefore it is derived. It cannot be absolute. Is it therefore relative? If so, it is changeable. Yet Paul (Galatians) speaks of the one Gospel. We need another conceptual category between absolute and relative. It would seem that the term "constant" might meet this need. Constant refers to that which, by nature, does not change though it may be derived . . . . Then it follows, God is absolute. That which he initiates and affirms to man in his covenant and redeeming acts is constant; however, the forms in which man responds to God are tied to his culture and therefore are relative. The absolute and the constant are supracultural but man's response is relative and thus can vary from culture to culture as each society expresses the supracultural in forms peculiar to its own cultural configuration.

Thus a relevant expression of the God-man relationship can preserve the integrity of a culture but in no way needs to compromise the essence and nature of the supracultural.[21]

This is, essentially, the meaning of Charles Kraft's usage of "transculturation,"[22] of S. R. Garcia's and William Wonderly's usage of "incarnation,"[23] of Louis Luzbetak's usage of "accommodation"[24] and of the Roman Catholics' general use of "adaptation." It is essentially what John Beekman means by "a culturally relevant witness,"[25] what William D. Reyburn means by "transformed symbolism,"[26] what Michael Green[27] and Ralph Winter[28] have emphasized with reference to the "flexibility" of the early church witness, and what Eugene Nida[29] and Kraft[30] call "dynamic (functional) equivalence translations." It is what J. Merle Davis meant by the title of his anthropologically oriented *New Buildings on Old Foundations*[31] which characterizes the approach of missionary authors such as Edwin W. Smith,[32] W. Stanley Rycroft,[33] John T. Dale,[34] and many others.

Last, and characterizing in a measure all of the preceding, is the principle recently dramatized vividly by Don Richardson's account in *Peace Child* — the principle of redemptive analogy.[35] In Richardson's words, "Redemptive analogies, God's keys to man's cultures, are the New Testament-approved approach to cross-cultural evangelism. And only in the New Testament do we find the pattern for discerning and appropriating them, a pattern we must learn to use."[36] The principle of redemptive analogy, he explains, is:

... the application to local custom of spiritual truth. The principle we discerned was that God had already provided for the evangelization of these people by means of redemptive analogies in their own culture. These analogies were our stepping-stones, the secret entryway by which the gospel came into the Sawi culture and started both a spiritual and a social revolution from within.[37]

Instructive comparable "redemptive analogies," although without specific theoretical context, may be gleaned from many other accounts of evangelistic breakthrough such as *The Dayuma Story* by Ethel Wallis,[38] *Cannibal Valley* by Russell Hitt,[39] *Christ's Witchdoctor* by Homer Dowdy,[40] and especially *For This Cross I'll Kill You* by Bruce E. Olson,[41] Redemptive analogies, whereby people in a non-Christian culture may suddenly comprehend certain aspects of the gospel explained in terms of familiar custom, myth, tradition, or ritual, constitute the very essence of inculturation. A beautiful example comes from the experience of the famous missionary-anthropologist Edwin W. Smith:

The most pleasant memories of my missionary life at Kasenga are associated with the weekly preachers' class, when half a dozen intelligent young men and I deliberately tried to find out how to relate our preaching to the actual life and thought of the people. I sat among them, not as a master but as a fellow-learner. We sought not illustrations merely, such as one might derive from fables and from the classics, but for *adumbrations of Christian truth in the native religious and social practices.* It was never difficult to teach about God — never necessary to prove His existence. Hundreds of times I have opened religious conversations, individual and public, by asking, "What are the praise-titles of Leza (the Supreme Being)?" With a little adroit assistance on my part it was always possible to get a list: "The Moulder," "The Creator," "The Great Giver," "The Guardian," and so on, from untutored pagans. These gave an excellent opening. Old traditions about Mwana Leza, "The Child of God," who came down to earth, preached good-will and was slain, formed a natural introduction to preaching about our Lord. The facts of slavery — how men and women became slaves and how they were redeemed by the self-sacrificing efforts of their clansmen — helped to bring home the truth about Him who gave His life as a ransom. Fireside tales of men who voluntarily died for others led our hearers to contemplate Calvary. I have before me now the notes of an address we produced in concert, on the text, "He taketh away the first that He may establish the second," drawing out the analogy between the Hebrews and the Ba-ila; *every point driven home by reference to native custom, worship, temples, sacrifices;* and all through no denunciation, but a sympathetic attempt to show how the new religion is the perfecting of all that was valuable in the old . . . . There are indeed some New Testament texts upon which it is easier to preach to Africans than to Europeans. "Your life is hid with Christ in God," e.g., is not perhaps readily comprehensible to modern English audiences; but by people who believe that it is possible to abstract one's life and hide it for safety, the great truth expressed by the Apostle is grasped with less difficulty.[42]

Dr. Barney's term *inculturation* is favored here because it denotes precisely what the varied usages seem to intend, and is aptly comparable to established anthropological terminology such as "enculturation," the socialization of a person within his own culture — the process by which a human infant becomes human culturally through interaction with his human environment — and "acculturation," the process of culture change resulting from the contact of two (or more) cultures, and the state of changed cultural characteristics or traits of a person or a society which has sustained the impact of such a process.

Acculturation (and variants of it such as "acculturized")[43] should be avoided as a synonym for contextualization because of its long-established special meaning in anthropological literature.[44] However, it should be employed whenever the actual interaction of peoples of different cultures and the dynamics of culture change resulting from such contact are in view. Thus the *inculturation* of the gospel would always be taking place in a context of *acculturation.*

Enculturation, on the other hand, is the experience of every human. It is the dynamic process of socio-cultural maturation. This takes place willy-nilly, with or without the complexities of acculturation. But in today's world there is hardly a place on earth where children are not being reared in the presence of some acculturative influence. The importance of this for the present concern with the inculturation of the gospel will be brought out more clearly below as we deal with the contextualization of the church.

As for "incarnation," it would be best to avoid this term as a synonym for inculturation. It is not entirely out of order because inculturation may be considered similar (but not identical nor exactly parallel) to the primal model of contextualization — the incarnation of Christ in human form. In the interest of increased precision the contextualization of the gospel, the church, and the Word should be dealt with in terms denoting the actual process and conditions involved. "Incarnation" certainly may continue to serve as an instructive metaphor.

Contextualization of the Church
And Its Leadership: Indigenization

Almost without exception, contextualization has been introduced in contrast to indigenization. But although there have been deplorable shortcomings in the name of indigenization, and although missiologists and anthropologists have come down hard on the "horrible example" cases of ethnocentric evangelism and culture-blind applications of the indigenous principle, there remain many examples of indigenous Christianity which resulted either from the wise application of what the earlier theorists meant by the indigenous principle, or from uninstructed but perceptive, Spirit-guided procedure which accomplished the same results.

I cannot accept the suggestion that contextualization expresses "a deeper concept than indigenization ever does,"[45] nor can I quite believe that "this new terminology . . . may also be the promise of the long-awaited end of a paternalistic relation between 'old' and 'young' churches."[46] Changes in this terminology cannot be counted on to change attitudes any more than in the case of the "native-national" switch.

We should also think twice before rejecting the terms *in-*

digenous, indigeneity, and *indigenization* on grounds that this is "a nature metaphor, that is, of the soil, or taking root in the soil" and that "because of the static nature of the metaphor . . . it is in danger of being merely past-oriented" in the face of "the new phenomenon of radical change."[47] Shoke Coe concludes: "So in using the word contextualization, we try to convey all that is implied in the familiar term indigenization, yet seek to press beyond for a more dynamic concept which is open to change and which is also future-oriented."[48]

In the first place, there is nothing necessarily static about the concept. Its etymology involves Latin morphemes meaning "to bear or produce within." Its English meaning, then, becomes "native; born, growing, or produced naturally in a country or region."[49] Now the beauty of "indigenous" for the label of a truly "contextualized" church is that the surest sign of such Christianity is its incorporation within the *enculturative* experience in the home! When the Christian home rears its children as Christians and the teachings and belief system of Christ are "born or produced within" the home, Christianity is *indigenous* within that culture. The Christianity thus established need not be thought of as tied to any particular traditions of the past. It becomes a part of the society and culture where it is, and may continue to be a part of that society and its culture as they change. Thus it may be as forward-looking as the people who accept it.

This is a perspective which has been missed by those missionaries who, in cases where the Christian church has grown up as a largely foreign, intrusive institution, have enthusiastically advocated a return to the traditional cultural forms of worship, of the calendar, of music and other aesthetic forms, only to have their suggestions rejected by the Christians within the very culture for which this "indigenization" was planned. Such plans have been rejected for two reasons. First, the missionary himself was too involved in making the decisions regarding the selection of forms from the traditional culture; second, the people themselves were *no longer there.* They had become acculturated to a point where many of the traditional forms no longer constituted indigeneity for them. At this point, Luzbetak's term *accommodation* applies to the contextualization of the church as well as to that of the witness. He points out that:

> The object of accommodation includes not only the whole culture and culture as a whole but also the actual and living culture — the ever-changing life-way . . . . Accommodation is not opposed to ac-

culturation or culture change as such. On the contrary, the object of accommodation is the culture as it actually is, today and now, and it supposes due appreciation of future foreseeable trends and needs . . . . If everything else would make sense, and if a tribe in a Central African jungle were to ask me to erect a Gothic cathedral for them, I would build a Gothic cathedral if that were what the actual culture appreciated and demanded.[50]

The indigenous principle to some is synonymous with the "Nevius Method," made famous by Dr. Nevius in his publications from Shanghai in 1885 in which he strongly advocated that the new churches should be self-supporting.[57] It appears that what Nevius originally meant by "self-support" was not limited to the financial, but included the spiritual aspect as well and individual leadership from within the new body of believers. This became, in the process of explanation and application, the self-supporting, self-governing, and self-propagating model. However, these elements were interpreted inevitably from the viewpoint of Western culture (for reasons elaborated below under a consideration of differences between Western and non-Western ethos). "Self-supporting" and "self-governing" were interpreted along Western lines and money became a primary consideration. A part of this was due to the forms of the transplanted church which centered initially in the salary of a pastor. At Lausanne, Michael Green pointed out that:

> The early church was not unduly minister-conscious. There is notorious difficulty in attempting to read back any modern ministerial pattern into the New Testament records. Today, everything tends to center around the minister. The paid servant of the church is expected to engage in God-talk, but not others.[52]

"Self-governing" at least had the biblical model of elders and deacons, but the many Western varieties of church polity along denominational lines tended with few exceptions to reproduce themselves on the mission fields as a matter of course.[53] Even the "self-propagation" tended to be imitative of the forms in which the gospel had been received from the West. As William Smalley has expressed it, "I very strongly suspect that the three 'selfs' are really projections of our American value systems into the idealization of the church, that they are in their very nature Western concepts based upon Western ideas of individualism and power."[54] Similar opinions had been voiced a generation earlier by Alexander King among others.[55]

Thus the denominational structure on the fields together with the Western forms of the churches made it necessary to undertake a delayed and gradual approach to indigenization as the value of the principle was realized. In 1931 Roland Allen commented upon the current interest in "devolution" from missionary to local control:

> The "Church" in the sense in which St. Paul established the church at once was not in their view: . . . in the New Testament there is no devolution in that sense, because no New Testament Apostle or evangelist was ever "in charge," as these missionaries were "in charge." . . . Action like that is simply in a different world from any Apostolic action, and reveals at once how far these missionaries were from Apostolic principles and practice.[56]

But let us devote our attention to some of the examples of missionary opinion and activity which have resulted in a Christianity truly indigenous in other cultures. In this way we perhaps may justify the preservation of the term for modern use. An early expression (1924) of the indigenous principle involved education:

> Secondary schools . . . whose curriculum was largely formed by transplanting a European or an American one to China or to India, should be regarded as of negative value. . . . Primary schools which alienate an agricultural people from the soil are non-cultural and as such are unsuitable for the mission. The mission should oppose by all possible means the government desire to exclude the native language from mission schools, because its aim is not to Europeanize or to Americanize but to Christianize. This does not mean transplanting unchanged into other races those forms of Christianity in which we have been brought up.[57]

A year later Diedrich Westermann expressed the same view: "We do not want Christianity to appear in the eyes of the Natives as the religion of the white man, and the opinion to prevail that the African must become a pseudo-European in order to become a Christian."[58]

The same sentiments had been clearly expressed at the World Missionary Conference in Edinburgh in 1910.[59] Also in 1925 a missionary work in Ceylon was reported as incorporating "all that is best in national feelings, ceremonies, music and art into the service of Christ and His Church."[60]

In 1931 a case was reported from New Guinea in which individuals were refused baptism until they obtained tribal consent. After two and a half years public consent was given and "the direct result was the further decision to recognize that Christianity had a right to exist within the tribe."[61] This case has marked similarities to the acceptance of Christianity among the Florida Seminole Indians in 1945.[62] They both constitute obvious examples of contextualized or indigenous churches widely known as "people movement churches" in contrast to "gathered colony churches," a distinction most notably emphasized by Donald McGavran in his book, *The Bridges of God,* and subsequent publications. Those making the personal decision to accept the initial witness, appropriately inculturated, do not always do so publicly. In many, if not most, societies of peasant or tribal varieties decision-making is by consensus or unanimity rather than by majority against a minority. Thus there is no place for individual independent decision-making not in conformity with tradition. Only when a consensus is achieved may one make one's decision known, and act upon it. "People movements" following in such a sequence of witness-decision-acceptance usually result in indigenously oriented churches with their leadership and growth formed in the patterns of the culture rather than being imposed from outside.

One further perspective is contributed by Charles Kraft as he adapts the Bible translator's concept of "dynamic equivalence" to the church.[63] Thus a contextualized or truly indigenous church should have the same meaning and function within its culture as the early church had for the people in the culture of that time.

Contextualization of the Word:
Translation and Ethnotheology

The Wycliffe Bible Translators, and many other comparatively solitary and unsung translators of the Bible have been doing authentic contextualization for a long, long time. In most cases the activities inevitably involve all kinds of contextualization: inculturation, indigenization, and not a little ethnotheology. The Bible translator in many places has been the first witness, the first missionary, the church planter, and stimulator of theological formulations.

On the basis of other anthropological parallels, "ethnotheology" is an eminently appropriate term for the contextualization of theology. As Charles Kraft points out,[64] there are ethnohistory, ethnomusicology, ethnolinguistics, ethnobotany, and ethnoscience, that is, special areas of study that focus on what Professor Kenneth Pike, in his signal contribution to scientific conceptualization, has called the *emis* viewpoint.[65] It seems to me that the interest that has flourished for several generations in the distinction between ethnocentric missionary activities and the indigenous principle, and now between Western theology and non-Western contextualized theologies may be most aptly expressed in terms of Pike's *etic-emic* distinctions. Coined "from the words phonetic and phonemic, following the conventional linguistic usage of these," Pike explains:

> The etic viewpoint studies behavior as from outside of a particular system, and as an essential initial approach to an alien system. The emic viewpoint results from studying behavior as from inside the system . . . .
>
> Descriptions or analyses from the etic standpoint are "alien" in view, with criteria external to the system. Emic descriptions provide an internal view, with criteria chosen from within the system. They represent to us the view of one familiar with the system and who knows how to function within it himself . . . .
>
> An etic system may be set up by criteria or "logical" plan whose relevance is external to the system being studied. The discovery or setting up of the emic system requires the inclusion of criteria relevant to the internal functioning of the system itself . . . .
>
> Two units are different etically when instrumental measurements can show them to be so. Units are different emically only when they elicit different responses from people acting within the system . . . .
>
> Etic data are obtainable early in analysis with partial information. In principle, on the contrary, emic criteria require a knowledge of the total system to which they are relative and from which they ultimately draw their significance.[66]

Unquestionably contextualization must be an emic approach. Christian ethnotheology is theology done from inside the system, rendering the supracultural Christian absolutes not only in the linguistic idiom but also within the particular forms that "system" takes within the system: concepts of priority, sequence, time, space; elements of order, customs of validation and assertion; styles of emphasis and expression. Charles Taber has pointed out that even our "option for philosophy as the medium for theological discourse" may be considered relative to the Western tradition. He further suggests, "Certainly, a theology developed in the non-Western world would not have been so nakedly cognitive, so deficient in affective impact, as ours. There would certainly have been more room for emotions and for imagination, for reliance on poetic rather than technical metaphors."[67] He and others have even brought up the necessity to rethink what is "proper" hermeneutics and proper exegesis. Methodology itself must also be emic.

There is not much question about the objectives of Christian ethnotheology. They are nicely expressed by Flond Efefe as he points out that

> to Africanize Christianity cannot be an occasion for prefabricating a new theology. Christian values are universal values. The purpose

of the Pan-African movement on African theology is to promote an African expression of the interpretation of the Gospel . . . .

It is in hearing the Gospel that the Christian faith is born and the supreme purpose of African theology is to facilitate for Africans the conditions for hearing it.[68]

Let us turn now to a brief description of some of the types of failures to contextualize Christianity, and an analysis of their causes and consequences.

CHRISTIANITY AS A FOREIGN RELIGION

In 1957 an Indian Christian church leader made the startling statement that (with the exception of scattered local instances) for 150 years it had not been possible to build a fully indigenous Christian church in India.[69] The same Indian churchman also pointed out that:

> The Church of India must be prepared to admit the criticism so often made against her, that she is a weak church. She does not exist in her own right. She is an appendage of the mission field. Is it not true that in some congregations the membership of the church consists almost entirely of those who for their livelihood depend upon the missionary societies? They are men and women employed to carry out the mission of the denominational churches from the West. It is a painful truth which must be accepted with grace.[70]

Missionary literature over the past twenty-five years reflects a tremendous, even desperate effort on the part of some Indian and Western Christians first of all to "see" this situation for what it is, and to accomplish consolidation under Indian auspices. Nevertheless there persist widespread conditions which characterize organized Indian Christianity as anything but indigenous.

Not quite twenty years ago, E. C. Bhatty, then Secretary of the National Christian Council of India, wrote, "Except for the urban congregations which support their own pastors, in all denominational mission fields evangelistic, educational, medical, and other work has been, and still is, the responsibility of the oversea missions."[71] Missionary George Leeder reported in 1961 that out of a list of twenty-nine Christian hospitals in India, twelve were under the auspices of nine different denominations; and of sixty-nine Christian high schools in one survey, sixty-seven — all but two — were managed by denominational mission societies.[72] A letter from Bishop Sumitra, then moderator of the Church of Southern India, read in part:

> With regard to the relationship between the Church of South India

and the supporting missions, you know what I think should be done. We want you to treat us as one church. Now we are divided. There is an L. M. S. field, a C. M. S. field, an S. P. G. field, etc. [73]

Whereas this may not have characterized every diocese in South India, nor in India as a whole, it is a condition which is still paralleled in far too many places. In 1969, John V. Taylor, General Secretary of the Church Missionary Society wrote that:

> The Indian Church desperately needs to put off her institutionalism, for it is that which is western through and through . . . . But the institutions, and especially their management by ecclesiastical committees, are symptoms of an institutional idea of the Church which impairs spiritual vitality and impedes true "Indianization." [74]

One of the important consequences of the foreign quality of Christianity in India and in many parts of the non-Western world is the limitation thus placed upon the ability of the local Christians to propagate the gospel among their own people. This lies at the heart of the need for the inculturation of the gospel everywhere it is preached, and is particularly hard for Western Christians to comprehend. Herbert C. Jackson, Director of the Missionary Research Library in New York, has offered striking examples of prominent Indian Christians who, having learned of their new faith only in terms of its Judaic-Hellenic expression, now experience great difficulty in communicating Christianity effectively to those in their own land. [75]

In 1970 Sabapathy Kulandran, Bishop of the Jaffna Diocese of the Church of South India, wrote:

> Modern Indian Christian theologians . . . . have one handicap, and that is their education and outlook are Western-oriented. This is the result of no one having paid heed to the advice . . . fairly early in the century that theological education in India should be oriented to the country. [76]

He further urged, "Indian Christian theologians must be willing to steep themselves far more in the spirit and atmosphere of living Hinduism." [77] In this regard, John V. Taylor puts it in even stronger language which could be applied in many countries: "And the Christ who is for all men is dishonoured by his Indian disciples so long as they present him to their fellow men as an alien . . . . Moreover, those disciples themselves will not really know him until they learn to be totally Indian in his presence." [78]

Joy Ridderhof of Gospel Recordings during a recent journey was asked by adult Christian converts in at least one culture to send them recordings of scriptural teaching in their language for their children. When asked why they needed recordings in view of the fact that both they and their children spoke the native language, they replied that they had learned all they knew of Christianity in English and found it very difficult to express the ideas and teachings for their own people. Similarly, William Bentley, a black American evangelical leader writes, "All of us who receive our [theological] training in white schools . . . upon our return to the communities which produce us . . . have to de-whitenize ourselves in order to speak meaningfully to the masses of our folk."[79] Otherwise there is the danger, as expressed in a current account from Bali, of the Christians being "foreigners in their own country."[80]

In many parts of Africa the same experience repeatedly occurs. William Reyburn discovered on his own that the actual reason for poor church attendance among the Kaka in the village of Lolo in the Eastern Cameroun stemmed from a basic cultural belief involving witchcraft. To his previous questions about the matter, the local catechist had offered merely that whereas the women liked to go to church on Sunday, the men wanted to stay home and drink wine. Even though the catechist knew about the beliefs of his own culture, he could not identify their present functions with reference to Christianity. As Reyburn explains:

> Missionaries had always relegated witchcraft to the trash can and the . . . catechist's training . . . had taught him to be naive about the most dynamic forces in his own life. His education was formed in the categories of the missionaries' experience only, and this had imposed upon him a sophisticated atmosphere which was irrelevant to the task of presenting the Gospel in Lolo.[81]

Roland Allen long ago described conditions responsible for many of the separatist movements among the target populations. They were in large part due to the Westernization (rather than indigenization) of church leadership.

> All authority is concentrated in the hands of the missionary. If a native Christian feels any capacity for Christian work, he can only use his capacity under the direction, and in accordance with the wishes, of that supreme authority. He can do little in his own way; . . . Consequently, if he is to do any spiritual work he must either so suppress himself as to act in an unnatural way, or he must find outside the Church the opportunity which is denied to him within her borders . . . . It is almost impossible to imagine that a native "prophet" could remain within the church system as it exists in many districts. If a prophet arose he would either have all the spirit crushed out of him, or he would secede.[82]

The failure to relinquish the church to indigenous cultural forms and leadership to native individuals may be explained in terms of the unfamiliar cultural context within which missionaries were working. Strong feelings of insecurity assail one when personal interaction yields unexpected and incomprehensible responses within unfamiliar social institutions. This widely experienced insecurity is the essence of culture shock. The antidote for culture shock might be to flee. When fleeing is impossible and one does not have any control of the situation, some symptoms of homesickness may result — a common experience on any campus early in the school year. When fleeing is impossible, but control exists, another antidote is to structure the institutions of social interaction in familiar cultural forms. Too many mission stations exhibit this pattern.

A fourth alternative, but one which requires strong trust, and an understanding of the principles of enculturation through which those unfamiliar institutions and the incomprehensible cultural ethos have become what they are, is to sit at the feet of the culture, so to speak, and patiently to learn as much as possible about it *before* trying to undertake any formal evangelism. It is true that to some considerable extent the term *convert* in India became synonymous with outcastes. It is not without significance that Christianity's major advances in the era of world-wide missionary activity with few exceptions have been among primitive tribal peoples, and, in civilized societies, among the lowest social classes. For as foreign missionaries we have always been better prepared to teach the illiterate and heal their bodies while addressing our evangelism to them through the correction and alleviation of the more obvious evils than we have been to live with and learn from them, in the face of culture shock, reserving our evangelism until it could be addressed to them through native ethos to the best minds as an acceptable and culturally relevant option. Like so many of the principles being urged upon the present generation of missionaries, this one is not new. It was eloquently expressed in almost the same terms in the account of the 1910 world missionary conference in Edinburgh: "Men who have to preach the gospel to minds to which its initial presuppositions are completely strange, what a knowledge should they have of those minds, with their interests, their traditions, their beliefs, and their whole ethos."[83] This method is based upon an attitude of trust, not only in the integrity and coherence of the target culture to sustain the inculturation of Christianity, but in the native Christian leaders' capacity to be directed by the Holy Spirit. Roland Allen wrote early in this century:

We have educated our converts to put us in the place of Christ. We believe that it is the Holy Spirit of Christ which inspires and guides us; we cannot believe that the same spirit will guide and inspire them.

The consequence is that we view any independent action on the part of our new converts with anxiety and fear.[84]

CHRISTIANITY: SUPRACULTURAL AND CULTURAL

This situation has been a problem in virtually every society and subculture where men and women have received the gospel or theological training from European or American teachers. One of the principal reasons for this is the twofold difficulty of, first, making the distinction between the supracultural content of Christianity, and its forms and expressions in *our own culture;* and second, once this crucial distinction has been made, attempting to disengage (decontextualize?) the supracultural or noncultural doctrines of Christianity from our Western cultural forms and expressions. *Only a supracultural message disengaged from any cultural context is free to be inculturated in another.*

Mokgethi Motlhabi, a director of the Black Theology movement in the Association of Black Churchmen in Johannesburg, puts his finger precisely on this facet of the problem as he points out that:

> Very little has been done to adapt and relate the Christian tenets to the African way of life and culture. Christianity was from the beginning brought to the black man wrapped in Western culture and Western values, and *no distinction was drawn between . . . Christianity and Western culture.* Thus any black man wishing to become Christian had to embrace the whole of the Western values . . . and had to renounce his entire background as paganism and superstition.[85]

Similarly Dr. Wayan Mastra, Chairman of the Protestant Christian Church in Bali, writes:

> When Christianity came from West to East . . . most of the missionaries identified Western Christian culture with the Gospel and tried to impose it on the people of the East . . . . They did not distinguish between Western culture and Christian culture, between Christian culture and the Gospel.[86]

An example of this may be found in a survey of ten years in Africa prepared in 1924:

> The increase in the African ministry during the decade emphasizes again the urgent need that theological preparation *enriched by the best experience of the West* should be made available for the future leaders of the African Church.[87]

> A great continent is at the crossroads of life; *it lies with the western nations to guide the destinies* of millions.[88]

It was also reported that colonial administrators and missionaries, demonstrating even for that day an astonishing naiveté regarding the concepts of race and culture, visited Hampton College and Tuskegee Institute "to study the educational principles which have borne satisfying fruit among North American Negroes."[89]

One irony in this history is that at the very time these sentiments prevailed there were advocates of a far more enlightened view whose published expressions of sound indigenous method and procedure appeared in the very same journals.[90] Forty-four years ago missionary Floyd Hamilton warned of "a 'foreignized' native church around the missionary centre" which tended "to increase the active antagonism of the non-Christian communities from which these native Christians came."[91] In the same year a German missionary to Tanganyika, a Dr. Gutman, warned: "Missionaries from the West . . . are in real danger of becoming, unconsciously, agents of civilization rather than of the Gospel."[92]

DIFFERENCES BETWEEN
WESTERN AND NON-WESTERN ETHOS

An explanation for this state of affairs, which had so much influence upon the lack of progress of Christianity in the non-Western world, involves a number of factors. Basic among them is the manner in which Western civilization, with its manifest advance along industrial and technological lines, structured the whole system of values of its constituent nations. Political power and technological progress were fused with Christian piety into an inevitably ethnocentric, if benevolent, ethos. All "uncivilized" societies were appraised by the power-progress-piety ethos as inferior *on all counts*. The great commission was responded to within the context of the approving benevolence of the ethos. So was the whole colonization complex. However, the philanthropies of the Western world, sincerely motivated as they were in both instances, were severely distorted by the ethnocentricity of the ethos.

In Christian missions this took the form of a marked disregard for the culture of the receiving societies. As late as the 1950s this was demonstrated in a forceful way in the astounding results of a survey conducted and reported by Henry H. Presler of the Leonard Theological College in Jabalpur, India. In order to study missionary opinion on the question, "What need a Christian worker in India know of Hinduism and Islam?" he recorded approximately five thousand personal conversations. According to Presler, "Almost half the number of Christian workers now active in India say that *nothing* need be known of the non-Christian faiths."[93] Presler stated that those who held that nothing need be known of the non-Christian faiths relied upon the verse of Scripture, "My Word shall not return unto Me void." Sadly enough, there are still some on the field today who believe that, say, the teaching of a women's Bible class in English, even though many of those attending understand very little English, will somehow be effective. "At least the true gospel has been given," was the concluding remark in a recent account from the field. Caring little for the customs and knowing even less of the culture, such people were described by Edwin W. Smith in 1924 as those who "have not got beyond the Elizabethan's description of native customs: 'Ye Beastlie Devices of ye Heathen.' "[94] Another example: a missionary to Madagascar, in the typical language of the early part of this century represented the culture as their "inevitable indecencies and idiocies," and "their childish, futile, and deplorable ceremonies."[95]

The current report from Bali cited above traces a similar history there. "When the Gospel came to Bali, it was not planted in the Balinese atmosphere and situation because it was felt that Balinese artistic expression belonged to the demons; new converts were therefore taught to shun Balinese art."[96] The conventional ethnocentricity of the power-progress-piety ethos of the Western nations imposed upon the minds of its citizens presuppositions regarding non-Western societies which are, even today, very hard indeed to overcome in the effort to advance the thesis of contextualization. The modern scene has become even more complex. In addition to industrialization, economic specialization and technological sophistication, the character of our urban ethos has made us more insensitive toward our neighbors, and the advance of secularization has made us more tolerant of sin. The greatest social cleavage so far known between the sacred and the secular characterizes our outlook on every contemplated change we offer or impose on foreign peoples or minorities at home. None of this characterizes the non-Western peoples. The further they are from the urban "civilized" pole toward the primitive or "folk" culture pole, the more their ethos diverges from that of the West. William Smalley has stated the problem most effectively in his classic paper on "Cultural Implications of an Indigenous Church":

Our distance from most other cultures is so great, the cultural specialization of the West is so extreme, that there are almost no avenues of approach whereby the work which we do can normally result in anything of an indigenous nature. It is . . . ironical . . . that the West, which is most concerned with the spread of Christianity in the world today, and which is financially best able to undertake the task of world-wide evangelism, is culturally the least suited for its task because of the way it has specialized itself to a point where it is very difficult for it to have an adequate understanding of other peoples.[97]

This shocking realization may, indeed, turn our attention to the need for a contextualization of the gospel even in our own urbanized, industrialized, technological democracy itself, which is, in many ways, a very difficult culture to address with the gospel. We have been told by American Indians for some time that their culture is more "Christian" than ours.[98] Granted the value of many of the major cultural themes in the American Indian ethos, the white man's culture today does seem less compatible with a Christian life-style.

Hinduism was significantly contextualized as it penetrated Western culture. Swami Nikhilananda, one of Vedanta's most distinguished apostles, described "the cardinal principles of Hinduism" as "the true basis of democracy" and offered the viewpoint of the Hindu as "the application of the democratic principle in religion."[99] Is this the Hinduism of a caste society?

The late W. A. Visser 'tHooft pointedly pleaded that an adjustment in the Christian approach is necessary if the misconceptions held regarding Christianity by the neo-pagans of our day are to be stamped out. We must include within our ministries to Americans, he said, a Christian theology of Eros and of human justice. There must also be a theology of nature for those who so widely charge that the exploitation of the habitat is supported by biblical teaching.[100]

There are, of course, voices in many quarters doing their best to inculturate the gospel to segments of American people. These witnesses include evangelical campuses[101] and pulpits[102] as well as countless Christian businessmen and women who are conducting truly emic testimonies for Christ.

FOOTNOTES

1. Byang H. Kato, "The Gospel, Cultural Context and Religious Syncretism," in *Let the Earth Hear His Voice*, ed. J. D. Douglas (Minneapolis: World Wide Publications, 1975), p. 1217.

2. Ibid.

3. Bruce J. Nicholls, "Theological Education and Evangelization," in *Let the Earth Hear,* p. 637.

4. Ibid.

5. Ibid.

6. Ibid., p. 647

7. Kato, "The Gospel," p. 1218.

8. Nicholls, "Theological Education," p. 647.

9. Ibid. Emphasis mine.

10. Quoted by Kato, "The Gospel," p. 1221.

11. Ibid., p. 1222.

12. M. Bradshaw and P. Savage, "The Gospel, Contextualization and Syncretism Report," in *Let the Earth Hear,* p. 1227.

13. Daniel von Allmen, "The Birth of Theology," *International Review of Mission* 64 (Jan. 1975), 37.

14. Ibid., citing *Ministry in Context: The Third Mandate Programme of the Theological Education Fund, 1970-1977* (London: Theological Education Fund, World Council of Churches, 1972).

15. von Allmen, "Birth," p. 50.

16. Ibid., p. 39.

17. "Culture and Identity: Report of Section I of the Bangkok Conference," *International Review of Mission* 62 (April 1973), 188.

18. Ibid.

19. G. Linwood Barney, "The Supracultural and the Cultural: Implications for Frontier Missions," in *The Gospel and Frontier Peoples,* ed. R. Pierce Beaver (South Pasadena, CA: William Carey Library, 1973), p. 51.

20. Ibid. Dr. Barney adds this footnote (p. 57): " 'Inculturate' is coined here to refer to that process or state in which a new principle has been culturally 'clothed' in meaningful forms in a culture."

21. Ibid., p. 51.

22. Charles H. Kraft, "Dynamic Equivalence Churches: An Ethnotheological Approach to Indigeneity," *Missiology* 1 (Jan. 1973), 56.

23. Samuel Ruiz Garcia, "The Incarnation of the Church in Indigenous Cultures," *Missiology* 1 (April 1973), 21-30; William L. Wonderly, "The Incarnation of the Church in the Culture of a People," *Missiology* 1 (Jan. 1973), 23-38.

24. Louis J. Luzbetak, *The Church and Cultures: An Applied Anthropology for the Religious Worker* (Washington, DC: Center for Applied Research in the Apostolate, 1963), ch. 13.

25. John Beekman, "A Culturally Relevant Witness," *Practical Anthropology* 4 (May-June 1957), 83-88.

26. William D. Reyburn, "Polygamy, Economy, and Christianity in the Eastern Cameroun," *Practical Anthropology* 6 (Jan.-Feb. 1959), 18.

27. Michael Green, "Methods and Strategy in the Evangelism of the Early Church," in *Let the Earth Hear,* p. 162.

28. Ralph D. Winter, "The Highest Priority: Cross-Cultural Evangelism," in *Let*

the Earth Hear, p. 237.

29. Eugene A. Nida, *Toward a Science of Translating* (Leiden: E. J. Brill, 1964).

30. Kraft, "Dynamic Equivalence Churches," p. 56.

31. J. Merle Davis, *New Buildings on Old Foundations* (New York and London: International Missionary Council, 1945).

32. Edwin W. Smith, "Social Anthropology and Missionary Work," *International Review of Missions* 13 (Oct. 1924), 518-31.

33. W. Stanley Rycroft, ed., *Indians of the High Andes* (New York: Committee on Cooperation in Latin America, 1946).

34. John T. Dale, "Anthropology," Part 3 of *Indians of the High Andes*, ed. Rycroft, pp. 97-153.

35. Don Richardson, *Peace Child* (Glendale, CA: G/L Publications, 1974), passim.

36. Ibid., p. 329.

37. Ibid., p. 4. It would appear that the presence of redemptive analogies is what Coe means by "contextuality," which he differentiates from the further process of *doing* contextualization. "Authentic contextuality leads to contextualization" — Shoke Coe, "Contextualizing Theology," *Theological Education* 9 (Summer 1973): 241, quoted by Peter Savage, "Discipleship in Context: The Challenge of 'Contextualization,' " Contextualization Study Group, January 29-31, 1976 (Abington, PA: Partnership in Mission [mimeographed]), p. 11. Reprinted (abridged) in *Mission Trends No. 3: Third World Theologies* ed. by G. H. Anderson and T. F. Stransky. (Paulist, and Eerdmans, 1976) 19-24.

38. Ethel E. Wallis, *The Dayuma Story* (New York: Harper, 1960, 1965).

39. Russell T. Hitt, *Cannibal Valley* (New York: Harper, 1962). See also Shirley Home, *An Hour to the Stone Age* (Chicago: Moody Press, 1973).

40. Homer E. Dowdy, *Christ's Witchdoctor* (New York: Harper, 1963).

41. Bruce E. Olson, *For This Cross I'll Kill You* (Carol Stream, IL: Creation House, 1973).

42. Smith, "Social Anthropology," pp. 529-30. Emphasis mine. See also Davis, *New Buildings*, p. 43.

43. C. René Padilla, "The Contextualization of the Gospel" (Abington, PA: Partnership in Mission, 1975 [transcript of oral presentation]), p. 1.

44. Robert Redfield, Ralph Linton, and Melville J. Herskovits, "Memorandum for the Study of Acculturation," *American Anthropologist* 38 (1936), 149-52. Since 1936 much has been written on the description and theory of acculturation. culturation.

45. Kato, "The Gospel," p. 1217.

46. von Allmen, "Birth," p. 37.

47. Coe, "Contextualizing Theology," quoted by Peter Savage, "Discipleship in Context: The Challenge of 'Contextualization,' " p. 10.

48. Ibid.

49. *Webster's New Twentieth Century Dictionary* (Cleveland: World, 1968).

50. Luzbetak, *The Church and Cultures,* p. 347.

51. Roland Allen, "The 'Nevius Method' in Korea," *World Dominion* 9 (July 1931), 252-58.

52. Green, "Methods and Strategy," p. 160.

53. Mahlon M. Hess, "Political Systems and African Church Polity," *Practical Anthropology* 4 (Sept.-Oct. 1957), 170-84.

54. William A. Smalley, "Cultural Implications of an Indigenous Church," *Practical Anthropology* 5 (March-April 1958), 55.

55. Alexander King, "Thinking in Tribal Terms," *World Dominion* 10 (Jan. 1932), 87-91.

56. Allen, "Nevius Method," p. 257.

57. Martin Schlunk, "Missions and Culture," *International Review of Missions* 13 (Oct. 1924), 543.

58. Diedrich Westermann, "The Place and Function of the Vernacular in African Education," *International Review of Missions* 14 (Jan. 1925), 26.

59. W. H. T. Gairdner, *Echoes from Edinburgh, 1910* (New York: Revell, 1910), p. 230.

60. J. Paul S. R. Gibson, "A Christian Experiment in National Expression," *International Review of Missions* 14 (Jan. 1925), 94.

61. Christian Keysser, "An Indigenous Movement in New Guinea," *World Dominion* 9 (Oct. 1931), 370.

62. James O. Buswell, III, "Social Dimensions of Revival: A Florida Seminole People-Movement" — paper read at Annual Meeting of American Scientific Affiliation, San Diego, August 1975.

63. Kraft, "Dynamic Equivalence Churches," p. 56.

64. Charles Kraft, "Toward a Christian Ethnotheology," *God, Man and Church Growth,* ed. A. R. Tippett (Grand Rapids: Eerdmans, 1973), p. 110.

65. Kenneth L. Pike, *Language in Relation to a Unified Theory of the Structure of Human Behavior* (The Hague: Mouton, 1966).

66. Kenneth L. Pike, "Etic and Emic Standpoints for the Description of Behavior," in *Communication and Culture,* ed. Alfred G. Smith (New York: Holt, Rinehart and Winston, 1966), pp. 152-54.

67. Charles Taber, "Anthropology and Theology," Contextualization Study Group, January 29-31, 1976 (Abington, PA: Partnership in Mission [mimeographed], p. 5.

68. Flond Efefe, "Revolution in Theology" *All Africa Conference of Churches.* Bulletin 5, Sept.-Oct. 1972, p. 7.

69. E. C. Bhatty, "Is the Church in India Thinking?" *International Review of Missions* 46 (July 1957), 257.

70. Ibid., p. 254.

71. Ibid., p. 258.

72. George Leeder, "The Staffing and Support of Institutions Under a United Church of India," *Occasional Bulletin from the Missionary Research Library,* New York 12 (Oct. 1961), 5-6.

73. Telfer Mook, "Western Responsibility to a United Church in India," *Occasional Bulletin from the Missionary Research Library,* New York 12 (Oct. 1961), 2.

74. John V. Taylor, *CMS News-letter* No. 327 (May 1969), p. 3.

75. Herbert C. Jackson, "The Forthcoming Role of the Non-Christian Religious Systems as Contributory to Christian Theology," *Occasional Bulletin from the Missionary Research Library,* New York 12 (March 15, 1961).

76. Sabapathy Kulandran, in a book review of M. M. Thomas, *The Acknowledged Christ of the Indian Renaissance* (London: SCM Press, 1970), *International Review of Mission* 59 (1970), 476.

77. Ibid.

78. Taylor, *News-letter,* p. 3.

79. William Bentley, "The Black Church: Origins, Direction, Destiny," *Inside,* September 1973, p. 21.

80. Wayan Mastra, "Christianity and Culture in Bali," *International Review of Mission* 63 (July 1974), 399.

81. William D. Reyburn, "Motivations for Christianity: An African Conversation," *Practical Anthropology* 5 (Jan.-Feb. 1958), 32.

82. Roland Allen, *Missionary Methods: St. Paul's or Ours?* (1927) (Grand Rapids: Eerdmans, 1962), pp. 81-82.

83. Gairdner, *Echoes,* pp. 220-21.

84. Allen, *Methods,* pp. 143-44. See also "Nevius Method," p. 257; "The Place of 'Faith' in Missionary Evangelism," *World Dominion* 8 (July 1930); Melvin Hodges, *The Indigenous Church* (Springfield, MO: Gospel Publishing House, 1953), p. 55.

85. Mokgethi Motlhabi, "Black Theology: A Personal View," in *Black Theology: The South African Voice,* ed, Basil Moore (London: C. Hurst and Co., 1973), p. 79. Emphasis mine.

86. Mastra, "Christianity and Culture in Bali," p. 396.

87. "The African Continent: A Survey of Ten Years," *International Review of Missions* 13 (Oct. 1924), 495. Emphasis mine.

88. Ibid., p. 497. Emphasis mine.

89. Ibid., p. 498.

90. E.g., Smith, "Social Anthropology"; Schlunk, "Missions and Culture"; Westermann, "Place and Function"; Gibson, "Christian Experiment"; W. T. Balmer, "Textbooks with an African Background," *International Review of Missions* 14 (Jan. 1925), 37-44.

91. Floyd E. Hamilton, "Christian Missionary Education," *World Dominion* 10 (April 1932), 126.

92. Alexander King, "Thinking in Tribal Terms," *World Dominion* 10 (Jan. 1932), 89.

·93. Henry H. Presler, "The Christian's Knowledge of Non-Christian Religions," *International Review of Missions* 50 (April 1961), 184.

94. Smith, "Social Anthropology," p. 518.

95. W. Kendall Gale, "The Witch-Doctor's House Becomes A Sanctuary," *World Dominion* 9 (April 1931), 172.

96. Mastra, "Christianity and Culture in Bali," p. 398.

97. Smalley, "Cultural Implications," p. 63.

98. The North American Indian ethos is characterized by the ethics of self-effacement, generosity rather than acquisition to guarantee security, noninterference, and harmony quite in contrast to the competitive selfishness which

prevails in the dominant culture of America.

99. Swami Nikhilananda, "Hinduism," *Religion in the Twentieth Century*, ed. V. Ferm (New York: Philosophical Library, 1948), p. 13.

100. W. A. Visser 'tHooft, "Evangelism in the Neo-Pagan Situation," *International Review of Mission* 63 (Jan. 1974), 84-85.

101. E.g., Marvin K. Mayers, "God in Man: A Systems Approach to Biblical Theology" (1969 mimeograph) Contextualizing Christianity for Today's Americans; Taber, "Anthropology and Theology," p. 6; Robert E. Webber, *Agenda for the Evangelical Church,* in press.

102. E.g., Bryant Kirkland, pastor of New York's Fifth Avenue Presbyterian Church, and winner of the "Minister of the Year" award for 1975, contextualizes Christianity to New Yorkers. Even missiology itself is being contextualized to today's Western world in view of the rise of missionary activity in the non-Western world, necessitating also attention to the contextualization of missiology within the non-Western church. Josef Glazik, "The Meaning and the Place of Missiology Today," *International review of Missions* 57 (Oct. 1968), 459-67.

RESPONSE / Samuel Rowen

It is clear from the presentations by Drs. Buswell and Ericson that the gospel has been revealed once for all and inscripturated. There are not different gospels for different places. Contextualization does not mean, as some would maintain, that every culture has its own Old Testament and the New Testament is to be shown as the fulfilment of the truth already revealed in each cultural context.

A second observation is the emphasis that truth as abstracted statements tends to be sterile. The purpose of truth is not merely right conceptual understanding, but right action. With this I heartily concur. However, in response, I would like to pose some questions and ask for further clarification.

(1) Do contextualization and indigenization involve the same set of concerns? If contextualization is the same as accommodation or adaptation then the answer is yes. However, the concern of contextualization is that the gospel must not simply root itself in the soil, it must also judge it. There has been a tendency to regard culture and the *status quo* as sacred and inviolable. But every culture is subject to the fall and needs to be brought under the judgment of the Scriptures. Since the context is constantly changing either by new expressions of the depravity of man or by the positive effects of the advance of the gospel, the *process* of contextualization is continual. It is expressed in the Reformation motto: *Semper Reformanda* (Always Reforming). The search for a more dynamic term led to the term *contextualization*. At the same time it is true, as stated, that new terminology will not necessarily issue in new attitudes or behavior — understanding is a necessary but not sufficient cause for change.

(2) What is to be contextualized? The definitions of contextualization in terms of communication fail to take into account that the concern is for the contextualization of something. The discussion of the contextualization of the Word, church and wit-

ness is legitimate, but still misses the heart of the concerns of contextualization, that is, the contextualization (as process) of the gospel and the contextualization of theology. The gospel is the *good news* in context. Theology is the application of the Word of God to the concrete realities of life. Thus *who* is to do the contextualizing is of basic importance. It must be those who are going to live out in obedience the gospel in that particular context. One cannot contextualize the gospel for another.

(3) Has the gospel been too narrowly understood? Is there such a thing as a noncontextualized gospel? The crucial question is: What is the gospel? The answer to this will determine the extent to which Paul was involved in matters of social and cultural change. In Colossians Paul contextualizes the gospel by saying that those who are raised with Christ (the gospel) act differently. Thus contextualization of the gospel radically affects the basic institutions of society (e.g., the family). Paul acts as a social critic in the application of the gospel. Liberation theology is an attempt to contextualize the gospel, but some of its exponents have an understanding of the gospel which differs from the evangelical view. A fundamental concern in contextualization is: What is the gospel?

(4) Implicit in the whole task of contextualization is the issue of hermeneutics. We must be able to determine what is normative and what is descriptive. What are the biblical norms for hermeneutics? Can hermeneutical norms be found within each culture? It is here that the critical differences between legitimate contextualization and syncretism will be determined.

(5) Does the fall affect different cultures in different ways? To ask the question more positively: Does each culture have within it some perspective which gives fresh insight into the understanding of the gospel? If so, the process of the contextualization of the gospel by the universal church is a necessary task in order that we may see displayed the manifold wisdom of God. Contextualization then is not to be the producing of theologies, but theologizing in such a way that reflection leads to action.

(6) If creeds and confessions are our contextualized expressions of the gospel, then what is their proper place in the continuing process of contextualization? In what ways do we legitimately build upon what the Spirit of God has done through the church in the past?

RESPONSE / R. J. Davis

The consideration of contextualization — even in these two thought-provoking papers — impresses us in small measure when we consider in contrast the infinite endeavor to which God Himself was put to reveal Himself to man. Time and space unfortunately limit the authors and respondents.

Dr. Buswell says:

> This situation has been a problem virtually in every society and sub-culture where men and women have received the gospel from European or American teachers. [One of the] principle reasons for this [is that] it is difficult to disengage (decontextualize?) the supracultural or noncultural doctrines of Christianity from our Western cultural forms and expressions. *Only a supracultural message disengaged from any cultural context is free to be inculturated in another.*[1]

The premise is correct in the broad sense but it is idealistic and beyond the range of possibility. It is great as our goal but even God's revelation of Himself with divine inspiration in operation was handicapped by man's inability to comprehend. Even so the wisdom of God provides that such perfection is not wholly essential. The gospel (Christianity) was and is communicated, and passed on cross-culturally, both verbally and behavioristically (by word and in person). God purposefully chose the time, place and manner of His revelation to man when He launched Christianity within the matrix of Greco-Roman culture.[2] The Judaistic background provided the scene of the revelation; the Greek and Roman cultures were the means of expressing and spreading the revelation. "The fulness of time" means more than the peace and tranquility which prevailed at the zenith of the Roman Empire. It includes the total cultural milieu of the then known world, composed as it was of many diverse peoples.[3] The revelation came from God to man in that total milieu. Let it continue to flow directly, not by Western or other bypaths. The genius of the gospel is its unique capability of adaptation and suitability to human need of whatever kind or class.

While it is clearly evident that linguistic communication presents problems, the Bible is the one verbal revelation of God. It is the only form that is inerrantly inspired. The wisdom of God determined the *modus operandi* — no warrant was given for human judgment in alteration or substitution of words, ideas or idioms. The Word of God in its given form must remain inviolate. God knew the problems involved in crossing cultures and hence gave the Holy Spirit to provide superhuman assistance to man to comprehend.

Contextualization as described in Dr. Ericson's concluding paragraph is an acceptable model. He emphasizes the necessity of casting the content of divine communication to man in the thought forms, ideas and decision-making processes with which the receptor is familiar. This is further stressed by reference to New Testament examples:

The limits and controls placed upon us in the endeavor to channel God's thoughts and message to man are inviolate. The gospel tradition cannot be changed but the situational expression of the Christian life — at the other end of the spectrum — must be as "fully contextualized" as is "compatible with Christian truth. There are also standards by which contextualization can be measured and evaluated — Scripture, the mature Christian mind, and the corrective force of the divine Word."[4]

In our desire to pass on to other peoples the Word of God we have no legitimate alternative to giving absolute allegiance to the text. A high view of inspiration requires that there be no deviation, however intense the desire to accommodate the words, the idioms, the thought forms. Adherence to the inspired text alone secures the message of Scripture. Let the exegetes grapple with it. A true and faithful hermeneutic will extract the truth from the text. The problem of "transculturalization" is best met by faithfulness to Scripture as given, and by reliance upon the Holy Spirit to do His work of breaking through into the heart and mind of man with the truth of God and "to render the full impact of the inspired" and inerrant "text for the new" hearers and their needs.[5]

To deviate from such a "process succeeds only in removing the heart from the gospel. Two steps are required of the exegete: mastery of the meaning of the text in its historical context and appreciation of the requirement of the culture . . . both skills are necessary for good interpretation."[6]

FOOTNOTES

1. Cf. John 14:26; 16:13.

2. Cf. Luke 4:18, 19; Galatians 4:4.

3. Byang H. Kato, *Theological Pitfalls in Africa* (Kisumu, Kenya: Evangelical Publishing House, 1975), p. 174.

4. C. H. Pinnock, "The Inspiration of the New Testament," — ed. Merrill C. Tenney *The Bible, The Living Word of Revelation,* (Grand Rapids: Zondervan Publishing House, 1968), p. 159.

5. Ibid.

6. Ibid.

RESPONSE / Charles M. Sell

My first reaction to these papers was sheer joy and delight mixed with a certain relief. Joy because the papers were rather comprehensive and complementary to one another. Relief caused by a new awareness that evangelical missions are giving fresh practical expression and effort to the previous insights of Allen, Pike, Nida and others.

We are indebted to Dr. Buswell for his comprehensive view of the issue and I especially appreciate his expansion of the term to include more than mere communication. And to Dr. Ericson, I would especially convey thanks for the discovery and analysis of New Testament passages relevant to contextualization.

My response takes the form of a three-pronged challenge for further study and application.

First, much attention should be given to the controls or limits of inculturation. Buswell has pointed out the threat: syncretism always peers from around the corner. All of us can recall gross alignments of pagan practices with Christianity. Remember that Karl Barth — at least the younger Barth — produced a contextualized theology. And Norman Vincent Peale claims to express the gospel to the American businessman in contemporary psychological terms.

Dr. Ericson has given us controls from the New Testament. But we can profit from formulations of limits within the framework of evangelical systematic theology. Hermeneutic formulations must be sharpened. Christian historians can help. And certainly in reference to the church forms, practical theology must take the lead.

Second, I urge us to concentrate more on what Buswell has termed "decontextualization." It is one of the major thrusts of his paper. Suppose you grant (though it is debatable) that Western Christianity is one of the most successful contextualizations of the gospel. Hasn't that become one of the most talked-about threats to the church? American Christianity finds it hard to adapt itself elsewhere. Most of the Asians I have met, for example, were not as dismayed by the fact that they weren't offered an Asian Christianity as they were by the fact that they got so much American baggage with what was offered! On this point, the Bible does speak, and when it does, it affirms that decontextualization precedes contextualization.

In speaking of decontextualization, I was not striking out at contextualization. I think the third thing we should aim for is "enlightened contextualization." In the modern world, there is no room for blind adaptation, or for people who relate the Word of God to their culture unthinkingly, regarding their contextualization as the last word. By enlightened contextualization, I mean helping people gain an anthropological view of themselves and others together with a firm understanding of absolute truth. (Roman Catholics, I recollect, gave as the excuse for their adaptation — which often was syncretism — the naiveté of the masses.) The "decontextualization individual" will be free to contextualize when he understands the relevance of cultures, even his own, as Ericson demonstrates was the case with Paul. If saints are grounded in God's Word and also aware of the temporal nature of their society, they will be in the best position to help contextualize in other places and in the changing future. We must help people discern the essence from the nonsense. Movements such as messianic Judaism, the Jesus people, and the renewal movement need careful scrutiny. They may be the symptoms of a vibrant body of Christ which is not *of the world* in order to really be *in the world*. That is the essence of contextualization.

REPLY / Norman R. Ericson

Answering the responses to the papers on contextualization leads primarily into matters of implementation. It is hoped that some avenues for further study of the right kind of contextualization will be opened.

First a statement regarding indigenization and contextualization. The difference seems to be a matter of chronology and degree. Indigenization was an early effort in (newly?) evangelized nations to utilize the nationals and to incorporate certain native cultural forms which were virtually consistent with Western Christianity. But contextualization is a later breakthrough aiming to adopt the new culture *in toto*. This means that not only people and acceptable cultural forms, but even the ideology and noncongruent culture must be examined with the hope that they too can be legitimized. Contextualization is acceptable, when it operates under the controls expressed in the paper. It cannot displace the "core" or change the "substance" of the gospel. Yet it must find full realization in "application" and "expression" to the degree that these do not contradict the core and substance.

Rev. Rowen emphasizes the dynamic question: "What is the gospel?" One wonders with him whether there is a noncontextualized gospel. And in the New Testament there are models dealing with this issue as well. Peter's sermon at Pentecost, Paul's sermon to the Jews and proselytes at Antioch of Pisidia, and to a pagan audience in Athens give us examples in oratorical form. The criterion seems to be the capacity of the receiving audience, that is, their familiarity with the canonical literature and the history of salvation. When the audience had knowledge of these, it was utilized. When the audience did not have knowledge of these, other culturalized appeals were made which led to the presentation of Jesus Christ. But an audience was not left uninformed. New Testament authors and speakers always taught and appealed to the history of salvation as the context in which God is working. This then was applied to the audience or church, as exemplified by the exhortations of the New Testament letters.

It must also be remembered that this question ("What is the gospel?") was a crucial problem in the early church, even in the presence of a Jewish canon and the living apostolic voice. Paul's letter to the Galatians reflects disagreement and debate over the circumference of the gospel. There is pertinence in the question: "How much of the traditional attitudes and performances must be carried to a new ethnic audience?" Paul's answer is implicit in his movement from Pharisaism (in the good sense) to the church of Jesus Christ. He emphasizes both continuation (appeal to Abraham) and discontinuation (the end of circumcision). On the one hand the message of the cross is a distinct development in the history of salvation. It is a new constant that cannot be modified. But its application and expression must be appropriate to the receiving context. Some *must not* be circumcised (Titus); others *should* be circumcised (Timothy). One of the evident messages of Galatians, then, is that each culture and every social change compel Christians to make re-examination of the application and expression of the gospel.

This brings us to a basic matter which demands a new dimension: hermeneutic. It seems that all hermeneutical studies have been monocultural: they are entirely Western. There is even a kind of inbreeding. Our Western hermeneutic has its roots in the origin of our Western society. We therefore fail to see that our applied hermeneutic may be based more on our Western cultural tradition than on the message of the New Testament. Let me give two examples. Requiring the same kind of submission to a prime minister or president that was demanded by an emperor or king is as inappropriate as saying that Jesus requires the use of organic fertilizers because he stated that the husbandman would use dung to restore the vine.

In contrast Peter made an appropriate cross-cultural application in I Peter 3:1-6. In discussing a wife's "submission" to her husband (only) he uses Sarah as an illustration. She was to Abraham what their culture required and exhibited this by calling him "lord." Peter does not direct Christian wives to call their husbands "lord," however. What he does insist upon is a gentle and pleasant disposition. The result will be the best wives possible for the first century. Here we have one of many patterns in the New Testament for a cross-cultural hermeneutic.

It is at this point that I am pleased to agree with Rev. Davis' emphasis upon "the inspired text alone" and a thorough knowledge of cultural backgrounds. His properly strong statements have equally strong implications. We cannot give the Third World an English Bible when the original text was delivered in Hebrew and Greek. Western ecclesiologists are not the ultimate authorities on contextualization. God in His Holy Word has already declared and interpreted His ways among mankind. The same Holy Spirit at work in the infant church is at work also in the minds of mature Christians in the Third World.

This emphasis upon the biblical text and the Jewish, Greek, and Roman cultures requires that we provide a *complete* education in these areas for any who are going to minister or administer. Without the language we lose the thought; without the setting we lose the message. We must be sure that all persons whom we train develop full skill and knowledge in both the original text *and* the original context. A high view of Scripture demands high standards for ministers.

What then about creeds, confessions, and Western church history? They cannot, of course, be ignored if only because much of this has already been transmitted to the Third World. But they also have illustrative value as case studies for contextualization. Basically a creed (or a confession) is a hermeneutic in propositional form. Creeds therefore reflect biblical truth and the particular concerns of a body of believers in a particular historical situation. By verbalization, inclusion/exclusion, and emphasis/de-emphasis, the creeds present minimal elements of contextualization. Creeds, then, can be helpful to us if we analyze them contextually as case studies. So also church history.

And thus Dr. Sell's phrase is attractive. "Enlightened contextualization" properly emphasizes the need for interdisciplinary seminars in our evangelical schools. Too often such study is only incidental, and is left up to the students. But the complexity of contextualization demands complexity of scholarship.

REPLY / James O. Buswell, III

I have nothing but positive reactions to what Dr. Sell says. I heartily endorse his emphasis upon "enlightened contextualization" *preceded* by decontextualization.

The response of R. J. Davis strikes me as a defensive attempt to oppose any excesses of the contextualization thesis. Such a stance in this case appears to be based on certain unwarranted assumptions. In his third paragraph Davis says (1) that the "Judaistic background" and the "matrix of Greco-Roman culture" within which the revelation was initially given included "the total cultural milieu of the then known world, composed as it was of many diverse peoples"; and (2) that because "the revelation came from God to man in that total milieu," it should be allowed to "continue to flow directly, not by Western or other bypaths."

Dr. Ericson's paper fully documented the fact that even *within* this Greco-Roman culture Paul contextualized his presentation of the gospel specifically and effectively. When it came to the communication of the gospel to the "many diverse peoples" of the then known world, of course many "other bypaths" both cultural and linguistic were necessary.

From the "then known world" to the present day the diversity of cultures to which the gospel must be taken has increased. Not only are there cultures in greater numbers, but cultures and languages vastly different from *any* in the "then known world."

Contextualization of the gospel begins with the very translation of the words, continues with the rendering of ideas into familiar idioms, and proceeds through the language and the rest of the culture to put the unchangeable gospel content into the thought forms of the receiving society. I think that perhaps Davis inadvertently confuses *form* and *content* when he expresses the opinion that "no warrant was given for human judgment in alteration or substitution of *words, ideas or idioms*. The Word of God *in its given form* must remain inviolate . . . . A high view of inspiration requires that there be no deviation, however intense the desire to accommodate the *words,* the *idioms,* the *thought forms"* (emphasis mine). I don't think that Davis means that no one should have the Scriptures in any form but the original Greek and Hebrew, as his words seem to be saying, because he also accepts Ericson's model of "casting the *content* of divine communication to man in the *thought forms, ideas,* and decision-making processes with which the receptor is familiar" (emphasis mine).

The questions of Samuel Rowen appear to reflect observations of previous expressions of contextualization within certain nonevangelical contexts. "Accommodation" as well as contextualization is concerned with a "judgment" of the receiving culture by the gospel. Louis Luzbetak, for example, in his elaboration of "The Limits of Accommodation"[1] by no means allows for any approach or attitude which would tend to regard culture and the *status quo* as sacred. Rather, he insists upon the "obligation of preserving the deposit of Faith in its entirety and purity" in the face of cultural traditions which might be incompatible with it.

Regarding Rowen's question two, my breakdown of contextualization into that of the witness, the church, and the Word made quite explicit the objectives "to make the gospel message intelligible in the idiom of the language and culture of the receivers," and to have an emic ethnotheology which would provide the target population with precisely what Rowen specifies, "the application of the Word of God to the concrete realities of life." The development of this threefold breakdown of contextualization also made explicit the necessity of members of the culture doing the contextualization for themselves. Moreover, this is implicit in the emphasis upon the emic approach. Rowen's point is well taken: in the writing of theology "one cannot contextualize the gospel for another."

Rowen's third question is essentially the same question that Davis asked: "Is there such a thing as a noncontextualized gospel?" This would seem to be related to Professor Barney's concern for the preservation of "the essential nature of these supracultural components" of the gospel, and his distinction between absolutes, constants, and relativities. The principle of contextualization is never, to my knowledge, expressed without the assumption that the operation is certainly more than a mere cultural transmission. Thus in principle there always is a noncontextualized gospel in the spiritual, supracultural sense, but because we are only finite human beings, it cannot be communicated outside of a cultural context. There seems to be no disagreement in any of the literature on that.

Finally, in response to both Davis and Rowen, a distinction should be made between contextualization as advocated and carried out by evangelicals, and contextualization as advocated and carried out by those who are less meticulous in preserving the essentials of Christian orthodoxy. Of course this depends upon one's definition of what constitutes "the essentials." Nevertheless, without entering into that debate, it is obvious that many of the reservations held by evangelicals regarding contextualization have their bases in the fact that nonevangelicals perhaps have advocated contextualization earlier and more prominently than evangelicals have. Most nonevangelicals have done so without mention of the theological or doctrinal safeguards (whether or not they believe them to be essential) which are usually expressed by more conservative missiologists. Some advocates of contextualization have taken these theological guidelines for granted and urged theoretical and methodological considerations of contextualization primarily upon evangelical mission agencies whose representatives, they assume, would also take the same theological guidelines for granted. But conservative Christians have been notoriously unwilling to entertain theoretical or methodological innovations advocated by nontheological specialists or by suspected nonevangelicals without some accompanying expressions of theological loyalty or identity couched in familiar terminology. Somehow, evangelicals must be more willing to appraise new procedures, methods, and theory in terms of their direct applicability to efficient and effective communication of the gospel no matter in whose camp they originated or who may be employing or applying them to less than evangelical ends.

Finally, it may be helpful to combine Professor Ericson's modes of presentation with my outline of contextualization:

(1) Contextualization of the witness: inculturation.
    (a) Informational presentation.
    (b) Evangelistic presentation.
    (c) Instructional presentation.
    (d) Hortatory presentation.
(2) Contextualization of the church and its leadership: indigenization.
    (a) Extensional presentation.
(3) Contextualization of the Word: translation and ethnotheology.

(a) Linguistic presentation (translation).
(b) Didactic presentation.

FOOTNOTE

1. Louis Luzbetak, *The Church and Cultures: An Applied Anthropology for the Religious Worker* (Washington, DC: Center for Applied Research in the Apostolate, 1963), ch. 13.

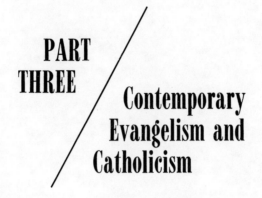

PART THREE

Contemporary Evangelism and Catholicism

**David F.
Wells**

CONTEMPORARY EVANGELISM
AND NEO-CATHOLICISM

It is now a decade since the Second Vatican Council celebrated the conclusion of its work. The changes which it ushered in, however, did not cease when the last bishop left the Eternal City. Through the traditional structures of the church there has since burst forth an extraordinary profusion of ideas and movements that has left some outsiders quite aghast. How do evangelical Protestants now relate to these new developments? Nowhere does this changed situation invite fresh, creative thought more insistently than in the question of salvation. And in few other matters is there less time in which to respond, for proposals are already being launched for joint evangelistic ventures between evangelical Protestants and gospel-minded Catholics. Do grounds exist for such cooperation?

NEW DIRECTIONS IN CATHOLIC THOUGHT

The task of describing the new trends in Catholic thought and piety is daunting for several reasons. First, Catholicism is a massive global synthesis of culture, religion and politics. In the wake of Vatican II, however, we are rapidly moving away from the notion that Catholicism means the same thing in all places at all times. It is far more appropriate today to speak of Catholic faith in this or that place. Generalizations about what Catholics think will, therefore, have to be both thin and unpretentious.

Second, the radical changes in the doctrine of the church effected at the council have produced a plethora of ideas and movements that are all jostling for acceptance; this mad jamboree simply defies description. The unprecedented freedom that Catholics now have is, however, of paramount significance, regardless of how it is used. New Catholics are no longer shielded and enclosed within the womb of the church. They are now ambulatory, enjoying the new sensation of life with few ecclesiastical controls.

Third, the relationship of the professional theologians to the church is more vexed and ill-defined than it has ever been. In certain respects their relationship to the church simply echoes that of the intellectual to society at large. In the last decade, deep if subtle changes took place in the exercise, influence and channels of knowledge in Western societies. It is clearer than it has been for a long time that what intellectuals write is by no means an index of what people are thinking. Furthermore, there has been a growing divergence between what some of the church's intellectuals have been saying and what the Holy See thinks ought to be said. The failure of the latter to discipline the more dissident members of the former such as Hans Küng and Edward Schillebeeckz has produced a situation that is very complex. It is evident, then, that what the laity believes is by no means identical with what the church officially teaches or with what its theologians publicly affirm.

These difficulties notwithstanding, my procedure now will be to analyze American Catholicism, since this has received detailed study by historians and sociologists. It is my hope that this limited analysis, which is not completely representative of Catholicism in other parts of the world, will nevertheless provide us with a paradigm from which principles can be adduced which will be applicable elsewhere.

It is undoubtedly too facile to say that one can divide Catholicism into two factions — "conservative" and "progressive." There are, nevertheless, tendencies in the church which roughly correspond to this division.[1] The old theology, for example, believes in an inspired Bible but subjugates it hermeneutically to the authority of the church; the new is more concerned to equate revelation with a Christian's religious perceptions or insights. The old affirms a structure of ecclesiastical authority, to which the laity is subject and over which the pope has full control; the new is opposed to rigid structures, questions papal authority, and looks for more democratic means of governing the church. The old sees salvation as bound up with church membership and participation in the sacraments, principally baptism and the eucharist; the new inverts the order, making salvation dependent, not on the church and its sacraments, but on subjective disposition. The old retains a strong transcendent or vertical dimension, even retaining prayers to the saints, monasteries and meditation; the new is open to seeing God working horizontally and immanently through social change and even revolution. The one equates Christianity with the acceptance of church teaching, submission to its authority, participation in its sacraments, belief in its divine founding and mission; the other identifies Christianity with commitment and subjective perceptions of God, both of which can occur outside of the structure of the church and lead to worldly involvement in society at the point through which the Divine is breaking in.[2]

These are but general tendencies whose concrete embodiment occurs in a multitude of different ways. The work of the sociologists in particular has shown that there is no such thing as "Catholic theology," if by that we mean a body of truth to which all assent. The Catholic Church consists of a series of partially overlapping layers, each one of which has its own peculiar, distinctive religious consensus. The theology of the laity is quite different from that of the priests; the priests' is different from that of the bishops; and theologians are a distinct group unto themselves. Furthermore, those who are younger in all of these categories tend to be more "liberal" than those who are older; this holds as a consistent pattern in each group. To speak, then, of new directions in Catholic thought is a complex and even dubious undertaking; to be precise, we need to limit the range of our purview. My concern here, therefore, is mainly with the laity and only secondarily with the priests.

In general it may be said that while certain traditional concepts have survived the last ten years more or less intact, dramatic changes have occurred both in the area of practical religious life and in the attitude to the official church.

Bearing in mind those concepts that are closely related to the issue of salvation, we note that change in theology has been relatively minor. More or less constant has been the belief in Jesus' divinity; 89 percent of Catholics affirmed it in 1952, 88 percent in 1965, and 86 percent in 1968.[3] The same can be said of immortality. In the three years cited, the figures for those affirming immortality were 85 percent, 83 percent and 75 percent.[4] The traditional attitude toward the doctrine of Scripture was more or less unscathed, too. In 1952, 88 percent declared it to be the revealed Word of God whereas the figure in 1965 was 82 percent.[5]

In the practice of piety, however, the old dicta and the familiar norms began to crumble under the pressure of new religious expectations. The practice of Bible reading suffered acutely. In 1952, 15 percent read it daily and 25 percent not at all; in 1965, 13 percent read it daily and those not reading it at all constituted 27 percent.[6] In the aftermath of the council, however, a precipitous decline took place. In 1968, only 2 percent read it daily and the percentage who never read it at all rose to 53 percent.[7] Throughout this whole period, furthermore, the laity has been increasingly less appreciative of the sermons it hears. Those who described the Sunday sermon as "excellent" in 1952 represented 43 percent. By 1965, this figure had declined to 30 percent and in 1974, it was down to 22 percent.[8] This falling interest was not arrested by the council's injunction to priests to inject more Scripture into their sermons; either the injunction was not heeded or, if it was, the laity showed no appreciation for the move. Prayer, which is the backbone of conventional Catholic piety, suffered, too. In 1952, 77 percent prayed each day; by 1965, this had fallen to 67 percent, and in 1974, it was down to 60 percent.[9]

The greatest changes, however, concerned the church itself. In 1964, 71 percent attended mass weekly whereas in 1974 this was down to 50 percent. The respective figures on monthly confession were 38 percent and 17 percent. In 1964, 70 percent stated that they believed that Christ had founded the church and established Peter as its first bishop to whom special powers were given which would be handed on to his successors; in 1974, this figure had fallen to 42 percent. In 1974, only 32 percent affirmed that the pope is infallible when speaking *ex cathedra* on matters of faith and morals.[10]

On the question of salvation itself, there was not a great deal of certainty when one of the surveys was completed in 1968. In that year, only 26 percent of Catholics enjoyed any sense of being saved despite the fact that 42 percent asked for forgiveness very often.[11] When listing the indispensable prerequisites of salvation, 65 percent mentioned baptism, 65 percent doing good to one's neighbor, 57 percent doing good to others, 54 percent cited prayer and 51 percent mentioned belief in Christ as Savior (although this was not defined). Membership in the church, a key element in the traditional doctrine, was mentioned by only 23 percent.[12]

The American laity, then, remains conservative in basic doctrine and is experiencing some changes in its practical piety, but its attitude toward the church is being transformed. Traditional ideas such as belief in the divinity of Christ, the Bible's inspiration, the necessity of good works and of baptism survived "the acids of modernity" more or less intact. Prayer and Bible reading, however, are declining; indeed, Catholics are less knowledgeable about the contents of the Bible than churchgoers in any of the main Protestant denominations. The doctrine of the church, especially as it relates to the saving of the individual, has been most seriously modified. Attendance at mass and confession is down, priests are viewed rather negatively, papal authority is openly questioned and only infrequently heeded, and being a member of the Catholic Church is seen only by a small minority as necessary to being saved.

The conservatism of the laity, however, was in striking contrast to the liberalism of their priests. This lends support to Jeffrey Hadden's thesis that the laity in general is drifting away from the priests and pastors.[13]

The divinity of Jesus was affirmed by only 54 percent of the priests in 1972, and only 45 percent thought that faith should be defined as believing what the church teaches. In addition, 65 percent argued that openness to the Spirit is as important as being receptive to the official teaching; 69 percent, furthermore, believed that an encounter with Christ is necessary for salvation, rather than merely accepting what the church teaches. What precisely is involved in such an encounter, however, is not clear, for 60 percent went on to say that God is found through interpersonal relations and 58 percent declared that His Word comes to us through contemporary "prophets" like Mahatma Gandhi and Martin Luther King.[14]

Once again, the traditional doctrine of the church, both in its authoritative functioning as well as in its role of bringing salvation to the individual, is clearly under assault by the priests. Correspondingly, there is a far greater stress on subjectivity, on relational theology, on faith as personal encounter rather than acceptance of ecclesiastical teaching, and on God speaking to man through secular movements and spokesmen.

Frictions between priests and laity have been evident for some time. How the newer concerns of the former will relate to some of the older concerns of the latter is not yet clear. But Andrew Greeley, who has been surveying Catholic opinions for a long time, believes that the views of the priests are continuing to filter down into the laity. He has found, for example, that the laity's interest in Christ's resurrection has quite changed. Formerly, he says, the laity's interest was in the historico-literary questions: Did the resurrection actually happen and are our records accurate? Now, he goes on, the interest has shifted to the interpretive-existential concern: "What does the resurrection tell us about the nature of reality and the purpose of human life?"[15] If Greeley is correct, this concern could be the harbinger of changes among the laity which will parallel what has taken place in Protestantism where interest has moved from *Historie* to *Geschichte*. What Catholicism will be like in the future could well turn on how this and related issues are finally settled.

POSSIBILITIES FOR DIALOGUE

Serious dialogue between evangelical Protestants and some Catholics is now possible, not least because of a changed psychology on both sides. Evangelical Protestants have discovered that there are Catholics who are nearer to their own position than are those Protestants who have been influenced by, say, the new secular and political theologies. By the same token, a Catholic with evangelical concerns may find more kinship with conservative Protestants than he does with "progressive" friends in his own church. Ideological differences are deeper and more important than denominational distinctives. Hitherto, the differences between evangelical Protestants and Catholics were at one and the same time ideological and denominational; in some instances they may now be denominational alone. How this convergence in ideology has taken place is not difficult to see.

First, the fundamental issue of the Reformation — whether it is right to see Christianity basically in terms of what the church teaches, what the church provides in its sacraments, what the church says is or is not permissible — has partly resolved itself. On a local, if not an official, level Catholics have been liberated from the matrix of ideas, rules and discipline in which they were formerly bound. Their emancipation, of course, also makes them vulnerable to those secular influences from which they were formerly shielded. The ebbing of the traditional doctrine of the church, then, merely establishes the possibility of a dialogue; it does not guarantee that Catholics will embrace a more biblical understanding of Christian faith.

A corollary to this change, however, has been the emancipation of the Bible. In this regard, it is important to recall that at the time of the Reformation the issue of authority was not focused on the problem of tradition.[16] It has been customary to think that the Reformers opposed Scripture to tradition, whereas their opponents subjugated Scripture to tradition. This is incorrect. It is true that the Reformers believed that an illegitimate use of tradition was being made by the Catholic Church but, on the other hand, they also appealed to tradition in support of their own views and they did incorporate some traditions into their worship and church life. The point that they did make unanimously, consistently and untiringly was that *the church* must be subject to Holy Writ. The basic tension was between the authority of the Bible and that of the church, and only occasionally between the teaching of Scripture and that of tradition. What they argued for — a Bible free from the smothering controls of the magisterium — now exists at a grass-roots level, regardless of the official doctrine on this matter. It is true that the response to Scripture of the Catholic laity has been somewhat unenthusiastic and its knowledge of what Scripture teaches is poor.[17] Nevertheless, an evangelical posing the question as to what Scripture says about salvation is not likely to be rebuffed with the observation that it is what the church teaches on this subject that is important.

Second, contemporary Catholics are recovering the personal, subjective dimension of faith which has been absent for so long. Faith is now more frequently defined as being open to the Spirit, or as encountering Christ, than it is believing what the church teaches. The pendulum, however, has sometimes swung too far, passing all the way from credence without commitment to commitment without credence. The one is as unbiblical as the other. But at least an evangelical Protestant can now often speak of a personal knowledge of Christ without encountering a look of blank incredulity.

Third, the theology of the sacraments which used to be a major obstacle to evangelistic work is undergoing modifications. First, the notion that the eucharist is so holy that only a priest can celebrate it while the congregation looks on from a respectable distance has been discarded. The twentieth century has seen a consistent movement away from this idea towards that of lay participation, a movement formalized by Pius XII's *Mediator Dei et Hominum* (1947). Second, the sacraments have been spiritualized. The Second Vatican Council insisted that a sacrament was constituted as such by its role in mediating the presence of Christ to people. Because of this broader understanding of the sacraments and the intention to move away from the rote, mechanical nature of the earlier conception, the gap has been closed between Catholic and Protestant views of the sacraments. Indeed, even the doctrine of transubstantiation was stated in an ambiguous way by the council.[18] Third, subsequent to the council there was a strong movement in Catholicism to establish a hierarchy amongst the traditional seven sacraments.[19] Baptism and the eucharist have been singled out as more important than the other five sacraments. Amongst the significant changes in Catholic conceptions of the sacraments we note, then, the recovery of something approaching the priesthood of believers, a concern to integrate the sacraments christologically, a desire to find a role for faith, and the movement toward having two major sacraments — baptism and the eucharist. These are significant changes which bring Catholic and Protestant theologies very close to one another.

TENSIONS IN COOPERATION

As the possibilities for dialogue have become more apparent, proposals for cooperation in gospel ministry are becoming more numerous. Are there grounds for thinking that the former can, or should, grow into the latter?

Evangelicals in the separatist denominations, be they adherents merely of first degree separation or enthusiasts for the second degree as well, will find all such proposals anathema. The mission field, however, has sometimes been preserved from the effects of the domestic quarrels of American Christians. But the issue of cooperation may not be settled so easily or simply. Where, then, are the areas of tension that are likely to exacerbate relations between evangelical Protestants and Catholics who are jointly engaged in evangelistic work? The two questions of greatest difficulty, I suggest, concern the so-called formal and material principles of Protestantism.

On the first question we note that the Second Vatican Council affirmed the traditional Catholic doctrine that Scripture is the inspired, inerrant Word of God,[20] but it then went on to qualify that statement by making special revelation broader than the scriptural form of it. Special revelation was seen as having derivative forms or channels. The council cited four such channels or media through which the revelatory Word comes: the laity's experiential knowledge of God, Scripture, tradition and the magisterium.[21] There are not, however, four sources of revelation. There is only one source, but it has four channels. Therefore, the possibility of conflict between, say, Scripture and tradition or Scripture and the teaching of the church was theoretically eliminated. Inasmuch as it is the *same* revelation which is mediated by both Scripture and tradition, Scripture and the church, Scripture and the whole people of God, the sources can only complement, never contradict one another. Revelation, therefore, can and does exist outside of Scripture, not merely in its "general" form — to use a Protestant designation — but in its "special" form, too.

The council's position, as it turns out, does offer a seedbed for radical ideas which some have chosen to exploit. On the basis of this broader understanding of revelation, a majority of American priests is now hearing the Word of God in the utterances of "prophets" such as Gandhi and King; by the same token, it is possible to see this same Word in the insights of secularists and revolutionaries. And this also accounts for the disconcerting ease with which Catholic charismatics have been housed within the overall structure of the church.[22] Despite David Wilkerson's pessimistic vision, Catholic charismatics have so far caused fewer problems in their church than have their counterparts in Protestantism.[23]

The official Catholic view on the nature of revelation, then, is broader and more encompassing than the evangelical Protestant belief which restricts it, in its "special" form, to Scripture. Catholics with an evangelical disposition are far less likely to be troubled by Protestants who have a gospel concern than are Protestants by these Catholics. The Catholic view embraces the Protestant; the Protestant view excludes the Catholic. This difference will not create problems if the two sides simply agree that in their evangelism the Bible will be authoritative. The question is whether it will be seen as the exclusive channel of special revelation and therefore exclusively authoritative.

The second point of tension concerns the material principle — the doctrine of justification — and is more serious. If there is not complete agreement on what constitutes the essentials of the evangel, it is difficult to see how cooperative evangelism can take place. It would be naive to imagine that both sides could agree merely "to preach the gospel" or "to preach Christ." What is entailed in preaching Christ and His gospel must be explored. To fail to do so would be an evidence, not of great Christian virtue, but of great Christian folly.

The kind of dilemma in which evangelical Protestants find themselves in this regard is well exhibited in a new volume bearing the title, *Catholic and Protestant Evangelicals on Common Ground*. Paul Witte, the author, was brought up as a Catholic, spent eight years in seminary training to be a priest, was converted and has studied with the Wycliffe Bible Translators. However, he remains a Catholic. Believing that Protestant and Catholic evangelicals are heirs to misunderstanding which has kept them divided from one another, Witte has written this conciliatory study, hoping to reunite the estranged parties.

In his opening chapter he touches on both the formal and material principles. "I acknowledge," he says, "Jesus Christ as my personal Savior. I consider Scripture to be the Word of God and the sole authoritative revelation."[24] No sooner has he said this, however, than he launches into an argument the upshot of which is that evangelical Protestants should not be disconcerted by the Catholic view that one of the channels through which revelation is given is tradition. "We are making a distinction," he affirms, "between revelation and Scripture, for although Scripture contains revelation, not all revelation is restricted to the Scriptures."[25] How, then, is Scripture "the sole authoritative revelation," as he affirms? Scripture clearly cannot be the "sole" revelation; moreover, it can be considered authoritative only if it is assumed that the revelation given through perceptive insights, tradition and the church's teaching does not contradict it. The fact of the matter, however, is that there are numerous manifest contradictions which are so glaring that not all of Witte's good will can conceal them.

On the material principle, the author is even less satisfactory. He affirms that Christ is his "personal Savior." Is it unreasonable to hope, then, that he will provide at least some biblical, doctrinal explanation of his experience? After all, the differences between Protestants and Catholics stem mainly from Luther's recovery of the biblical doctrine of justification, *sola fide, sola gratia*; that being the case, Witte has a golden opportunity to show that despite his Catholic allegiance, his experience of Christ as Savior is precisely what Protestants have in mind when they talk about justification. The truth of the matter, however, is that Witte gives not the slightest indication that he has even heard about justification. When his mind turns to salvation, he talks instead about changes in the mass and the spiritual benefits of the liturgy![26] This phenomenon of experiencing Christ as Savior in the absence of any clear understanding of justification requires closer scrutiny if we are to establish whether there is common ground between evangelical Protestants and Catholics who care for the gospel. What needs to be examined in particular is the way in which the atonement is interpreted.

There are three main theories of the atonement, although in the modern period some novel permutations on these have taken place.[27] The basic interpretations, however, are the Latin (or penal), the Greek (or mystical), and the so-called classic, a designation provided by Gustav Aulén.[28] The Latin view conceives both of sin and of Christ's death in legal terms, makes much of sacrificial imagery and generally presents Christ as the victim who paid the penalty (sometimes stated as debt) for the sins committed by the world. Although this theory was besmirched by its incorporation into schemes of merit and penance in the Middle Ages, it forms the basis, in its pure biblical form, of the doctrine of justification. It is this theory — this understanding of sin, judgment and Christ's death — which is almost completely lacking in contemporary Catholic thinking. In its place is a mixture, in varying proportions, of the other two views. The Greek view sees mankind as a universal whole to which Christ joined Himself in the incarnation, into which He injected the principles of incorruption and immortality with the purpose of overcoming sin in its main effects of corruption and mortality. The focus of this theory is the incarnation rather than the cross; the flavor of it is decidedly mystical and the outcome unquestionably universalistic, for it is argued that Christ joined Himself not to the man, Jesus, but to mankind through Jesus. The classic theory, which has become the peculiar property of the Scandinavian theologians, sees the cross in terms of its cosmic conquest.[29] Sacrificial images are rejected; the intent, rather, is to see Christ as the victor not the victim. At Calvary, He overcame the hosts of darkness throughout the universe. The theory's strength — its objectivity — is also its weakness, for man's fate is settled with little reference to his subjective involvement in sin and his need for personal faith. The battle is waged over his head and he is seen as the spoil which the victor takes. There is some biblical support for seeing the cross in terms of a cosmic duel between God and the devil, but this constitutes only a minor theme in Scripture. It subserves the major one of Christ's sacrificial death. The theory, finally, lends itself to an unbecoming universalism.

In 1964, Hans Küng shocked the theological world by arguing that Karl Barth's doctrine of justification is identical with that held by traditional Catholic theology.[30] This is significant because in *Church Dogmatics* Barth develops the classic view although modifying it slightly by his own reinterpretation of the Latin view. He sees the basic conflict to be between God and nothingness (or chaos). At creation God overcame nothingness and at the cross it is unmasked and shown to be an illusion. This does not mean that evil does not still infect mankind. Rather, its power is only that of any illusion; an illusion is powerful if it is believed or feared, but powerless if it is not. An illusion has no capacity to force itself upon men's minds. Barth, it needs to be remembered, does not believe in the devil as a personalized source of evil who has the intelligence and power to insinuate evil into men's lives. The upshot of this is that since evil has been pressed into nonexistence, mankind has been liberated and saved. It is only the intrusion of some elements of the old penal theory that slightly modify a thoroughgoing universalism in Barth's thought.

Küng was apparently correct in discerning that these ideas were widespread and had enjoyed long acceptance in Catholic theology. At the council, there is tacit consent given to the key elements of the Greek theory and the classic view is everywhere assumed. Its inescapable universalism is also evident. It is seen, on the one hand, in the absence of any teaching on man's lostness and the danger of God's judgment to which he is exposed; on the other hand, it is seen in the wholly positive evaluation that is made of non-Christian religions. The Logos is perceived as savingly lighting all men, even atheists. Response to this light does not necessarily involve rejection of non-Christian religious faith or even of atheism. It is conceivable for an atheist to be saved in spite of his atheism.

In terms of both the Greek and classic theories, Christ's death can be affirmed as necessary to man's salvation, as central to theology and proclamation, as indispensable to Christian life without any understanding, as Luther put it, that He bore the sins of men, "not because he committed them, but because he took them committed by us, upon his own body to make satisfaction for them with his own blood."[31] Indeed, the Greek and classic views of the atonement can be personalized. The necessity of commitment, of openness to the Spirit, of encounter with Christ can be affirmed in the absence of any understanding of the biblical doctrine of faith. The appearance, therefore, of evangelical Protestant language among Catholics need not necessarily indicate a recovery of what evangelical Protestants think is biblical Christianity. The task of looking behind religious words for their real theological meaning cannot, therefore, be passed off as of little consequence; it is this task to which we are now being called.

Martin Luther rightly declared that the church stands or falls by its success or failure in understanding the gospel as it is focused on justification, originated in grace and received by faith. These, I believe, are still the doctrines by which every mission, every evangelistic venture, every individual will likewise stand or fall.

CONCLUSION

The turmoil of the last decade has significantly changed the face of Catholicism. On a practical level ecclesiastical authority has been weakened, subjective religious concern has been reintroduced, and the theology of the sacraments has been modified. New doctrinal relationships between evangelical Protestantism and the varieties of Catholic belief must now be developed; it is a task which will be made all the more difficult by the desire for cooperative ventures, especially in evangelism. Contrary to ecumenical wisdom, I propose that it is doctrine which unites and service — if performed in the absence of commonly agreed doctrine — which divides. It would be unfortunate, indeed, if the desire for common service were to precede common doctrinal understanding and, in fact, vitiate it. And until the situation clears, especially with respect to the multiple changes in Catholicism, it is difficult to offer any clear rules for joint service, since as yet there is no common understanding of biblical doctrine. The cart is coming before the horse.

The pressure of circumstances may be such, however, that in this case the cart must come before the horse. As undesirable as this may be, evangelical Protestants will still have to insist that there be agreement on two issues and that the terms of these issues be developed with theological clarity.

First, the biblical Word must be seen as exclusively authoritative both for the content of the evangel and for the methods of evangelism. The conflict today is not so much between authority which is biblical and that which is ecclesiastical; rather, it is between revelation which is biblical and that which is not. Unless it is agreed that special revelation comes to man, not through tradition, the magisterium, the insights of Christians or the perceptions of non-Christians, but only through Holy Writ, any joint venture is bound to flounder. Worse than that, it will become a monument to our disobedience.

Second, the nature of divine forgiveness, its means and its method, must reflect faithfully the apostolic teaching. Can that forgiveness which the gospel declares is man's deepest need be found through a theology that understands Christ's death merely in mystical and classic terms? I doubt it. Only those evangelicals in a Platonic tradition would feel any inclination at all to embrace the mystical view, and the classic represents but a minor theme of New Testament teaching. That line of ideas, however, which emerges in New Testament words like "lawbreaking," "blood," "sacrifice," "wrath," "judgment," "Judge," "advocate," "propitiation," "justification" and "forgiveness" constitutes such an essential part of the apostolic view of the Cross that its elimination would mean the destruction of the Christian gospel. And tied into this teaching are concepts such as "repentance" and "faith" which have at best only a strained relation to the classic view and almost none to the mystical. The widespread failure of the New Catholicism to come to terms with these ideas is disconcerting.

It may be replied that the evangelist is in no position to dictate to God the quanzity and quality of the minimum knowledge with which He can savingly work in anyone's life. Undoubtedly this is true. It is important, however, not to draw fallacious conclusions from this proposition. Because God might work off a slender epistemological base in some cases, it should not be concluded that agreement between evangelical Protestants and gospel-minded Catholics on justification is unimportant or unnecessary. The Bible offers no comfort to those who dispense with its teaching, most particularly its teaching on the atonement and the sinner's reception of its benefits. To replace clear biblical teaching on the evangel by faltering experiential perceptions as to how God seemingly might work is to overturn the apostolic teaching. This reveals a Christian mind, not at its best, but at its worst.

The apostolic injunction to hold forth the truth in love is sometimes excruciatingly difficult to enact, for love's desire to conciliate, to put expressions such as "encounter with Christ" and "openness to the Spirit" in their best possible light flies in the face of truth's demand for doctrinal sharpness and clarity of understanding. Truth can no more be bartered away than Christian character can be violated. It is through love of people that we should be willing to eschew the battle cries of former days and seek to explore our relationships within the framework of Holy Scripture; it is through love of the truth that we will insist that God's gospel must be preached on His terms and only on His terms. If we fail to meet this challenge creatively, these new opportunities might slip through our fingers; if we fail to meet it biblically, the new opportunities will bring about our own undoing. We risk much by failing to explore the relationship with Catholicism; we risk much when we do so.

FOOTNOTES

1. According to Cornelius Van Til, there are different understandings of man which lie beneath the two theological tendencies in the church; but with his penchant for verbal obscurity, he has almost succeeded in denying this insight to his readers: "In

the synthetic teleology of history that is found in the documents of Trent and Vatican II the relation of God to man is largely expressed by an intermingling of the Parmedian notion of pure static being and the Heraclitian notion of being as pure 'flux. In this notion of the analogy of being pure determinism and pure indeterminism, pure rationalism and pure irrationalism seemed to be given equally ultimate standing" *A Christian Theory of Knowledge* (Philadelphia: Presbyterian and Reformed Publishing Co., 1969), p. 188.

2. These doctrinal antitheses in contemporary Catholicism are explored in my study *Revolution in Rome* (Downers Grove, IL: Inter-Varsity Press, 1972). I acknowledge the seeming poor taste in referring to my own work. Unfortunately, serious analysis by evangelical Protestants of Catholic thought is exceedingly scarce. Indeed, the only substantial study on Vatican II by an evangelical is G. C. Berkouwer, *The Second Vatican Council and the New Catholicism,* trans. Lewis B. Smedes (Grand Rapids: Eerdmans, 1965).

3. Martin E. Marty, Stuart E. Rosenburg, and Andrew Greeley, *What Do We Believe?* (New York: Meredith Press, 1968), p. 224; Rodney Stark and Charles Y. Glock, *Patterns of Religious Commitment,* Vol. I, *American Piety: The Nature of Religious Commitment* (Berkeley: University of California Press, 1968), p. 33.

4. Marty, Rosenburg, and Greeley, *What Do We Believe?,* p. 246; Stark and Glock, *American Piety,* p. 33.

5. Marty, Rosenburg, and Greeley, *What Do We Believe?,* p. 228.

6. Ibid., p. 230.

7. Stark and Glock, *American Piety,* p. 110.

8. Shirley Saldahna et al., "American Catholics — Ten Years Later," *The Critic* 33 (Jan.-Feb. 1975), 17.

9. Ibid., p. 15.

10. Ibid.

11. Stark and Glock, *American Piety,* pp. 133, 113.

12. Ibid., pp. 43-44.

13. Jeffrey Hadden, *The Gathering Storm in the Churches* (Garden City, NY: Doubleday, 1969).

14. National Opinion Research Center, *The Catholic Priest in the United States* (Washington, DC: United States Catholic Conference, 1972), pp. 93-97. The reasons for and significance of the different theologies in Catholicism I have explored further in an extended essay, "Recent Roman Catholic Theology," in *Tensions in Contemporary Theology,* ed. Stanley N. Gundry and Alan F. Johnson (Chicago: Moody Press, 1975), pp. 287-324.

15. Andrew Greeley, "The New Agenda," *The Critic* 30 (May-June 1972), 39.

16. For further analysis see Van Til, *A Christian Theory of Knowledge,* pp. 161-68, 194-220; Berkouwer, *The Second Vatican Council and the New Catholicism,* pp. 89-111; David F. Wells, "Tradition: A Meeting Place for Catholic and Evangelical Theology?" *Christian Scholar's Review,* V (1975), 50-61.

17. In a rating on biblical knowledge, Catholics in 1968 scored 13%. Figures in some of the Protestant denominations were as follows: Methodists, 27%; Congregationalists, 28%; Episcopalians, 30%; American Lutherans, 31%; United Presbyterians, 39%; Missouri Synod Lutherans, 43%; American Baptists, 48%; Disciples of Christ, 55%; Southern Baptists, 67%. Stark and Glock, *American Piety,* p. 155.

18. The Council stated that Christ "is present in the sacrifice of the Mass, not only in the person of His minister . . . . By His power He is present in the sacraments, so that when a man baptizes it is really Christ Himself who baptizes." No explanation is offered as to *how* He is present in these sacraments. The possibility that His presence might be a little less than traditional theologians have stated, and might come about in a different way, is brought to the fore in the sentences which follow: "He is present in His word . . . . He is present, finally, when the Church prays and sings" *Con. Sacred Liturgy,* 7. Christ's presence in the church and through His word is not by means of transubstantiation.

19. See, for example, *Concilium*, Vol. 24: *The Sacraments: An Ecumenical Dilemma* (New York: Paulist Press, 1967); *Concilium,* Vol. 31: *The Sacraments in General: A New Perspective* (New York: Paulist Press, 1967).

20. Although the wording of Vatican I on biblical inerrancy was adopted, it is not without loopholes. See Wells, *Revolution in Rome,* pp. 29-33. Cf. the essay entitled "The Approach of New Shape Catholicism to Scriptural Inerrancy: A Case Study for Evangelicals" in John Warwick Montgomery, *Ecumenicity, Evangelicals, and Rome* (Grand Rapids: Zondervan, 1969), pp. 73-96.

21. See the use of terms such as *Dei verbum* and *Dei locutio* in *Con. Revelation,* pp. 1, 2, 3, 8, 10, 13, 14, 17, 21, 26.

22. Apparently in 1975, 6 percent of Catholics had at least attended a charismatic meeting. Saldahna et al., "American Catholics," p. 15.

23. The point at which most difficulty arises is that of reconciling the traditional notion of the impartation of divine life through the sacraments with the sudden in-breaking of the Spirit. The former is a slow process, the latter a sudden experience. Catholic charismatics now seem to favor the view that the taking of the sacraments carries with it all the implications of later charismatic experience. The sacraments are like time bombs which explode subsequently.

24. Paul B. Witte, *Catholics and Protestant Evangelicals on Common Ground* (Waco, TX: Word, 1975), p. 13.

25. Ibid., p. 23.

26. Ibid., pp. 50-56.

27. See, for example, Sydney Cave, *The Doctrine of the Work of Christ* (London: University of London Press, 1937).

28. Gustav Aulén, *Christus Victor: An Historical Study of the Three Main Types of the Idea of Atonement,* trans. A. G. Hebert (New York: Macmillan Co., 1972).

29. See Nels Ferré, *Swedish Contributions to Modern Theology, with Special Reference to Lundensian Thought* (New York: Harper & Row, 1967).

30. Hans Küng, *Justification: The Doctrine of Karl Barth and a Catholic Reflection* (New York: Thomas Nelson, 1964).

31. This is substantially the translation found in Martin Luther, *Luther's Works,* 51 vols., ed. Jaroslav Pelikan (St. Louis: Concordia Publishing House, 1963), vol. 26, p. 277.

Harold O. J. Brown

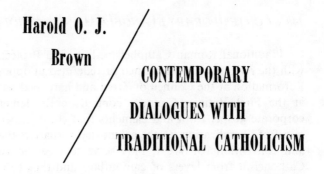

CONTEMPORARY DIALOGUES WITH TRADITIONAL CATHOLICISM

The difficulty of dialogue with Roman Catholicism in the 1970s remains that noted by the English Roman Catholic modernist George Tyrell in 1907: "We can never be sure exactly what Catholicism is."[1] Not only is it difficult for veterans of decades of controversy with Rome such as Gerrit C. Berkouwer to identify with assurance exactly where "Catholicism" is today, to what it holds fast, and where it is going; even younger evangelical scholars with a great measure of sympathy for the church in its ferment, such as my colleague David Wells, bear witness to the difficulty of accurately hitting so fast-moving a target. For me, however, the task is made easier by the fact that despite all the changes, a very substantial portion of the world's approximately six hundred million Roman Catholics remain as they were before Vatican II. One cannot say that they are unaware of the transitions within their church, but one will be correct in saying that they have not changed with them.

Change within the vast and complex structure of world Catholicism must necessarily be a many-sided phenomenon. Simple generalizations about so extensive a process involving so many cultures, subcultures, races, languages, and varying stages of political, economic, and social development are risky, but necessary. In the midst of a bewildering profusion of trends, movements, reactions, and counterdevelopments of all kinds, we can discern two chief motifs of change. To each of these motifs evangelical Christians will naturally respond differently, with varying degrees of sympathy, encouragement, and dismay. Although both are often labeled in the secular press — and sometimes even in religious circles — as "liberalization," they are clearly significantly different. Both involve a departure from the genuinely or supposedly monolithic unity of pre-Vatican II Roman Catholicism, but in different directions and for different reasons. We may call these two motifs "liberalization" and "biblical trans-

Traditional Roman Catholicism, linked in Protestant thought with the religious system defined or redefined in opposition to the Reformation at the Council of Trent and hardened and reinforced at the First Vatican Council, contains both elements that incorporate gospel truth and elements that stifle or pervert it. The motif of liberalization, to the extent that it shatters the definitions and conventions of Trent, may serve to free the gospel within Catholicism from layers of camouflage and thus to make it perceptible and acceptable to masses of people who are Catholic and may even be (in the words of the apostle to the Athenians) "in all things very religious," but not in fact Christians in any sense recognizable by Bible-believing evangelicals. This liberalization has made it possible for increasing numbers of Catholics in the 1970s to do within their church what only two decades ago they found hard to achieve without leaving it: come to a simple, straightforward gospel faith in the free salvation earned once for all in the finished work of Jesus Christ, and to the attitudes of trust and assurance and the practices of piety that are appropriate to that faith. At the same time, as a general movement involving challenge to authority, questioning of received traditions, and the abandonment of the sense of absolutes both in the area of truth and of morals, liberalization within world Catholicism can and does have the effect of sapping not only the old certainty based on confidence in ecclesiastical authority but also the evangelical assurance that properly results from turning from a form of Christian religion to the living Lord and Savior Jesus Christ. The very liberalization that makes it possible for Catholics to read the Bible and comprehend the gospel may also make it hard for them to heed the claims of the Bible and the gospel and more than those of discredited ecclesiastical authorities.

The second motif, that of biblical transformation, has expressed itself in an intensity of biblical study and faith that only a few years ago must have seemed impossible in circles where — despite formal papal exhortations to study it — the Bible was generally thought confusing, dangerous, and better left unread. And yet from the evangelical perspective even the process of biblical transformation is not without problems. Until recently Roman Catholics, while leaving the Bible largely unread, regarded its authority with that sense of total and unthinking submission that supposedly typifies Protestant fundamentalists. Today, however, along with the Bible itself, Catholics have also appropriated the whole phantasmagoria of "biblical" criticism and hermeneutics, bringing the same varieties of relativism, reductionism, and existentialist reinterpretation that have so exsanguinated most traditional Protestant communities.

Over against the two modern motifs, liberal and biblical, we have that which for many Protestant critics represented — and still represents — the quintessence of Catholicism: a rigid traditionalism and authoritarianism. And while tradition may pervert biblical doctrine, it also may preserve it. In fact, a major part of that which is *traditum* — handed over — from generation to generation in modern Catholicism as in early Christianity is precisely the Scripture and its message. For countless American Catholics of our own generation, the experience of personal confrontation with Jesus Christ has given light and power to a previously existing intellectual and moral structure that, though the vital structural elements were there, contained no true life and little spiritual joy. Because such evangelized Catholics had learned something of the meaning of absolutes, of authority, and obedience in a less than evangelical context, they joyfully made the transference to a gospel that is genuinely true, not just "religiously" true, to a God who is living Author, not merely deduced First Cause, and to an obedience that endures beyond the high points of emotional self-surrender.

Yet it goes without saying — certainly before a Protestant audience — that the same traditionalism that can ideally cherish and preserve biblical teachings can also conceal and deaden them. Thus for the evangelical Protestant, as for the evangelically-moved Catholic, traditionalism, like liberalization, has two faces. Much attention, justifiably, has been devoted to the positive aspects of liberalization and biblical transformation within Catholicism. Because an inestimably large number of serious Roman Catholics remain more firmly attached to traditionalism than to liberalization or biblical transformation, and because this attachment can have either positive or negative effects, it is appropriate to consider the question of evangelical dialogue with traditional, conservative Catholics and Catholicism.

TWO TYPES OF "DIALOGUE"
During the early days of the Reformation, there was little that corresponded to what we now mean by dialogue — an exchange of views tending towards mutual appreciation and understanding with

no real expectation that the views of either party will be substantially modified. The age of the Reformation was less concerned with finding a *modus vivendi* than with finding truth. The great encounters of that age were polemical and ended more often with anathemas than with "joint communiqués." They were termed "disputations" or at best "colloquies," and only in rare cases did they end on a note of mutual felicitation. Although in some cases the ostensible purpose of the disputation or colloquy was to convince one's counterpart of his error in order to be reunited with him, in most cases it was simply to show the wrongness of the opponent's views and hence to justify one's own view and separation from him. To the extent that our understanding of gospel faith corresponds to its rediscovery in the Reformation era, and the traditionalist Catholic's religious system to its rejection, or at least substantial modification in Tridentine Catholicism, there remains a legitimate place for evangelical Protestant-Roman Catholic disputation today. Dialogue in the form of disputation can certainly be abused, or become abusive, but it can also serve two legitimate purposes. To the extent that contemporary traditional Catholicism still exhibits the characteristic of its Renaissance predecessor, namely, an intolerable adulteration of biblical content with more or less poorly Christianized humanism and rationalism of pagan origin, disputation is necessary to set forth and protect what is specifically evangelical and therefore vital in our own religious thought and life. And to the extent that the traditionalist Catholic genuinely seeks truth that is intellectually defensible on the basis of authority worthy of respect, he may be challenged, helped and perhaps even persuaded by a clear contrast between biblical and traditional Catholic views.

Dialogue as Disputation

Nevertheless, dialogue in the sense of disputation remains largely concerned with defending one's own position or forcing one's opponent to surrender his. In this sense, its value is largely intellectual and educational. We disdain neither the intellect nor the educational process. Yet, while proclaiming their importance, we would acknowledge their limits. One may intellectually grasp the content of a truth being propounded and yet not "know the truth"; indeed, one may even know the truth in some sense and yet not obey it.

Dialogue as Evangelization

To the extent that what a practicing Roman Catholic believes falls short of being evangelical, in the sense that it is not true to the gospel — and surely the most common divergence on the part of active Catholics is what we may call the Galatian error, that is, adding works to faith as a condition of salvation — then the desired result of an effective "disputation" with him would not be his "refutation" but an evangelical awakening and conversion. Formerly such awakening and conversion seemed automatically to require the Catholic to leave his old church and join an evangelical fellowship. This was clearly evangelization. Indeed, in past decades it was not at all unusual for a Catholic who began to entertain an evangelical understanding of the Christian faith to be forced out of the Roman church. Today, very little such pressure is put on evangelically awakened Catholics by their church. If the Roman Catholic Church is not in a position to discipline priests, or even professors of theology who appear to be theological liberals and moral relativists and to reject some of the fundamental truths and most basic moral obligations of Christian faith, it is not apt to take steps against those who are merely evangelically inclined.

And were they to leave, where would we wish them to go? Many of the churches that grew out of the Reformation have moved so far away from biblical authority and the central doctrines of Scripture that to join one of them might prove far more dangerous to an evangelically converted Catholic than to remain within his own "Catholic" fold. (In this context, as a practical matter we should note that most serious Roman Catholics, even the more sophisticated ones who have a fair notion of Protestant theology, simply are not aware of the way Protestants differ from one another. They know that there are "liberals" and "fundamentalists," and may even recognize "evangelicals," but tend to think that the differences are to be found in denominational labels, rather than where they are really to be found — in congregations or even individual believers.) Thus today dialogue can have an evangelistic impact on the people involved, even though the Catholic participants may never see the need of formally repudiating the Roman Catholic doctrinal structure or of breaking with the Roman church.

DIALOGUE AS DISPUTATION:
PERSISTENT CONFLICTS

One reason for continuing the "old" dispute with Catholicism is that so many — perhaps the great majority — of today's

Catholics are spiritually neither "liberalized" nor "evangelized" but simply old-fashioned Catholics. They may not believe very intensely or practice very consistently, but what they do vaguely believe or sporadically practice is not the religion of Karl Rahner, Hans Küng, or Leslie Dewart. So we continue the dialogue in its old form in part because so many Catholics — not the *avant-garde*, but quite possibly the main force — will still be affected by it.

Secondly, Roman Catholicism did not become the most pervasive interpretation of Christianity simply through a series of historical accidents. It represents a natural, albeit subevangelical, response to the concreteness of the gospel message. Even if the Catholic Church as it exists today were to vanish, the religious phenomenon of Catholicism would probably reappear, precisely for this reason.

The fundamental differences raised between Roman Catholicism and evangelical Protestantism over the centuries remain with us today. As has been repeatedly emphasized, there have been no official changes in Roman Catholic doctrine as a result of Vatican II.[2] Indeed, post-Vatican II Catholicism has not repudiated the two nineteenth- and twentieth-century developments that, formally speaking, moved the modern Catholic Church farther away from biblical Protestantism than it was in the Reformation era: papal infallibility (1870) and Mariology (immaculate conception, 1854; bodily assumption, 1950). Admittedly most Roman Catholics have greatly modified their stand on these doctrines, and disregard them or minimize their importance. However, what was wrong in both the papal and Marian developments remains a feature of Catholicism today: the excessive humanizing of authority on the one hand and of the work of redemption on the other. Indeed, these tendencies are also found among evangelicals. Hence it cannot be irrelevant to continue to examine them and seek to counteract them. We cannot make the mistake of viewing them merely as intellectual problems of historical analysis; they are spiritual problems affecting our faith and obedience today.

Authority

The spark that ignited the Reformation was John Tetzel's hawking of indulgences on Martin Luther's doorstep. The conflict Tetzel aroused quickly came to focus not on the indulgences as such, but on the source of the power to grant them, that is, on the authority of the church, and more specifically of the pope, as opposed to the sufficiency of Scripture alone.

The conflict took place on two levels: on the theoretical level, it was *sola Scriptura* against *Scriptura et traditione* as the source of revelation. On the practical level, Scripture stood against the institutions of the papacy and hierarchy, specifically against their interpretation of the "power of the keys" to bind men's lives and determine their destiny. The mere statement of these two aspects of the conflict illuminates both the attraction and the weakness of the simple evangelical position vis-à-vis the complexity of Catholicism: one Protestant constant, Scripture, against two Catholic variables, tradition and hierarchy. The Reformation is often described — particularly by evangelicals in democracies owing dues to secular conceptions of liberty — as a struggle for "freedom of conscience." In one very important sense, this description fits. Man is free indeed only when the Son has made him free, and the Reformation made possible direct access to the Son through the Word. But in another sense "conscience" was precisely *not* freed, but made captive — in Luther's terminology, "captive to the Word of God." Vis-à-vis Catholicism, this recourse to "Scripture alone" must appear austere, uñimaginative, and constricting. The thin line of biblical relevation is opposed to the amplitude of tradition and the human expansiveness of papacy and hierarchy.

1. Scripture and Tradition

The Council of Trent saw itself forced to oppose the Reformers' emphasis on the sovereign authority of Scripture by distinguishing between Scripture and tradition and placing them on a level of equality as sources of doctrine. This constituted a drastic mutation of the early church view of tradition. Then tradition meant "faithful handing over," and its chief task was precisely the transmission of the authentic Scriptures. When the Roman church, in 1517 and afterwards, faced the need to defend nonscriptural beliefs and practices, it was forced into a downgrading of Scripture to second place as the source and norm of truth. To illustrate, note that even its apparently clearest statements, such as the command for all to partake of both elements (Matt. 26:26-28), could be — and were — subjected to an ecclesiastical "interpretation" that effectively undid them: communion in only one element became and remains Catholic practice. Particularly during the twentieth century, now that it is no longer so necessary to defend themselves against Protestant attacks, Catholic writers stress the uniqueness of Scripture, saying, for example, that "only" Scripture constitutes "intrinsic and immediate evidence of God himself."[3] Yet nowhere in modern Catholicism, and certainly not in traditional Catholicism, is Scripture really the *norma normans*; it remains the norm that needs another norm to interpret it. The increasing Catholic interest in the Bible and acknowledgment of its authority still fall short of acceptance of Luther's principle, *sola Scriptura*. It remains *"Scriptura et...."*

In our day, a paradoxical situation has arisen: Catholic interest in the Bible has grown to an unprecedented extent, but the result is not what evangelicals expected. It has not produced widespread defection among Catholics or mass conversions to Protestantism in any form. Thus the time-honored Protestant conviction that the way to win (proselytize) Roman Catholics is to "get them into the Bible" is not proving true. At least it is not working out that way. Catholics are regularly urged by their church to read the Bible and to adopt other formal and informal devotional practices previously typical of Protestantism; they join Bible studies and prayer groups, but not Protestant churches.

In the past, Catholics imagined that they could not be gripped by the authority of the Bible without losing confidence in the authority of their church. Today they have lost the sense that *sola Scriptura* necessarily means *dum non per traditiones ecclesiae*. In this sense the very openness of contemporary Catholics, their new willingness to hear authorities besides their own after centuries of jealous sole allegiance, makes it hard for them to recognize the exclusive claims of Scripture as the "only perfect rule of faith and practice." In effect, they accept its claim to be "supreme" as they now accept the papacy — as one "supreme" among many.

From this perspective, it seems that the Scripture-tradition argument is hard to "win," either in the disputational sense of persuading the Catholic to abandon extrabiblical authorities, or in the evangelistic one of leading him to a confident trust in the full sufficiency — a necessary pleonasm — of the truths the Bible proclaims. Today, instead of downgrading the Bible, the authorities of Catholicism exalt it. This makes it hard to use the Bible to discredit them with the charge that they set themselves up in opposition to it. Furthermore, within Protestantism — taken in the general sense — the authority of the Bible is so widely disregarded that evangelicals must appreciate the high (if not altogether supreme) place Catholics have always accorded it in theory and now increasingly in practice. Today, Catholics are generally losing their zeal for the absolute, monarchial authority of the pope and the ecclesiastical magisterium in matters of doctrine. At the same time the concept of tradition is being modified to accord at least a relative pre-eminence to Scripture. It seems unproductive to engage in a major struggle for the sole sufficiency of Scripture against tradition when Catholics themselves seem unwilling to fight for tradition. Instead, it is increasingly important in dialogue with contemporary conservative Catholics to guard against the danger that they may accept biblical authority as too many Protestants do: as culturally conditioned, relative, and fallible. Persuading Catholics to abandon Scripture-and-tradition as authoritative may not give them the more trustworthy authority of Scripture alone: it may just leave them without authority. The argument, Scripture alone or Scripture-and-tradition, generally will not be perceived by Catholics as a matter of principle worth fighting about. Most contemporary Catholics, like most other late-twentieth-century men and women, do not think in such abstract categories. If they can once be persuaded that Scripture is reliable and sufficient, they may come to see that to add tradition to Scripture is superfluous, long before understanding — if ever they do — that such addition in essence negates the principle of the authority of Scripture.

2. Scripture and Ecclesiastical Authority

Tradition is too vague and ill-defined today for a sharp conflict with Scripture. The primary area in which contemporary conservative Catholics are apt to feel the conflict between divine, that is, biblical authority, and the authority of human ecclesiastical institutions, is the place at which those institutions seek to bind one's conscience and to treat indifferent or doubtful matters as vital, certain, and required. The Roman church, which in principle has abandoned not one of its fundamental theological or ethical positions, has softened much in practice. It now seldom places the serious Catholic in a situation such as the young Luther faced when he felt that the demands of his church were beyond him and when, far from assurance of forgiveness, he was sure that God condemned him.

It would no longer correspond to the experience of most Catholics to charge Catholicism in general, as Jesus did the Pharisees in Matthew 23:4, with laying unbearably heavy burdens on those most eager to be disciples. The easing of the obligations placed on the serious Catholic by his church (for example, the relaxation of church laws on Sunday worship and Friday abstinence) reduces the old tension between the relative simplicity of the gospel and the complexity of the Catholic way of salvation. The present situation may incline many Catholics to wonder why evangelicals persist in holding to moral absolutes explicitly set forth in Scripture, when in the name of liberalization they have relativized their own standards. Evangelicals are challenged to learn how to argue against the observance of unnecessary and un-biblical standards without accidentally persuading Catholics that no absolute standards exist at all.

3. Catholic Appreciation of Authority

The positive feature in all this is that despite the weakening in-fluence of modern trends, a traditional Catholic often is better prepared to understand biblical concepts of authority than is a typical European or American Protestant. He habitually thinks of God as a person, not as a philosophical postulate, and understands that if such a person is really there, He has the inherent right to command absolute obedience and unadulterated worship. The traditional Catholic's sense of awe and even plain fear before the majesty and justice of God are great assets in an age that trivializes everything. When a Catholic through faith in the sufficiency of the finished work of Christ learns to see the God he instinctively dreaded as a loving Father, he has understood something magnificent, something that liberal Protestants may have much more difficulty in grasping. The Protestant brought up on the com-fortable platitudes of liberalism naturally regards both God and himself as too good and tolerant to have a serious and lasting disagreement: hence he may never possess that fear of the Lord which is the beginning of wisdom. The difficulty in dealing with the Catholic who has been brought in great fear of God is to get from fear to wisdom and from wisdom to love.

Justification

Older and more recent treatments of the controversy between evangelical and Catholic religion virtually all have in common a major emphasis on the Catholic versus the Reformation (or evangelical) concept of justification. All Christians agree that "all have sinned, and come short of the glory of God," and all acknowledge that the work of Christ gained for us the possibility of forgiveness and restoration. But do we appropriate this work and apply it to ourselves? Classical Reformation polemics saw in Catholic teaching and practice a nonevangelical view of human merit. (Such teaching assumed that if it was not possible to earn salvation outright, it was at least possible to cooperate in a significant way in gaining it.) The gospel doctrine of salvation is precisely that it is free, not earned or merited.

The evangelical concept of justification by faith, even in the sharpened formulation of Luther, "by faith alone," is not altogether foreign to Catholicism at any period in its development. As Vittorio Subilia points out in his discussion of Barth's criticism of the Catholic doctrine of justification as "another gospel," the Council of Trent explicitly followed Augustine in stating, "None of the precursors of justification, either faith or works, merit justification."[4]

Although justification is the theoretical problem, the point at which to challenge conservative Catholicism probably lies for us today with the problem of whether man even wants to try to merit justification. Church historians know that both early and later Catholicism repeatedly rejected Pelagianism, at least formally. Yet it is undeniable that modern popular Catholicism, like some forms of liberal Protestantism, in practice stresses good works to the extent of making them appear a means of earning grace (if we may use such self-contradictory terminology) rather than a grateful response to it. At an earlier stage in religious history, the requirements of Catholic obedience were so heavy, but yielded so little assurance, that Catholics could turn to the Reformation's *sola fide* as a liberation. Today, by contrast, the fact that *sola fide* requires clarity about faith seems a burden rather than a blessing.

1. The Objectivity of Justification

In the Reformation era, and in the naive Protestant understanding of the Reformation struggle, Catholicism often seemed earthy, legalistic, corporeal, while Protestantism appeared transcendent, generous, spiritual. To the countless exercises, prayers, confessions, absolutions, and penances the Catholic associated with becoming justified in God's sight, the Lutheran and the Calvinist posited justification by faith. But the Reformation idea of justification was precisely that of a *substantial* change: man, a sinner, becomes something that he was not, just and acceptable in God's sight. The fact that this transformation is God's work, not man's, means that we can rely on it. In the sixteenth century, the Catholic was afraid of hell, which he felt was his probable destination. Evangelical teaching about objective justification gave believers assurance of salvation. Today the Catholic, especially if he is more or less observant, tends to feel that most people will "make it" somehow — a logical consequence of the implicit or explicit universalism of much contemporary religion. At this point the evangelical may find it necessary to preach the full severity of the law as part of the gospel in order for people to recognize that as their fallen condition is objective (not just a way of looking at reality), so too their restoration must be objective.

2. The Process of Sanctification

The attempt to obey God and to lead a life of recognizably Christian tenor comes, in evangelical theology, under the heading of consequences of or responses to forgiveness. The relative simplicity of the biblical moral precepts should not obscure the difficulty of keeping them. Traditionally, Catholics — who regarded such obedience as in some sense a prerequisite of grace, rather than its product — have made the effort to obey a complex set of rules. Today, with an increasing awareness of the evangelical contention that one is "justified by faith, apart from the works of the law," Catholics may entirely overlook the fact that while justification is simple, sanctification is a complex process constantly requiring their best efforts. Contrasted with the Pelagian optimism of an earlier era, the modern Catholic may feel that a life of true obedience is beyond his capacity. Such a sentiment is more akin to the passivity of mid-century neo-orthodoxy than to the dynamism of evangelical faith, which sees liberation from dead works as freedom to serve the living God.

Other Mediators

In sixteenth-century Catholicism, there was a great struggle to preserve the legitimacy of the saints as mediators (literally, *intercessors*, a distinction that does not resolve the problem). The culmination of this struggle came in the promulgation of the dogma that Mary, because her flesh was too pure to warrant corruption, was assumed bodily into heaven. Various teachings that have encouraged and confirmed the idea that access to God is complex and dangerous, and not to be lightly ventured, promoted a reliance on mediators and intercessors. Unfortunately the generalized Catholic devaluation of the idea that such mediators are necessary may lead to a downgrading of the concept of the mediator as essential. Here the problem is to get rid of a host of unnecessary intermediaries without losing sight of the one who *is* necessary. Mary, the saints, papal and hierarchical authority may be considered under this heading of unnecessary intermediaries.

DIALOGUE AS EVANGELIZATION

A comprehensive list of the *quaestiones disputatae* would far exceed the scope of this presentation. In addition, it would detract from consideration of what must be the concluding element in any discussion of evangelical-Catholic dialogue. If we look away from the legitimate desire to defend the faith against misrepresentation and attack, and from the understandable although uncommendable desire to vindicate one's own position and contest one's opponent, we will see that while other categories may be added, the headings of authority, justification, and other mediators cover many of the most important conflicts between Roman Catholicism and biblical Protestantism.

For the purposes of our discussion, these three headings also serve admirably to indicate the points at which the evangelical in dialogue must persuade — if not "refute" — his Catholic partner in order to achieve the evangelistic purpose of which we have spoken.

The great charm of Catholicism vis-à-vis Protestantism lies in its richness. But it is precisely this richness — some human beings as vicars or vice-gerents of Christ, heavenly intercessors and earthly absolvers, stand between the sinner and the anger or forgiveness of God — that prevents many Catholics from grasping the fact that the gospel gives us not merely the one thing needful, but the one thing adequate: personal access to Jesus Christ, "advocate with the Father," and "the only Mediator between God and man."

With an awareness of the availability and adequacy of such mediation may come a perception of the unconditional graciousness of justification through the finished work of Christ — recognition that the initial, crucial stage in the process of restoration is accomplished, and that the believer may have assurance concerning the ultimate outcome.

This narrowing of the Catholic field of vision to one Mediator (Christ) and to one effective justification may facilitate concentration on a sole source of authority — the austere but constant Scripture (in contrast to the many voices of a millennia-old teaching authority). Again, what is at stake is less the legitimacy of biblical authority, which Catholics have always recognized, than its sufficiency. And it is precisely in this narrowing and concentration, if it is achieved, that dialogue with Catholics will be evangelistic. The goodness of the news of the Reformation rediscovery of the gospel lay precisely in its dependability, regardless of the distractions of a rich, complex and subtle religious tradition. Catholics who today discover the uniqueness of the only Mediator, the definiteness and completeness of justification through Him, and the sufficiency of a sole, circumscribed, and yet altogether trustworthy and adequate authority, will have experienced effective evangelization regardless of how they respond in terms of doctrinal reformulation or denominational realignment.

FOOTNOTES

1. George Tyrrell, *Through Scylla and Charybdis* (London: Longman, Green, 1907), p. 73.

2. E.g., Wolfgang Dietzfelbinger, *The Roman Catholic Church Today: A Protestant View* (London: Lutterworth, 1970), p. 13. Cf. Vittorio Subilia, *The Problem of Catholicism* (London: SCM, 1964), p. 31.

3. Hans Küng, *Rechtfertigung — Die Lehre Karl Barths und eine Katholische Besinnung* (Einsiedeln, Johannesverlag, 1957), pp. 116ff., cited in Subilia, *Problem*, p. 37.

4. Subilia, *Problem*, pp. 39-40, citing Heinrich Denziger, *Enchiridion Symbolorum* (Freiburg im Breisgau, Barcelona: Herder 1952 ed.), p. 801.

RESPONSE / Wade T. Coggins

Dr. Wells articulates two very sound and valid concerns about possible cooperative evangelism with neo-Catholics who are "gospel-minded":

(1) "The biblical Word must be seen as exclusively authoritative both for the content of the evangel and for the methods of evangelism."

(2) "The nature of divine forgiveness, its means and its methods, must reflect faithfully the apostolic teaching."

Clear guidance on how to apply these fine ideals at the cutting edge of evangelism fails to materialize, however, as the paper concludes with the question still unresolved: "We risk much by failing to explore the relationship with Catholicism: we risk much when we do so."

Perhaps part of the dilemma lies in the nature of the opening proposition of the paper. What kind of "joint evangelistic ventures between evangelical Protestants and gospel-minded Catholics" is envisioned? If the proposition speaks of formal relationship, the cautions are realistic and can be discussed by the parties seeking to form the relationship.

It seems probable, however, that most missionaries, national pastors and laymen will come at the question of evangelism and neo-Catholicism from a wide range of situations, few of which will allow for discussion with church officials about the nature of forgiveness. Much of the concern arises rather at the personal level as the worker asks, "Shall I accept an invitation to teach a Catholic study group, knowing that the chances are high that they will continue to be Catholics?" Or, "Is it an acceptable goal to evangelize them without insisting that they sever relations with the Catholic Church?" Or, "What should my response be to a 'gospel-minded' priest who wants help in planning and leading Bible study groups related to his parish?" Opportunities of this informal variety are extremely widespread today. Missionary Paul Lewis in Anapolis,

Goias, Brazil surveyed a class of college-level young people (94 percent Catholic) and found that 97 percent had an interest in studying the Bible in small groups.

Dr. Wells observes that "Catholics are less knowledgeable about the contents of the Bible than churchgoers in any of the main Protestant denominations." This need for greater Bible knowledge and the interest in Bible study groups combine to offer a great opportunity for those in a position to teach. The missionary, pastor or layman who sees interest and need will likely accept the challenge to teach a study group. This tends to happen without any formal arrangement or any attempt to understand the theories of justification and forgiveness. Of course, it is hoped that this will lead to a practical acceptance of justification.

After acknowledging the reality of the dilemma with which Dr. Wells closes, we need to press on to think of the many directions in which cooperation between evangelism and neo-Catholicism might lead. It is a day of great opportunity. The combination of need and interest present in the new Catholic reality might well lead evangelicals to pour great effort and resources into teaching Catholics in Bible study groups.

Paul Lewis (the missionary in Brazil referred to earlier) reports that Catholic leaders put on a drive to encourage Bible reading in the state of Minas Gerais. They succeeded so well that 20,000 Bibles stocked in the local bookstores were sold out during the opening days of the campaign.

Wells rightly warns that Catholics who transfer their loyalty away from an authoritarian church to the Scripture may be highly vulnerable to secular influences. Studies which acquaint them with the Bible and its claims can serve them well in weathering this storm.

While Bible study groups have been used to illustrate some of the points of this discussion, it is obvious that efforts in a multitude of fields are having a great evangelistic impact on neo-Catholics: literature, broadcasting, campaigns, cooperative city-wide efforts, to name only a few.

Perhaps we can seek to provide some guidelines for informal situations as well as for formal "joint evangelistic ventures." These guidelines could help the front-line Christian who must work through such problems without the counsel of theologians.

RESPONSE / Philip E. Armstrong

Let us apply the studies on evangelism and neo-Catholicism to the Philippines as an example of the issues faced by evangelicals engaged in church planting in a Catholic country. The Philippines called itself the only Christian nation in Asia, yet the quality of religious devotion was almost medieval. Since Vatican II, however, the climate has totally changed. Outsiders cannot conceive the present open attitude toward non-Catholics and toward Bible reading which was virtually forbidden before the council. That same openness has produced a theological spectrum that often outstrips the liberalism of ecumenical Protestants. Along with a genuine spiritual awakening have come new theological conflicts involving, among other things, the secularization of a church isolated from society, the humanization of Marcos' "new Filipino," and liberation theology.

Protestant reaction has varied. Some feel Rome will never change; some are actively working with and within the church. Most are looking for guidance. These are the issues we face:

(1) Numbers of Roman Catholics are experiencing the new birth and a deep assurance of their salvation that was unknown before. Previously one could assume their ignorance of biblical conversion. But, now that there are born-again believers within the Roman Catholic Church, the spiritual state of each individual must be evaluated separately. Though this is going to be difficult, it is essential.

(2) Evangelizing individual Catholics presents no problem. But difficulties arise when a missionary engaged in church planting intends to gather a group of converted Roman Catholics to form an evangelical church.

(3) We must look carefully at true Protestant distinctives if we expect the Catholics to find a biblical basis for separation from their church.

(4) Dialogue, which prior to Vatican II was impossible in coun-

tries where Catholics constituted a majority, is now essential.

(a) Dialogue will force us to sharpen our own biblical perspective of unbridgeable differences, helping us to avoid the syncretism that has characterized Catholicism's missionary strategy in the past three hundred years.

(b) Dialogue will provide a platform for proclamation based on current needs felt by the Catholic people at a time when the monolithic viewpoint of Catholic theology is no longer realistic.

(c) Dialogue will enable us to identify error, against which we must speak out if we are to point men to Christ with integrity. We must be set for the defense of the gospel as well as for proclamation.

(5) The average Catholic is confused by the erosion of unquestioned authority within the Catholic hierarchy. Previously he was not allowed to read the Scripture; now that it is available there are nagging questions as to its authenticity. Tradition, upon which much of Catholic commitment was based, is being constantly re-examined. Our confidence in the authority of the Scripture demands a new commitment to integrity in biblical interpretation as well as preaching. With such a commitment an uncompromising message could produce a significant impact on the whole of Catholicism.

(6) Evangelicals have a present occasion for aggressive evangelism that may not come again. By the next generation the theological confusion and liberal thought of the younger clergy may well spoil the present hunger of masses of Catholic people throughout the world.

(7) Recognizing the present work of the Holy Spirit within the Roman Church, and the opposition of the enemy to that work, the entire evangelical church should in this unique age pray that the Word of God may have free course and that the Holy Spirit may guide the Catholics into all truth.

RESPONSE / Gilbert A. Peterson

The deep desire of many evangelicals is to multiply the number of outreaches in evangelism. They are seeking new opportunities to develop every avenue of discussion with those who appear to be receptive. Further, many evangelicals are increasingly weary of the dividing of ranks that has taken place over the years, many times over personal and political concerns rather than over serious doctrinal differences.

Against this backdrop arise apparent opportunities for greater rapport and rapprochement with those who are sounding what appear to be new trumpets in the land. The trumpets, however, have an uncertain sound as the players are not united under a common director, nor do they seem to be playing the same tune.

In his incisive paper, Dr. Wells analyzes the issues by providing a carefully documented account of the historical developments and trends in American Catholicism since Vatican II. Next, he appropriately raises both the historical precedents and doctrinal issues that are determinative in this contemporary consideration.

The authority of Scripture is rightfully seen as a primary issue. Unless there is true common ground on this subject, all other discussion becomes subjective and relativistic. Finding that common ground will tend to be difficult for laymen because of well-established tradition, behavioral habits, and the very spirit of the present age which tends to foster rebellion against all forms of authority.

The doctrine of justification is also correctly identified by Dr. Wells as a stumbling block to effective dialogue, cooperation, and spiritual fellowship. Without unequivocal agreement on the historic orthodox position of this key doctrine there cannot be meaningful dialogue or even basic communication. Semantics must not be taken lightly at this juncture, as the meaning of the terms used is the difference between true agreement and supposed agreement.

Dr. Brown's presentation reaffirms both the difficulty and danger of anticipating that the dramatic changes occurring in Catholicism signal a coming together of evangelicals and modern-day American Catholics. In fact, the opposite appears to be occurring. New freedom within Catholicism is not making it easier for evangelicals to "win" Catholics to a knowledge of the truth. Rather, new freedom appears to be causing Catholics to find new expressions within the general framework of Roman Catholicism, and most often without the benefit of a grounding in biblical doctrine. Brown shows that this freedom may be leading in the wrong direction. Liberation from strict adherence to a set of regulations handed down from above and unquestioningly obeyed may not produce freedom in Christ, but rather freedom from Christ.

The shifting sands of Catholic theology may well call for evangelicals to reassess their actual or intended approaches to Roman Catholics and to do their homework even more carefully. Opportunities for evangelism do exist, but like Alice going through the looking glass, evangelicals may well find that the present distortions and modifications in Catholicism are more difficult to understand and to handle than the situation prevailing in the past.

My colleagues are to be commended for their insightful, persuasive, and scholarly approach to this critical question. The winds of change are indeed blowing across the land and we are indebted to these scholars for showing us the direction of these changes.

REPLY / David F. Wells

I am most grateful for the kind reception accorded my paper both by the respondents and the audience. Their comments and questions have been helpful in focusing attention on how to translate theory into practice as well as the problems involved in so doing.

I could wish, too, that there were some simple rules resulting in a set form of procedure which would cover each and every situation in which Protestant meets Catholic. Unfortunately such rules no more exist than does the pot of gold at the end of the rainbow. What we are therefore obliged to do is to apply the principles of Scripture to each situation in which we find ourselves, treating each case on its own merits. To this end, may I clarify a little more some of the ingredients which should become a part of our reflections?

(1) It is important to remember that the church is Christ's and not our own, bought with His blood and not paid for by our efforts. We are but His co-workers. Our task, then, is not to tell God what He can or cannot do, but in humility to ask Him what He is doing and to make us a part of it. I imagine that the Holy Spirit might be more adventurous than some of us who believe that a person almost has to become a Protestant to be saved and less adventurous than those who see salvation under every green bush in the land.

(2) It is with the truth question alone that we are concerned. Our task is to bring Catholics to Christ, not particularly to Protestantism. Northern Ireland is a standing reminder of the folly of "converting" Catholics to Protestantism and Protestants to Catholicism, for I suspect that Christ is no better known than He was before the strife. I believe that we ought to do our utmost to prevent the truth of the gospel from becoming just another part of the sectarian differences.

(3) We cannot assume that our love of truth and of God's people is greater than His. If He has indeed regenerated a Catholic

it would be unwise to think this was an error. On the other hand, we should not assume that the work of the Spirit within some Catholics is a divine validation of Catholicism. We must maintain a balance between these two positions.

(4) That new converts are prone to make errors, believe falsehoods, and fluctuate in their faith even to the point of backsliding, should be taken as axiomatic. The task of the missionary, then, is no different from that of the pastor. Once a person has crossed the threshold of justification, the missionary is to bring him prayerfully to a greater Christian self-consciousness through the use of the biblical Word. As a Catholic grows in his Christian life, he will become more aware that there are contradictions between the teaching of Scripture and that of his church. The tension will be resolved only by his leaving the church or deliberately working for reform within it. I therefore assent to the paradox that while there are Catholics who are Christians, there are few Christians who are Catholics.

(5) Jesus declared Christians to be the salt and light of the world. The question arises: How can we be salt and light to Catholics? A convert might find more support and nourishment for his faith in some Catholic churches than he would in some Protestant churches. There is no difference in principle between the problem faced by the missionary and that faced by Christians at home. There are no formulae that comprehend all situations, no rules of thumb that guarantee an effective communication of biblical truth without antagonizing the audience or exposing the Christian to the danger of compromise. The awkward choice into which we are sometimes forced is that some would prefer to suffer the hostility of others than to compromise, while others would prefer to compromise slightly in order to avert antagonism. Neither of the alternatives is a happy one: we have to find ways of holding forth the truth so winsomely that it provokes no justifiable ill will, despite the fact that it is unvarnished and undominished biblical truth that we are proclaiming. Reverend fathers, do you know of any rules of thumb that would guarantee the success of this difficult venture?

REPLY / Harold O. J. Brown

Gilbert Peterson's comments on both papers are so kind and irenic that the only appropriate response is a word of gratitude. Wade Coggins draws attention to the possibility of outreach through Bible study groups involving Roman Catholics but leaves open the serious question as to how to handle those Catholics who may be awakened to an evangelical faith in such an ecumenical group. No doubt the greater tolerance of Roman Catholicism to nontraditional ways of religious expression within its own ranks will make it easy for such evangelical Catholics to remain within the Catholic fold. But at some point there must be a biblically-based doctrinal critique of unreformed, subevangelical elements in Catholicism.

Philip Armstrong, from the perspective of work in a non-Western, yet heavily Roman Catholic culture, sees conflict arising when evangelicals seek to plant new evangelical churches rather than simply create an evangelical base within the Roman *ecclesia*. He addresses himself to the need for separation, a question with which I feel the rest of us have failed to deal. However, this is an unresolved problem within Protestantism as well — many Protestant denominations are no more evangelical and scriptural than the Roman Church as a whole. Armstrong also has properly registered the progressive deterioration of much of Catholicism as it slides past evangelicalism into liberalism and secularized theology.

In retrospect I think that we have too much neglected the question of potential conflict between evangelical church growth through proselytism of Catholics and "revival" within Catholicism. To go from a commitment to church planting and church growth to satisfaction with giving a more evangelical tone to existing Catholic institutions would be to abandon one of the major standards by which we can check and secure our progress in the propagation of the gospel. It also would undermine missionary enthusiasm and, to a lesser extent, the evangelistic efforts of local churches. There can be no doubt that the Holy Spirit is at work within the Roman Church, but it is often hard for us as non-Romans to separate the wheat from the chaff.

Both David Wells' paper and mine were tentative, yet cautiously optimistic, an attitude also mirrored in the responses.

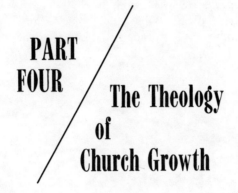

PART
FOUR

The Theology
of
Church Growth

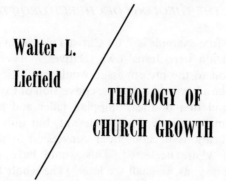

**Walter L.
Liefield**

THEOLOGY OF
CHURCH GROWTH

THE IMPORTANCE OF BIBLICAL FOUNDATIONS

The significance and contribution of the church growth movement are so well known, and its theological principles so often challenged and defended, that any further discussion must either be comprehensive — and, hence, far beyond the limits of this paper — or extremely selective. Obviously the latter course must be followed here. Further, the discussion over the past years has resulted in modifications and corrections so that some earlier assumptions need not be addressed. The term *people movements* has, for example, come under criticism and, therefore, has been largely displaced by the term *multi-individual conversion*. This lessens, though it does not eliminate, the need to discuss the problems inherent in the former term. Nevertheless, certain assumptions tend to persist even through such modifications, and whether or not the present construction is satisfactory there still remain basic biblical issues to be considered.

This paper addresses itself not so much to the church growth movement or even to its "theology," as to the underlying biblical issues. It has been observed that the best church growth literature has sought the support of Scripture, although it has been charged that "most of Church Growth missiology's theological bases have been worked out *after* the methodological insights and mission principles were arrived at through field observation and experience."[1] A recent small work by J. Robertson McQuilkin, *How Biblical Is the Church Growth Movement?*, is oriented, as the title indicates, to an evaluation of the movement rather than to a study of the basic biblical data.[2] I do not wish to criticize this book or its approach. Nevertheless, it illustrates what I see as a basic problem, namely, that even in such a work there is a tendency to *use* Scripture rather than to *study* it. For example, in dealing with the concept of "multi-individual interdependent decisions," Scripture is introduced in support of the proposition that God deals with groups. The first example is: "Of Christ's twelve disciples, a rather large proportion were Jesus' own relatives."[3] This assertion and its application to the present issue would be difficult to support biblically. The author next cites the conversion of Cornelius and his household and that of the Philippian jailer and his household. These examples are indeed very relevant, but unfortunately, the further implications of household conversion in the context of Roman society are neglected. This would have supported the author's premise, as we shall see later. (The whole background is available in Michael Green's *Evangelism in the Early Church.*[4]) Again I must emphasize that I am not offering a criticism of McQuilkin's work but rather trying to indicate the need to go further and study the biblical data in their own context.

A final example from the same paragraph in McQuilkin's work is his statement that Paul did not bring the message to a city "on an individual house-by-house visitation program but by approaching the synagogue." Acts 20:20, where Paul says that he had taught "publicly and from house to house," is not mentioned. It is possible that McQuilkin does not consider teaching to be evangelism, and therefore thinks this verse is irrelevant. If that were his assumption, however, it could be challenged biblically.

My first conclusion, therefore, is simply that much work needs to be done in the primary study of biblical texts which relate to church growth. This study must take into account the social and cultural background of the biblical context. I urge this not so as to find the movement or its literature in error, but rather in order that the work of God might proceed on a biblical foundation.

The balance of the present study will be structured around several major topics relevant to the church growth movement. If, on occasion, criticism is offered of the exegetical conclusions of church growth leaders, it is with the humble realization that they have been caught up in a great movement for which they have sought biblical points of reference. Those who have written are not primarily exegetes, as I am not a missiologist. This paper is only an attempt by one member of the body of Christ to help other members for the ultimate glory of the Head of the body, Christ our Lord.

MULTI-INDIVIDUAL DECISIONS
Terminology
Several issues seem to have risen to the surface. They are intertwined with each other and, hence, difficult to discuss in

isolation. Some also are connected with the older term *people movements*. Although some of the misconceptions associated with that term have been cleared up, a seemingly erroneous understanding of the great commission has persisted. In his pioneering work, *The Bridges of God,* Donald McGavran said, "The Greek word translated 'nation' in the English Bible means exactly 'people' in the sense in which we are using that term."[5] He earlier defined people as "a social organism which, by virtue of the fact that its members intermarry very largely within its own confines, becomes a separate race in their minds."[6] Unfortunately this idea, which we consider to be a misunderstanding, was perpetuated some fifteen years later in McGavran's work, *Understanding Church Growth.*[7] There he says:

> Coming to the New Testament, we note that Matthew 28:19 instructs Christians to *disciple the tribes.* In Hindi, the national language of India, the words read *jatiyon ko chela karo,* i.e., "disciple the castes" — a much more accurate rendering of the Greek than the common English version "to make disciples of the nations."[8]

McGavran goes on to further define the term as "the castes and families of mankind," and the "multitudinous peoples of the Gentiles."[9] This last description is closer than the others. The term translated "nations" in various versions of Matthew 28:19, including the recent New International Version, is not the anthropological kind of term which McGavran supposes. The word, of course, is *ethnē.* In the Septuagint it often simply means "Gentiles" and may be simply "used non-sociologically to describe all the individuals who do not belong to the chosen people."[10] This does not exclude its use to refer to a "people" in the singular, but of the terms used in the New Testament it is "the most general and therefore the weakest."[11] Had the great commission been intended to convey the meaning McGavran assigns to it, some other word would almost certainly have been used. One thinks primarily of *genos,* which means a race or nation or people, but also of *phulē* (people as a national unit of common descent), *laos* (people as a political unit with a common history and constitution), and *glōssa* (people as a linguistic unit).[12]

A further point must be made. The consideration of the relevant biblical passages should include not only specific word studies, such as sketched above, but also contextual study. The issues of particularism and universalism are strikingly important in the Book of Matthew. The disciples originally were to go only to the "lost sheep of Israel" (Matt. 10:6). In the context of Matthew, therefore, the great commission is of special importance. It does not indicate that the Christian mission is to be carried out "people by people," but that the mission is to go far beyond the confines of Judaism to the Gentile world.

It might be noted also that the "people" terminology in the New Testament has been the subject of recent study. "Jesus' Audiences According to Luke," an article by Paul S. Minear, for example, investigates the terms *laos* (people), *ochloi* (crowds), and *mathētai* (disciples) from a theological perspective.[13] A recent monograph, *Luke and the People of God* by Jacob Jervell, deals theologically with the identity of God's people.[14] I cite these works only to illustrate that it is precarious to deal with such terms merely from an anthropological or even lexical viewpoint. Contextual and theological study are absolutely necessary.

Biblical Examples

While an appeal to Matthew 28:19 to support the concept of "people movements" has its weaknesses, references to household conversions in the Book of Acts (e.g., Acts 16:29-34) seem to me not only justified but worthy of greater emphasis. Michael Green has shown that the household was a basic and large sociological unit in ancient Greco-Roman society.[15] He points out that a household included far more than the immediate family and also that "Roman households were united in a common religious cult (the *Lares*) irrespective of age or personal beliefs."[16] Missiologists will immediately see the significance of this and will recognize the difference between the typical American household and the larger cohesive sociological unit which is characteristic of many societies today in common with those of ancient times. It should be mentioned in passing that the conversion of a household was hindered if the initial convert was not the husband and father, and further it is obvious that once a household was converted it became a means of reaching others.

Since the word *conversion* has been used in the preceding comments, it might be useful to digress for a moment to comment on the importance of that term. It is, I believe, generally agreed among those involved in the church growth movement that one must distinguish between superficial conversion of masses of people and individual conversions made in interdependence with others. This is touched on by Michael Green in his study on evangelism.

But there may have been a further reason which led the early Christians to eschew mass evangelism for the most part. Did they, perhaps, realize the dangers which a shallow, widespread scattering of the seed could bring in its wake? No sooner do we hear of mass movements than we hear of the baptism of heathen ideas and customs into Christianity. Tertullian complained of it in Africa; Anne Ross has recently shown how it took place in Britain. Indeed, it happened all over the Empire as soon as Christianity was adopted as the official religion under Constantine.[17]

I should like to suggest further that it is important to distinguish not only between superficial mass conversion and multi-individual conversions but also between types of individual conversion. One may be genuinely "converted" from any one of many points of view — religious, political, and so forth. A. D. Nock has illustrated many types of "conversions" in the Greco-Roman world.[18] "Conversion to Christianity" may not, as we all know, signal regeneration. While it is well argued that no human can determine unerringly who is genuinely regenerated, and that, practically speaking, during great times of mass turning to God it is impossible to spend the time one should with each professed convert, nevertheless the biblical standard of the purity of the church must be maintained. This is not to say that a pure "gathered" church must insist on some overt sign of true conversion.

We are now ready to draw some preliminary conclusions. Our consideration of Matthew 28:19 led us to the conclusion that the great commission does not command or even suggest the evangelization of "peoples" as such, but rather of the whole world outside the community of believers. On the other hand, our brief observation of the conversion of households in the Book of Acts would indicate that the gospel did indeed spread within homogeneous units. We must now ask whether we can establish from that fact the further assumption that the gospel should be primarily preached, and the church primarily built, within larger homogeneous units rather than across their boundaries. McGavran is obviously correct when he says, "Men like to become Christians without crossing racial, linguistic, or class barriers."[19] Volumes of church growth publications have substantiated that this is indeed the case.

At this point, however, we must address ourselves not so much to the missionary principles and experience of the contemporary church as to the teaching and examples of the New Testament. The obvious example of the receptivity of the gospel among a homogeneous racial group is the large-scale conversion of Jews described in the early chapters of Acts. It is very easy to assume that we have there a paradigm of (to use the older term again) a "people movement" or of "multi-individual conversion." While it is not my intention to dispute that this may be the case, in the interest of sound hermeneutics and theology it is important to note several facts. First, the approach to the Jewish people, whether on the Day of Pentecost or by Paul's repeated visits to the synagogues, was based on theological, and not on merely anthropological or missiological, reasons. "To the Jew first" was a theological imperative, and this was true for Paul even though he himself was the "apostle to the Gentiles." It would be difficult to prove from Scripture that Paul went to the Jews because he expected a multi-individual response from the Jewish congregation or community as a homogeneous unit of society. His basic motivation was clearly theological.

There may be insufficient recognition in the church growth literature of the fact that there was considerable pre-evangelism of the Jewish people. Pre-evangelism — especially if it involves many years of "preparation" of a community or society for the reception of Christianity — might even be thought antithetical to rapid church growth. But the fact is that the examples in the New Testament most frequently used to support the church growth position — the Jews and the "God-fearers" — were precisely those segments of society which *had* been prepared and pre-evangelized! Several facts cry out for recognition. First, the Jewish synagogue was an educational center. In it both the Jews and those Gentiles who because of their interest in Jewish ethical monotheism were known as "God-fearers" heard the teaching of the Word of God Sabbath after Sabbath. In fact, the prevailing opinion of rabbis in the early centuries concerning the best means of proselytizing Gentiles was that the synagogue was the ideal place for their conversion.[20]

The second fact which tends to be overlooked is that both Jew and "God-fearer" were prepared in mind and heart for the gospel by virtue of the fact that the Word of God was taught in the familiar Greek of the Septuagint. Here again is a clear illustration of pre-evangelism. Through both means — the synagogue services and the hearing of the Greek version of the Scriptures — Jew and "God-fearer" alike acquired a familiarity with a theological terminology which was later employed by the early Christian missionaries in their preaching of the gospel. It cannot be stressed strongly enough that this situation was totally different from that which prevails on mission fields today. It does not do justice to the Scriptures to assume that Jews and "God-fearers" provide examples of homogeneous units of society and bridges for the gospel unless we also emphasize the lengthy process of preparatory evangelism which made these groups so responsive.

Third, it must be recognized that the Jewish people and the "God-fearers" were not the sole factors in the early spread of the Christian gospel. Due recognition must be given to Paul's methodical use of his evangelistic "team." Adequate attention has been given to this factor in mission literature but its importance may not have been emphasized sufficiently in discussions about church growth. Paul's team, while varying in composition from time to time, generally consisted of an assortment of Christians with mixed racial, linguistic and class backgrounds. Paul seems to have regarded the work of his associates as an extension of his own. This may be indicated by his reference to the "good deposit that was entrusted to you" (II Tim. 1:14; cf. v. 12 and I Tim. 6:20).

Still another element is the importance of the city in Paul's missionary strategy. When Acts mentions Paul's extended evangelistic work in a given locality, it is always within a city, rather than in a region. The stress, therefore, seems to be upon the city with its complex social structure rather than upon an ethnic group resident in an area as a homogeneous unit of society. Furthermore, Paul always seems to have sought a city which had a combination of specific characteristics: a city located on a major route oriented towards Rome, important commercially, possessing a Jewish synagogue, and having a Roman army camp and possibly a Roman colony.[21] Paul's abortive attempt to evangelize northern Asia Minor should probably not be seen as a change in strategy, that is, to visit sparsely settled areas, but rather as a determination to preach in several cities which lay on the northern trade route.

Incidentally, Paul's preaching at Athens should never be taken as an example, either positive or negative, of his missionary strategy. The reason for this is that it was not in his plan to go there; rather it was a place of refuge following his hazardous experience in Thessalonica. Further, he was not accompanied by his team. Silas and Timothy stayed in Berea, and those who went with him to Athens were unnamed "brothers" who did not remain with him (Acts 17:14, 15). While Athens is thought of today as an outstanding city in the ancient world, it actually lacked commercial importance and certain other characteristics which Paul normally looked for.

Paul, then, did not choose fields or ethnic groups but rather cities which were intercultural centers. Also, while he found many converts among the "God-fearers," it must not be supposed that they constituted a homogeneous community. Nevertheless, they were indeed "bridges" and through them the gospel passed from Jews to Gentiles.

A word should be added about the natural tendency in New Testament times, as well as today, to avoid a religious conversion which will take one out of his own family or socio-cultural group. Acknowledgment should be given, however, to the fact that the call to discipleship has always involved at least a willingness to break with one's own group. This is certainly clear in three examples of responses to Jesus' call (Luke 9:57-62). Whereas the issue in the first conversation in these verses is the lack of security characteristic of the daily life of an itinerant disciple, the issue in the second and third conversations is the radical break required with one's family. We observed briefly near the beginning of this paper the importance and strength of family unity, and how this could provide a vehicle for the spread of the gospel. Now we observe that the disciple of Christ may be required to take the difficult step of breaking with his family. Jesus addressed Himself specifically to this terribly shattering experience when He commended those that had left their families and assured them of an infinitely greater reward (Mark 10:29-31). It should be noted, then, that while the conversion of a number of Jews at the same time entailed mutual support, one cannot ignore those other circumstances when individual Jews had to break with the group. While too much stress must not be placed on Hebrews 13:13 because its significance is basically theological, we must not overlook the fact that many Jews found it necessary to "go to him outside the camp, bearing the disgrace he bore."

Large Numbers of Converts

This brings us to the matter of the large numbers of people who were converted in the early days of Christianity. One of the important characteristics of the church growth movement has been a new optimism regarding the possibility of multitudes turning to the Lord Jesus Christ in our day. Some, however, have been skeptical, and their reservations have probably been due to two primary reasons. One — already noted in the work of Michael Green — is the fear that the emphasis on numbers may lead us to accept as converts those who have not been genuinely regenerated. The other is a pessimism based on the assumption that the end of the present age will find few, rather than many, true believers on earth.

The first of these reasons for skepticism about large numbers of converts involves false motivation and its consequence, false profession, problems which have certainly been faced squarely by the church growth leaders. These problems have existed from the early days of the Christian church. The story of Simon in Acts 8 stands as a constant reminder that the heart of man "is deceitful above all things and desperately wicked." Naturally the problem is multiplied in proportion to the numbers of people accepted into the church. Unfortunately it has become commonplace, particularly in America, to advertise large numbers of converts to the supporting Christian public. It is true that there is ample precedent in the Book of Acts for noting multiple conversions (Acts 2:41, 47; 4:4; 6:1, 7; 11:21; 16:5; 17:4, 12). Those who are nervous about reporting numbers would claim that in Acts we have a unique historical circumstance, but others insist that Acts should provide us with a norm. It is perhaps more important to note the fact that in many of these cases the converts had been pre-evangelized, as we observed above. It should also be recognized that the numbers in the Book of Acts were recorded under the inspiration of the Holy Spirit, and are therefore certainly more reliable than judgments we might make today. Further, one purpose of Luke in writing Acts was to provide an apologetic for the Christian faith and the number of converts was important to that purpose. (It seems to me that reference to the sin of David in numbering the people is irrelevant because of the different circumstance and meaning of his act.)

We must stress here the importance of the purity of the church. In the parable of the wheat and tares in Matthew 13, the field is not the church of true believers nor even the larger professing church, but the world (v. 38). Likewise the parable of the dragnet in verses 47-50 should not be taken as justification for indiscriminate acceptance of all who profess conversion. On the contrary, the solemnity of the warning should caution us lest we allow any to think that they have been regenerated, justified and saved from God's wrath when, indeed, such may not be the case.

The second reason some are skeptical about large numbers of converts is that the Scripture does give some basis for questioning whether the end of this age will see a large world-wide church of genuine believers. The doctrinal position of the dispensational school of thought is well known, and will not be discussed here. One passage in particular may be especially relevant. In his interpretation of the parable of the importunate widow Jesus refers to those who languish waiting for vindication. After promising that

God will indeed bring vindication and justice speedily, He adds, "However, when the Son of Man comes, will he find faith on the earth?" (Luke 18:8). This is a most difficult verse. Because it is in the form of a question rather than a statement it is impossible to be dogmatic as to its meaning. The question must be taken seriously, but surely is not meant to discourage our evangelistic efforts.

Discipleship and Discipling

There is another major consideration which must be brought into this discussion. I would like to introduce it from its setting in John 8. Verse 30 tells us that as Jesus spoke "many put their faith in him." In the next verse the Greek construction is slightly different, and this difference is expressed in the New International Version by a change from "put their faith in him" (*episteusan eis auton,* v. 30) to "believed him" (*pepisteukotas autō,* v. 31). The group in verse 30 may have been true believers while those in verse 31 constituted a larger group who had merely accepted what Jesus had told them to that point. It may be arguable as to whether or not the slight change in Greek will bear this interpretation. But the context does seem to substantiate the inference. The wording in verse 30 usually describes true faith in Christ, whereas the context in verses 31 through 47 indicates that this group were not yet true believers (e.g., "You belong to your father, the devil," v. 43). The affirmation we want to note is in verses 31 and 32: "If you hold to my teaching, you are really my disciples. Then you will know the truth, and the truth will set you free." The words translated "hold to" represent the Greek for "abide" or "remain in." The concept of "abiding" is very common in John, and it is used here to stress the importance of continuity and obedience as a test of the genuineness of faith. This teaching must be compared with that in Matthew 7 where Jesus warns against the false profession of those who say, "Lord, Lord." To these He will say, "I never knew you" (Matt. 7:23). These verses teach us how precarious it is to assure people that they are regenerate before there is sufficient evidence that this is indeed the case.

More than that, it should be apparent from the verses just quoted that what we call "follow-up" is a part of discipling. The goal is that those who are evangelized become "disciples indeed" (KJV), that is, "real" or "true" disciples (*alēthōs mathētai*). A distinction is made in church growth literature between the work of "discipling" and the work of "perfecting."[22] It is rightly charged that all too often Christians have been so occupied with the work of building up converts that they have delayed and minimized the work of evangelism. It seems to me, however, that there is a theological danger in minimizing the teaching content in the work of discipling. In the great commission "teaching" is a participle parallel to "baptizing," and is too close syntactically to the main command, "disciple the nations," to be isolated from it. There are those who are disciples only in the sense of an initial interest and belief in the truth of Jesus' teaching. But as a disciple grows in knowledge, he should come to the point where he puts his personal faith in the Lord Jesus Christ and is regenerated. He should go on in an ever-deepening commitment as a "real disciple," following the teachings of the Lord Jesus on the cost of discipleship. It is clear that the evangelist should be concerned about the end product, that is, he should see the individual through to the point where he is unquestionably a true believer.

Moreover, Ephesians 4:11 identifies the evangelist as one of the gifts to the church. As such his work has some connection with the edification and maturity of the church. While there is certainly a difference between the work of evangelism and the work of pastors and teachers in the context of the local church, we must be careful not to divide these two aspects of the work so sharply that we miss the importance of the continuity involved. When Paul reported to the Ephesian elders on his work of evangelism, he affirmed, "I have not hesitated to proclaim to you the whole will of God" (Acts 20:27). Acts 14:21-23 describes Paul's total concern. After an unspecified period of time in Lystra and in Derbe he had made disciples in each city (vv. 21, 22). The verb translated "won disciples" in verse 21 is the same as "make disciples" in Matthew 28:19. After evangelizing Derbe he returned to Lystra and other cities to strengthen the disciples and appoint elders. Clearly the "follow-up" is part of discipling and a part of the evangelist's responsibility.

SELECTIVITY AND "WINNABLE PEOPLE"

The concept of selectivity or "winnable people" will occupy us only briefly. Without question we have been given a universal mission (Matt. 28:19; Mark 1:37, 38; Luke 24:46, 47; Acts 17:30; Rom. 1:14-16; 15:19-21). At the same time the New Testament seems to support a certain selectivity under the providence and will of God (Matt. 10:14, 23; 13:57; Luke 13:6ff; Acts 13:46, 51). Matthew 7:6 is often quoted ("Do not throw your pearls to pigs") but this is a command to be discerning, a balance to the "judge not" of verse 1. Matthew 13:10-16 indicates God's mysteries are disclosed to some but not to others, but the only application made is to the unique parabolic teaching of Jesus. The disciples were to shake off the dust of any town which rejected them and their message (Matt. 10:14). In that case, however, the Jewish residents had known the Old Testament message and were responsible to accept the message of the kingdom. Verse 23 of the same chapter has been used to uphold selectivity: "When you are persecuted in one place, flee to another." There, however, the issue is not mere unresponsiveness but persecution. More positively Paul stayed where God had "many people" (potential believers?) (Acts 18:8-11). In the oft-quoted verse of John 4:35 attention centers on the fields which are ripened for harvest, and Jesus said we should pray for God to send laborers into His "harvest" (Matt. 9:37f.). The emphasis clearly seems to be on those people who are ready for conversion. In New Testament times they were largely the Jewish people and the "God-fearers" who had been pre-evangelized. This emphasis on selective evangelism may need to be balanced by some less explicit data, such as the parabolic portrayal of a broad scattering of seed (Matt. 13:1-9, 18-23 and parallels). The ancient method varied, but seed was sometimes scattered first and then plowed in, with some seed remaining where the soil was unproductive.

I would conclude that while there is a biblical principle of selectivity, we must be careful lest we too easily turn away from people who are unresponsive, not because they understand and reject, but because they have not yet had sufficient time to absorb the semantic and theological significance of the new message. To turn away from them too soon is not in the best spirit of the church growth movement. Also it would seem that some portion of the missionary force should continue to scatter seed where none has yet been sown (e.g., unreached tribes, translation work, and so forth). With such balancing factors kept in mind, the basic principle of concentrating on winnable peoples seems to have biblical support.

CHURCH UNITY AND SOCIAL BARRIERS

Our final major topic is best introduced in the words of the following question: "How can we resolve the tension that exists between biblical norms for expressing the unity of the church and the anthropologically-defensible validity of a people's desire to become Christians without crossing linguistic, class or racial barriers?"[23] The desire for a homogeneous religious fellowship is seen in the separate synagogues which existed in Greco-Roman times for Jews of various backgrounds.[24] Church growth literature abounds with contemporary examples. How then are we to understand and apply the obvious biblical principles of unity? We must ask whether unity is an ideal or an imperative. In other words, does the New Testament mean only that if a local church happens to contain a mixed group they should live in harmony together, or that a church in a socially mixed area should deliberately try to include and to unify believers of various classes?

In approaching the Scriptures we must try to determine the force of any relevant text in its biblical context. We should ask what sort of unity is actually required by the theology of each passage. Galatians 3:28 is a well-known text on the subject. "There is neither Jew nor Greek, slave nor free, male nor female, for you are all one in Christ Jesus." This is the culmination of the argument that one is justified and reconciled to God by faith apart from the law. This law was, of course, a distinctive of Judaism. Paul's argument that Jew and Gentile now come to God by faith in Christ apart from the instrumentality of the law reduces that distinctive to the point where Jew and Gentile can mingle and even blend together in the church. The principle of unity thus established is further applied to groups where the particular distinctive under discussion, the law, does not play a role. Three examples are given: one racial, one social and one sexual. No further theological basis is offered for the second and third of these examples; for further comments on this we must go to Ephesians 2 and John 17.

Ephesians 2 establishes that through the cross of Christ we have been reconciled not only to God but also to one another. The immediate groups in mind are, of course, believing Jews and the Gentiles. These believers are not only reconciled to each other but are actually blended together in one body. This is described in Ephesians 3 as God's "mystery." It thus has extraordinary theological significance. The purpose of this unity, so contrary to human tendencies, is that "through the church, the manifold wisdom of God should be made known to the rulers and authorities and the heavenly realms" (v. 10).

The union of Jew and Greek in the church had particular significance for the Hellenistic world. Nevertheless, there is certainly a principle here which ought also to be followed today: the cross of Christ reconciles people of totally diverse backgrounds, races, and cultural distinctives. One cannot stress strongly enough the theological importance of this unity in the local church. Churches which are not monolithic in this respect lose an opportunity to demonstrate as they should the "manifold wisdom of God" and the reconciling work of Christ. How can the world know the validity of our claim to have been reconciled to God, an unseen reality, if they cannot observe its visible manifestation in the local church? (Is the answer to be found in some periodic demonstration of unity through conferences in the name of Christ? I think of cooperation between racial and organizational groups on the American scene, for example.) In John 17:23 also the matter is presented strongly: "May they be brought to complete unity to let the world know that you sent me and have loved them even as you have loved me." In this section of Jesus' prayer the reference is to future generations. The background of Judaism in Jesus' day is left far behind. It is a comprehensive statement about all subsequent believers. We must accept this therefore as applying to various racial, social and economic groups today. Unity is not simply for the sake of peace and harmony in the church, but is a visible testimony to the love of God and the reconciling work of Christ.

CONCLUSION

This final section was introduced by a question beginning with the words, "How can we resolve . . .?" The answer with respect to this topic is undoubtedly to be found in terms of balance rather than of an exclusive choice between alternatives. This principle will probably apply to the previous topics as well. The purpose of this paper has not been dogmatic, but to break up some ground which may have been solidified into clods of assumptions and to encourage the planting of new seeds of inquiry.

FOOTNOTES

N. B. Bible quotations are from the New International Version unless otherwise noted.

1. Roger S. Greenway, "Reformed Missions and the Theology of Church Growth," submitted to the Consultation at Westminster Theological Society, Philadelphia, March 14-26, 1976, p. 5.

2. J. Robertson McQuilkin, *How Biblical Is the Church Growth Movement?* (Chicago: Moody Press, 1973).

3. Ibid., p. 35.

4. Michael Green, *Evangelism in the Early Church* (Grand Rapids: Eerdmans, 1970).

5. Donald McGavran, *The Bridges of God* (New York: Friendship Press, 1955), p. 13.

6. Ibid.

7. Donald McGavran, *Understanding Church Growth* (Grand Rapids: Eerdmans, 1970), p. 310.

8. Ibid.

9. Ibid.

10. G. Bertram in *Theological Dictionary of the New Testament,* 9 vols., ed. Gerhard Kittel, trans. and ed. Geoffry W. Bromiley (Grand Rapids: Eerdmans, 1964) s.v. *"ethnos, ethnikos,"* vol. 2, p. 367.

11. Ibid.

12. Ibid.

13. Paul S. Minear, "Jesus' Audiences According to Luke," *Novum Testamentum* 16 (1974), 82-109.

14. Jacob Jervell, *Luke and the People of God* (Minneapolis: Augsburg, 1972).

15. Green, *Evangelism,* pp. 208-10.

16. Ibid., p. 210.

17. Ibid., p. 279.

18. A. D. Nock, *Conversion* (Oxford: University Press, 1933).

19. McGavran, *Understanding,* p. 198.

20. Walter L. Liefeld, "The Wandering Preacher as a Social Figure in the Roman Empire" (Ph.D. dissertation, Columbia University, 1967), pp. 206ff.

21. Ibid., p. 150; cf. pp. 212f.

22. Donald A. McGavran, *How Churches Grow* (New York: Friendship Press, 1959), pp. 93-101; Alan R. Tippett, *Church Growth and the Word of God* (Grand Rapids: Eerdmans, 1970), pp. 61-64. Both authors are careful to note the importance of a continuing work of perfecting. I am in complete agreement with this, and seek in my text only to enlarge the concept of discipling.

23. Arthur F. Glasser, *Church Growth Theology,* Reformed Missions Consultation, Westminster Theological Seminary, 1975 (mimeographed).

24. Acts 6:9. See F. F. Bruce, *The Acts of the Apostles* (Greek text) (London: Tyndale, 1951), p. 156.

**Arthur P.
Johnston**

CHURCH GROWTH THEOLOGY
AND WORLD EVANGELIZATION

INTRODUCTION

The theology of church growth is intimately related to the strategy of world mission. It understands that the New Testament teaches the primary task of the apostles and the church between the two advents of Jesus Christ is the expansion and extension of His church upon the earth — and that the historical inauguration of this task is recorded in the Acts of the Apostles. This theology centers around the *visible* manifestation of the church and its *numerical* increase both in its membership and in the number of churches upon the earth.

The Acts of the Apostles records the planting and growth of churches throughout the Roman Empire. The missionary work of the apostle Paul outlined the normative principles regulating evangelism, mission, and ecclesiology. The supernatural work of the Holy Spirit (Acts 2 and 16) and the dynamic of the Scriptures (Heb. 4:12) made possible effective evangelism, the discipleship of believers, and growing churches. Human forces such as the Roman Empire and persecutions played a significant and providential role in the growth of the church.

The legitimacy of church growth is founded upon the historical revelation that "God so loved the *world*." Furthermore, Jesus Christ died for *all*. The fact that His death is sufficient for all transmits to the church responsibility for world evangelization. The church is the *end* wherein God is glorified and she is also the *means* by which the billions of the world are to be evangelized. God is glorified and the death of His Son is vindicated by those who believe. Growth may be seen as a normal function of the church. Nongrowth represents a denial of her nature and role "between the times."

189

DYNAMICS AND STRATEGIES
OF THE GROWTH OF THE CHURCH
IN HISTORY

Church history and mission history reveal many influences that have fostered or hindered the growth of the church. Of particular interest in our day are those selective theological foundations relating to church growth. Some are important but cannot receive more than mere mention. The apostolic and postapostolic church, for example, clearly believed in the lostness and eternal punishment of men who are without personal faith in Jesus Christ. Unquestionably, the imminency of Christ's return also provided motivation for mission. These basic doctrines undergirded early missionary expansion and extension of the church. Other factors require greater attention.

The Place of the Scriptures

The Scriptures were used by the early church as the divine instrument provided by the Holy Spirit for evangelism. A. M. Chirgwin calls the Bible an "indispensable tool" in the expansion of the early church: "It seems beyond dispute that the early Christian preachers and writers constantly used the Scriptures as a means of persuading non-Christians to accept the faith. The Bible was the regular tool of their evangelism."[1] Eusebius (A.D. 260-340) recorded that the postapostolic believers inspired "by the Holy Word" sacrificially went out to evangelize and committed to their converts "the books of the divine Gospels."[2] The prominent place and use of the available Scriptures enabled the growth of the church within and beyond the boundaries of the Roman Empire.

The Planting of Churches

The geographical extension of the gospel necessarily involved the planting of local churches. Augustine[3] and Calvin both wrote of the "churches the Apostles planted."[4] Voetius (1589-1676) was concerned about planting new churches in his day. Shortly thereafter pietism developed and started to plant churches. Even though Zinzendorf's motto was "to win souls for the Lamb," eighteenth-century pioneers such as Ziegenbalg made an early contribution to methods of fostering indigenous church growth by seeking to establish an Indian church with its own Indian ministry *as soon as possible.*[5] There seems to be adequate evidence that the planting of indigenous churches has been a general characteristic of missions since the apostolic age.

Revivalism

While the Reformation brought a renewal of church life and

theology, it was Philip Jacob Spener who ignited the sparks of revival amid dead orthodoxy by teaching the centrality of the Scriptures, the return of Christ, and the necessity of Jewish evangelism. Renewed attention was given to personal faith and holiness of life based upon the ministry of the Holy Spirit and the Scriptures.[6] The urgency of these emphases gave impetus to evangelism, revivalism and foreign missions so that the nineteenth century has been called the Great Century or pietistic century of missions. The evangelical church grew and was planted upon all continents of the world through Western missions. Historically, pietistic missions have been concerned with the planting and growth of indigenous churches, not only with "souls."

The Autonomous Church

During the first part of the nineteenth century, the successors of William Carey gave special emphasis to the planting of churches which would become indigenous and autonomous as soon as possible. Henry Venn and Rufus Anderson believed that "heathen nations must be rendered independent of Christendom for their religious teachers as soon as possible."[7] While considerable diversity in nineteenth-century methodology may be discerned, the planting and growth of local churches were the focal point of missionary work. It was believed that the establishment of self-governing, self-supporting and self-propagating churches would enable the foreign missionary to go to new areas.

Titus Coan, a collaborator of Charles Finney, characterized this spirit in his mission to Hawaii which began in 1835. He planted churches by the use of methods contemporary specialists can admire. In 1870 the American Board withdrew from Hawaii, leaving behind sixty self-supporting churches with a total of 15,000 members and with 30 percent of their ministers engaged as missionaries on other islands. Arthur T. Pierson described Coan as a man who "depended on the Word, borne home by the Spirit."[8] Kanwealoho, one of the elderly Hawaiian missionaries, testified of the heritage left to his church: "Not with powder and ball and swords and cannon, but with the living Word of God and His Spirit, do we go forth to conquer the islands for Christ."[9]

The growth of the church is not a contemporary novelty or innovation, but a continuous, normal concern of mission leading to the "great new fact" of our times — the autonomous church in all continents and in almost all countries of the world.

The Christianizing Church

Gustav Warneck linked world evangelization with the Christianization of the nations. The congregation of converted individuals became God's school to instruct and familiarize the nation with the gospel. Making disciples was a step toward the establishment of a Christian society.[10] This Christianization of the nations by the "Christian" colonial powers characterized the theology of mission in the era of the Edinburgh World Missionary Conference (1910). The Western churches were to make the rest of the world "Christian" nations by evangelism and incorporation of Christian principles into the life of the colonies. The outbreak of World War I among "Christian" nations disillusioned many holding to this view of the growth of the church. It has postmillennial and "world-and-life-view" overtones which are in opposition to some aspects of pietism.

The Ecumenical Church

At the Edinburgh World Missionary Conference attention shifted toward the organization of the missionary forces to produce a Christian world. World evangelization required Christian unity and Christian education which would contribute toward the Christianization of the nations. The goal of missions became directed more toward the ethical and social aspects of the gospel as a result of the erosion of belief in the inspiration and authority of the Scriptures in previous decades. The diminished confidence in the Scriptures increased the emphasis upon ecclesiology, organization, methodology, technology, and so forth.

The "social gospel" of the first three decades of this century influenced missiology in two ways. First, the authority of the "church" replaced the authority of the Scriptures.[11] The visible church as an institution clearly eclipsed the invisible church: concern for "souls" fell into disrepute along with evangelism and revivalism. Second, evangelicals tended to emphasize the invisible church because of their disillusionment with the deviations from the Scriptures in the institutional churches. Until new denominations were established at home and abroad, evangelicals emphasized the individual and de-emphasized the visible church.

Many contemporary nonevangelicals see the mission of the church as "for the world," not "to the world." Church growth theology is a "morphological fundamentalistic" imprisonment of the past. It has structures that impede the *missio Dei*, a partnership with God in history wherein He transforms the world from the "old," before Christ, to the "new." "Christians therefore understand the changes in history in the perspective of the mission of God and so, trusting in God's promises, they dare to risk involving themselves in actual history, ever ready to adopt new forms of responsibility for the world."[12]

This theology sees the strategy of the church as giving up all ideas of self-aggrandizement, refusing to engage in proselytism and "adopting the pattern of messianic life — the form of the servant — without concern for success in terms of church membership and church activities."[13] It does not see the church as the mediating center of salvation nor does it expect men to emigrate from the world into the ecclesiastical structure. The goal of mission for Hoekendijk, Hollenweger, Margull and others has come to be the establishment of *shalom* in all aspects of human life and the full realization of human potential. The church has become the "sign" of the kingdom to come and, as such, must be concerned for the justice and the development of the world. Hence dialogue with non-Christian religions and contemporary ideologies and involvement with the *missio Dei* in the world become the methodology of mission. Church growth becomes incidental, irrelevant or unimportant.

In reaction to these developments among nonevangelicals the growing conservative evangelical movement engaged extensively in evangelism and mission without either clear ecclesiology or a definite methodology. Parachurch evangelism grew taking forms ranging from the Bible institute movement to philanthropic missionary agencies. Some believed world evangelization would be accomplished by the multiplication of missionaries and mission stations alone. Others believed there should be concentration on establishing a small national church with well-discipled leaders who, as the disciples of Christ did, would carry the gospel to the entire country. Still others attempted to get a small indigenous church going and to get out as soon as possible: they hoped leadership and training would be as spontaneous as growth. Into conflict with this nonbiblical orientation of the Christian mission and the differing viewpoints of conservative evangelicals came the post-World War II school of church growth led by Donald McGavran.

The Indigenous Church

In the view of Roland Allen the mission church should be autonomous from the very beginning. Following the three-stage pattern of self-governing, self-supporting, self-propagating hinders the work of the Holy Spirit. "Christians receive the Spirit of Jesus, and the Spirit of Jesus is the missionary spirit, the Spirit of Him who came into the world to bring back lost souls to the Father. Naturally when they receive that Spirit they begin to bring back others as He did."[14] This liberty from mission domination promotes "spontaneous growth of the church" through the indigenous church.

Allen's "conception of the Holy Spirit influenced his missionary principles more than did his High Church background, although he laid much stress on the efficacy of the Sacraments, which, he believed, guaranteed that the Church remained a visible Body."[15] Melvin Hodges popularized Allen's theology of church growth with a view toward the establishment of the indigenous church.[16] Based upon the Nevius principles, emphasis on the indigenous church was instrumental in the amazing growth of the Korean church.[17]

The Church Growth Movement

The present church growth movement represents a revival of the historic emphasis upon soul-winning and the planting and growth of the local church. Church growth proponents speak to both divisions of Protestantism. They remind nonevangelicals of the high place of evangelism and church growth in the Scriptures and in history. To the evangelical who has resisted the modernism and liberalism of his day, and who has long reacted against the institutional church, they issue a renewed call to plant the church. The July 1968 issue of the *International Review of Mission* expressed the general reservations of the nonevangelical conciliar movement while J. Robertson McQuilkin's *How Biblical Is the Church Growth Movement?* (Moody Press, 1973) represented a qualified general acceptance by conservative evangelicals.

The most significant contributions of the movement to contemporary evangelical thought seem to be the revival of churchmanship, the integration of the social, anthropological, and communication sciences into missiology, the emphasis on multi-individual conversions, and a concentration on responsive peoples and homogeneous units. Allen Tippett has complemented the insights of McGavran by stressing the biblical foundations for church growth[18] and by contributing anthropological insights.

THE CONTEMPORARY CHURCH GROWTH MOVEMENT

Church growth is unquestionably a significant strategy in contemporary missiology, and evangelicals in general are committed to it. Is this strategy justifiable from a biblical point of view?

The Prominence of the Church Growth Movement Today

The church growth movement has swept through the ranks of evangelicals since Donald McGavran's initial work, *The Bridges of God*, was published in 1955. The movement attained great popularity and continues to exert its influence upon many streams of world Christianity, in North America and elsewhere. Missionaries as well as mission professors are earning advanced degrees in church growth with the result that its teachings proliferate at home and abroad. Church growth was a featured subject at the Lausanne Congress of 1974 and therefore will, no doubt, exercise an even greater influence upon the growing missionary agencies of the Third World. Evangelical churches and missions everywhere are beginning to "think church growth."

Criticism of the Church Growth Movement

The church growth movement, however, has critics as well as advocates among evangelicals. Some Lausanne participants from lands where there are growing churches expressed criticism of American church growth methodology. More recently C. René Padilla, a Latin American, while recognizing the importance of *quantitative* or *numerical* church growth in Latin America, asserted that *qualitative* growth has been neglected:

> An analysis of the situation, however, shows the undeniable concentration of evangelical work on the multiplication of the number of churches and the number of church members. This becomes the real criterion for measuring the growth of the Church. The harm that this emphasis has caused is incalculable.[19]

Padilla's socio-political concerns influence his perspective. Very little, if any, approval of church growth comes from nonevangelical and official World Council of Churches sources.

Evangelical Appreciation of the Church Growth Contribution

Few evangelicals question the great contributions of the church growth movement to contemporary missiology. The massive evangelical post-World War II missionary effort has shifted slowly but certainly from a parachurch and institutional emphasis toward a heart-searching consideration of the church — visible and invisible. Evangelicals have learned to differentiate presence, proclamation and persuasion evangelism, and E_0, E_1, E_2 and E_3 evangelism. Missionaries and national pastors have begun to think about "measuring" the growth of their ministries (sometimes an embarrassing and challenging exercise), to set goals, and to glorify the Lord by an increased concentration on, and dedication to, productive efforts. The needs of the world have been seen in terms of "responsive" peoples to be "discipled," and "Eurican" agencies have become increasingly aware of the Third World churches and missions in "Latfricasia" when prayerfully planning their strategy.

The Development of Contemporary
Church Growth Theology

The leading spokesman of church growth continues to be Donald McGavran but he does not stand alone. The pioneer research of J. Wascom Pickett's *Christian Mass Movements in India* (1933) resulted in *Church Growth and Group Conversion* (1936), authored by Pickett, Warnshuis, Singh and McGavran. A foreword written by John R. Mott suggested that because of new insights the time had come for "a major shift in the emphasis and a marked reallocation of resources of men and money."[20]

Pickett preceded McGavran in proposing that "rural group conversion" avoids misunderstanding of the gospel and enables converts to understand the message in their own culture. This contrasts with "gathered" converts at a mission station who look on Christianity as foreign. Pickett says that because of group conversions Christianity is now seen

> as the adoption of a superior Indian way to God. Most of the customs and traditions, the institutions and relationships which make up their lives are preserved and transformed by this type of Christianization. What was ours, that, redeemed, remains ours. Though we are new creatures in Christ Jesus, still we can recognize ourselves and our neighbors as the very people who have been redeemed.[21]

Pickett sees this method as "a way of life which is going to redeem an entire people." As people movements grow there will be "a constantly widening stream of families" pouring into the kingdom of God.

Pickett's optimism probably reflected the viewpoint expressed at the Jerusalem Conference in 1928 that secularism would slowly but surely disintegrate the non-Christian religions and that only

Christianity could withstand it. The Christian mission, it was concluded, should no longer wrestle with the non-Christian religions (as Edinburgh proposed) but with secularism. Evangelicals, however, were more pessimistic concerning the future of society in the end times. They did not expect a large harvest. By contrast the World Council of Churches today seems to advocate dialogue as an ultimate long-range means of converting not only the non-Christian religions but also non-Christian ideologies such as Marxism.

In *The Bridges of God* McGavran developed Pickett's method into a strategy for today: "The era has come when Christian Missions should hold lightly all mission station work, which cannot be proved to nurture growing churches, and should support the Christward movement within Peoples as long as they continue to grow at the rate of 50 percent per decade or more."[22] He insisted that the nineteenth-century concept of individualistic "gathered" churches alienates converts and hinders further growth. This concept belongs to a later stage of evangelism:

> By "growing churches" we do not mean churches which are primarily recruited through the one-by-one process. As long as accessions from the non-Christians are one-by-one, from different levels of society, and result in no People Movement, any considerable growth will be rare and, even when achieved, temporary. Such a system can operate successfully only in a discipled society. By "growing churches" we mean organized cells of the movement of a people. Folk join these cells without social dislocation.[23]

McGavran is optimistic that large populations will become "responsive." "The missionary enterprise has not yet experienced the degree of growth which is possible . . . . As concentration of resources on growing points comes to be the strategy of missions, we shall find ourselves in a new era of advance."[24]

In 1965 McGavran submitted a strong critique of "presence" theology and its detrimental influence upon mission strategy in the 1950s.[25] Under the new editorship of Philip Potter, the *International Review of Missions* in July 1968 published extensive and intensive critiques of the church growth movement but also gave McGavran an opportunity to reply. In this 1968 presentation McGavran rightly identified as the crucial issue "the authority of the Bible and of those passages which command discipling or makes it the *esse* of mission." Then he asked, "Does it make an eternal difference whether a man believes in Jesus Christ as God and Savior and becomes His disciple and a responsible member of His

Church?"[26] In answer to this question McGavran clearly repudiated universalism and affirmed the necessity of personal faith in
Christ as eternally essential for man's immortal soul. He identified
with those who "are praying and working that every man on earth
may have the chance to say yes to Jesus Christ and become a faithful member of His Church."[27] Even though there may be differences regarding the means toward the accomplishment of this
goal, McGavran expressed the belief that "fantastic church
growth" is possible and necessary for there are two billion in the
world for whom Christ died who do not yet know His name!

McGavran disassociates church growth from those who, while
using biblical words, do not believe the Bible is God's infallible
Word and resort to humanistic terms: "They cannot but oppose
church growth strategy: their theology allows them to take neither
the Church nor the salvation of men's souls seriously. They use the
right words but with such a radical interpretation of meaning that
they no longer speak about historic Christianity."[28] Of course,
this characterization is not meant to include the entire membership
of the World Council of Churches — or even some of those who
have voiced some of the strongest objections to church growth. In
1963 the Department of Missionary Studies of the World Council
of Churches convened a Consultation on Church Growth at Iber-
ville, Quebec. With I John 1:3 as background it was stated that
"the Church must therefore seek to be ever growing in numbers, as
well as in the grace and knowledge of her Lord and Savior — not
for reasons of self-aggrandizement, but in pursuance of God's
desire that all men should be saved."[29]

Nevertheless, delegates at the Nairobi convention of 1975, after
consideration of the fact that there were almost three billion outside the church, deleted the number from their final report and
made no mention of church growth.[30]

After a penetrating theological survey of numerical growth J.
Robertson McQuilkin affirms that numerical growth is part of the
missionary task and that statistics have a valid use as an indication
of the church's primary responsibility of evangelism to the world.[31]

> Inasmuch as Scripture does not teach that large response to the
> gospel is impossible and does affirm that God does not will that any
> should perish, Christians are under obligation to work and pray and
> believe toward large response . . . . If it is the will of God, certainly
> it is His will for us to use all possible means to reach His goal.[32]

The Lausanne Congress of 1974 implicitly endorsed church
growth strategy. In his paper on the "Dimensions of World
Evangelism," McGavran wrote:

Awakening multitudes are often basically receptive to the Gospel
. . . . The masses have built a receptivity to the Good News. Oppressed and ground down, they, like ancient Israel, are looking for a
Savior! Their ears are attuned to him who cries, "Come unto me all
you who labor and are heavy laden." For the foreseeable future, the
masses will continue to be receptive.[33]

In agreement with McGavran, the Lausanne Covenant recognized
the value of church growth. To neglect the masses was seen as a
"surrender to secularism."[34] Pentecostal growth in South America
indicates the world-wide receptivity of the "awakening masses."

Church growth theology has been classified and refined as it has
met the scrutiny of both evangelical and nonevangelical
missiologists. If McGavran's earlier theology conveyed the impression of a mass approach in opposition to individual conversion, his later statements strongly support the need for personal
faith in Christ as essential for the salvation of individuals:
"Revivals, gathered-colony congregations, people movements, and
web movements are all the doing of God. So is any conversion
whatsoever. Men cannot make the Church grow — only God's
Spirit can do that."[35]

THEOLOGICAL FOUNDATIONS FOR
THE GROWTH OF THE CHURCH

Three historical dynamics have influenced the growth of
churches since the apostolic era. The first dynamic relates to the
sovereign work of God in the world through the ministry of the
Holy Spirit. God is providentially working with His servants in
world evangelization. As King of the universe He is immediately
operative so that His servants are not working independently but
are directed and controlled by the will of God. By the direct
operation of the Holy Spirit God governs His creatures according
to the way in which He has created them. He uses every aspect of
life: circumstances, motives, instruction and example. He also
works directly on the intellect, emotions and will of the heart by the
personal operation of the Holy Spirit.[36] Great things and small accomplish God's eternal purpose so that His servant in evangelism
must recognize what Jesus said as applicable in every endeavor,
"Without me ye can do nothing" (John 15:5). Whatever true
growth the church experiences will have God as the first cause,
causa prima, but the result is the product of both God and man for
God works by man for man.

God has commanded prayer for the miraculous and super-

natural restoration of His creative work in the hearts of men who
are by nature irresponsive to the gospel (Rom. 3:10-12; Eph. 2:1-3).
Prayer is the primary means ordained by God for pre-evangelism
and harvest. So Lydia's heart was opened by the Lord (Acts 16:14).
Paul urges prayer for divine aid against the supernatural forces of
darkness (Eph. 6:12, 18). The sovereign will and work of God are
immediately linked to and concurrent with the work of the Holy
Spirit and prayer in the Spirit. Prayer, Hodge says, is necessary so
that God will make His Word effective and "multiply his converts
as the drops of the morning dew."[37]

The second dynamic relates to the Holy Scriptures and the Holy
Spirit. The Reformers returned the theology of the Scripture to its
apostolic perspective and thus opened the door for pietistic
missionary expansion. Luther spoke of the Holy Spirit working *by*
or *through* the Word (*per verbum*); Reformed theologians spoke of
Him working *with* the Word (*cum verbo*). Berkouwer concludes
that there is as yet no real solution to the question of how to
describe the relation between the Word and the Spirit.[38] Modern
theology with its lower view of inspiration and authority describes
the Holy Spirit as working *without* the Word (*sine verbo*) — the
work of the Holy Spirit in the accomplishment of the "salvation"
of men is not limited to the use of the Bible.

Spener, the father of pietism, reintroduced to the modern
missionary movement the use of the Scriptures for evangelism and
sanctification by affirming that "the Holy Spirit is always with, by,
and in the Word [*allezeit mit, bei, und in dem Wort*]."[39] Consequently, the Scriptures possess the inherent power of God to en-
lighten man's reason and so to act upon his will that he will be
brought to conversion. God opens hearts as the Word is proclaimed.[40]

The lesson for the evangelical is clear. The growth of churches is
related intimately and primarily to the proclamation of the Scriptures. For this reason Paul exhorts Timothy to "preach the Word"
(II Tim. 4:2); for the Bible is living (*zōn*), and active (*energēs*)
(Heb. 4:12). The Bible is God's appointed instrument and means
for the salvation and sanctification of men. Appropriate texts are
to be read or quoted. But the power of mission does not lie in the
nature of the truths contained in the Scriptures even though there is
more moral power in the doctrine of God "than in all the systems
of moral philosophy."[41] The Holy Spirit must be invoked to help
in the effectiveness of this ministry. Though the disciplines of
sociology, anthropology, communication sciences and psychology

are helpful to understand the growth of the churches, they do not possess the power to make them grow. Rather the Holy Spirit is that power.

Christians may "make" converts to Christianity as a system of thought, to Christian culture, to the institutional church, to the local church fellowship, or to themselves as leaders, but only the Holy Spirit and the Holy Scriptures have the supernatural power necessary to convert men to Christ Himself (Rom. 10:9, 10, 17).

The third distinctive dynamic relates to the ministry of the Holy Spirit in the personal life of the witness. Unquestionably, there is a relationship between the work of the Holy Spirit in the lives of believers and the growth of the church. Hodge along with Spener does not believe that the Holy Spirit is a power "imprisoned" in the truth. Rather, acting with the Bible or without it as He pleases, He prepares the way for the truth.[42] At Pentecost the Spirit gave the apostles utterance. He enlightened their minds; He reminded them of what Christ taught. In like manner the witness today is to be filled with the Spirit and conscious of the divine resources that are his. It was the concern of Jesus that His disciples bear "much fruit" and that the Father be glorified as the work of the Son in the atonement is vindicated. Today (as throughout history) churches are growing because witnesses have recognized the Holy Spirit and prayerfully depended upon Him as they totally surrender themselves to the lordship of Christ.[43] In view of this McGavran has reminded us that the word revival needs to be restored to its proper usage.[44] Church growth in the final analysis depends upon the servants of God in the church. They must be "led by the Spirit" (Rom. 8:14).

REFLECTIONS ON THEOLOGY AND CHURCH GROWTH

While there are a number of theological details and nuances concerning which evangelicals may differ, the church growth movement has provided to nonevangelical missiologists and the missionary movement in general a strong case for a return to the historic evangelistic mission of the church. It has also reminded the parachurch movements of evangelicalism of their ultimate responsibility to contribute directly toward the growth of visible local churches. If the theology of the church growth movement retains its present biblical orientation, its contribution to the work of world evangelization may be even more significant in the future than it has been in the past.

Authority

The continual development of the church growth movement will not depend as much on its research into the social and behavioral sciences as on deepening theological insights. These insights are in turn dependent upon two foundations. The first is the solid bedrock of a "verbally inerrant" Scripture as the basis of sound hermeneutics. It will become more and more difficult simply to appeal to an "infallible" Bible because of the breadth of interpretation the word *infallible* permits. Anything less than "verbal inerrancy" may easily destroy the principles undergirding the movement. This very thing happened before the Edinburgh conference, swiftly undermining the healthy growing churches and mission movement of the nineteenth century.

The second foundation is a continual subordination of the findings of social, anthropological, psychological and communication sciences to the rigorous evaluations of Scripture. The Bible must be read and studied for what it is — the revealed Word of God. The sciences, as well as other disciplines, must remain under the judgment of Scripture lest the supposedly "assured" findings of science subjugate the Scriptures and missiology. These disciplines must be seen through the grid of Scripture, not Scripture through the grid of these disciplines. Some theological guidelines need to be established for rightly relating these disciplines to church growth.

Ecclesiology

The rising emphasis upon the place of the church between the conferences of Edinburgh (1910) and Madras (1938) tended to put the responsibility for world evangelism upon the institutional church.[45] In the pre-1950 era one spoke of the "growth of the church." The use of the phrase *church growth* indicates the influence and predominance of the visible institution. For some this emphasis has certain negative implications because biblical authority was eroded by higher criticism of the Bible (Barth) and replaced by the church and its tradition (the conciliar movement). To them, it speaks of the demise of missions in favor of the mission of the church. It speaks of a rejection of pietism and individualism and the concern of laymen to personally disciple other men and women for Christ. It speaks of the renewal of spiritually dead ecclesiastical superstructures that historically have encumbered the mission of the church. A rising emphasis on the institutional church can consequently undermine present church growth methodology and change it from an instrument that helps to one that hinders world evangelization. In an era of rising ecclesiology and the institution-alizing of church mission, renewed emphasis needs to be given to the spiritual nature of the local church. It is in its spiritual nature alone that the visible institution possesses validity.

Bibliology

While a few justifiably fault the church growth movement for not supporting and substantiating church growth principles from the Bible,[46] it has also been noted that historically the movement has neglected consideration of the content of the gospel to be com-municated.[47] Tippett gives an essential place to the Holy Spirit as the "noncultural" or divine factor at work in the growth of the church,[48] but could it not be that more attention to the recom-mended *use of the Scripture* in evangelism would elevate the movement to a place of even greater service? It is obvious that churches were planted and grew prior to the rise of the present movement. Was not the historical expansion of the church due primarily to the preaching of the Word?[49] Can a correct analysis of growth or nongrowth avoid this delicate but essential con-sideration?

Contemporary missiology must not beguile missions into that scientific morass wherein the essential proclamation of the Word is diminished. While the pietism of previous centuries and the Bible institute movement of this century have had their weaknesses, this has not been one of them. Thriving, growing churches with their own Third World missions have dotted the earth's surface as a result of simple proclamation borne supernaturally, but not magically, into unbelieving hearts by the power of the Holy Spirit.[50] While McGavran rightly believes that the Nevius method was not the only cause for church growth in Korea, was it not a primary consideration?[51]

Samuel H. Moffett was recently asked what made the church in Korea grow. He responded with the answer his father, Dr. Samuel A. Moffett, had given more than a half-century ago:

> Since the first dramatic leap in church growth had occurred in my father's area of work in North Korea, they (a commission of inquiry sent to study the methods) came to ask him the secret. I think his an-swer disappointed them. It was too simplistic. Too pietistic. But I think he was right.
>
> "For years," he said, "we have simply held up before these people the Word of God, and the Holy Spirit has done the rest."[52]

FOOTNOTES

1. A. M. Chirgwin, *The Bible in World Evangelism* (New York: Friendship Press, 1954), p. 21.

2. Stephen Neill, *A History of Christian Missions* (Baltimore: Penguin Books, 1964), p. 40.

3. "Contra Cresconium" 3.64, cited by Marc Spindler, *La mission, combat pour le salut du monde* (Neuchatel: Delachaux & Niestlé, 1967), p. 42.

4. John Calvin, *Institutes of the Christian Religion*, 2 vols. (London: James Clark Publishing Co., 1957), vol. 2, p. 318.

5. Neill, *A History of Christian Missions,* p. 228.

6. Philip Jacob Spener, *Theologische Bedencken* (Halle: Verlegung des Waysen-Hauses, 1700), pp. 159-62.

7. Quoted by Peter Beyerhaus and Henry Lefever, *The Responsible Church and the Foreign Mission* (Grand Rapids: Eerdmans, 1964), p. 11.

8. Arthur T. Pierson, *The Miracles of Missions* (New York and London: Funk and Wagnalls, 1902), p. 46.

9. Ibid., p. 52.

10. Beyerhaus and Lefever, *The Responsible Church,* pp. 45-49.

11. This has been somewhat modified since the conference in New Delhi (1961) added the phrase, "according to the Scriptures." A "consensus" within contextual theologies anticipates a conciliar plurality of churches (World Council of Churches, Accra, 1974, *Faith and Order Minutes,* p. 73; also, World Council of Churches, Bristol, 1967, *New Directions in Faith and Order,* pp. 32ff.).

12. *The Church for Others* (Geneva: World Council of Churches, 1967), p. 14.

13. Ibid., p. 19.

14. Roland Allen, *Missionary Methods: St. Paul's and Ours* (Grand Rapids: Eerdmans, 1962), p. 93.

15. Beyerhaus and Lefever, *The Responsible Church,* p. 36.

16. Melvin Hodges, *On The Mission Field* (Chicago: Moody Press, 1953).

17. See T. Stanley Soltau, *Missions at the Crossroad* (Wheaton, IL: Van Kampen Publishers, 1954).

18. See Allen Tippett, *Church Growth and the Word of God* (Grand Rapids: Eerdmans, 1970).

19. C. René Padilla, "The Contextualization of the Gospel" — a paper presented in June 1975 to a seminar on "Evangelical Literature in the Latin World" and published by Partnership in Mission, Abingdon, Pennsylvania. Padilla continues to explain that "in addition to creating a regrettable spirit of competition that is more related to the capitalistic system than to the Word of God, it has caused almost the whole evangelistic effort in the 'mission field' to be thrown into the spread of a simplistic version of the Gospel, of a message that perennially excludes the deeper dimensions of faith, of a 'culture Christianity' that remains impervious of the need to let the Word of God speak from within the human situation. What matters is to multiply the numbers of 'believers' even though in order to do this it may be necessary to leave out everything that cannot be made to fit into a completely individualistic, other-worldly system. Evangelism becomes little more than a technique to 'win souls,' and for this, theological reflection is unnecessary; it is enough to use canned methods and imported formulas of salvation" (p. 11).

20. J. W. Pickett, et al., *Church Growth and Group Conversion* (South Pasadena, CA: William Carey Library Publishers, 1973).

21. Ibid., p. 25.

22. Donald A. McGavran, *The Bridges of God* (London: World Dominion Press, 1955), p. 109.

23. Ibid.

24. Ibid., p. 112.

25. Donald A. McGavran, "Wrong Strategy: The Real Crisis in Missions," *International Review of Mission* 54 (Oct. 1965), 451-461.

26. Donald A. McGavran, "Church Growth Strategy Continued," *International Review of Mission* 57 (July 1968), 337.

27. Ibid., p. 338.

28. Ibid., p. 339.

29. "The Growth of the Church: A Statement," *International Review of Mission* 57 (July 1968), 330-34.

30. Fifth Assembly of the World Council of Churches, Nairobi, Kenya, November 23-December 10, 1975. Plenary Document 48, p. 11.

31. J. Robertson McQuilkin, *Measuring the Church Growth Movement* (Chicago: Moody Press, 1974). This was first published in 1973 as *How Biblical Is the Church Growth Movement?*, p. 30.

32. Ibid., p. 76.

33. Donald A. McGavran, "The Dimensions of World Evangelization," in *Let the Earth Hear His Voice*, papers and responses from the International Congress on World Evangelization, Lausanne, Switzerland, ed. J. D. Douglas (Minneapolis: World Wide Publications, 1975), p. 103.

34. "The Lausanne Covenant," in *Let the Earth Hear His Voice*, p. 7.

35. Donald A. McGavran, *Understanding Church Growth* (Grand Rapids: Eerdmans, 1970), p. 175.

36. Louis Berkhof, *Systematic Theology* (Grand Rapids: Eerdmans, 1939), pp. 165-178.

37. Charles Hodge, *Systematic Theology,* 3 vols. (Grand Rapids: Eerdmans, 1946), vol. 3, p. 475.

38. G. C. Berkouwer, *Sin* (Grand Rapids: Eerdmans, 1971), p. 213. Hodge takes a more trenchant position (*Systematic Theology,* vol. 3, pp. 465-85).

39. Spener, *Theologische Bedencken,* p. 159.

40. See Arthur P. Johnston, *World Evangelism and the Word of God* (Minneapolis: Bethany Press, 1974), pp. 30-32, 259-64.

41. Hodge, *Systematic Theology,* vol. 3, p. 471.

42. Ibid., p. 484.

43. A. J. Gordon, *The Holy Spirit in Missions* (Harrisburg, PA: The Christian Alliance Publishing Co., 1944), p. 79.

44. McGavran, *Understanding Church Growth,* pp. 163-80.

45. "Findings and Recommendations" of the Meeting of the International

Missionary Council, Tambaram, Madras, India, December 12-29, 1938, p. 41. The meeting also responded to the new "mass movement or group approach to Christ" (pp. 57-58).

46. Tippett, *Church Growth and the Word of God,* briefly and concisely supports the essential church growth principle by biblical texts.

47. McQuilkin, *Measuring the Church Growth Movement,* p. 56, 58. Stephen Neill records how the change in the Moravian missionary message in Greenland brought a remarkable response from a hitherto unresponsive people.

48. Tippett, *Church Growth and the Word of God,* pp. 42-46. McGavran has the same thrust in speaking of the work of the Holy Spirit as "authentic spiritual fire" in *How Churches Grow* (London: World Dominion Press, 1963), pp. 55-59.

49. Allen, *Missionary Methods, St. Paul's and Ours,* pp. 62-77. Roland Allen among others has noted the basic elements of Paul's preaching in the synagogue and to the Gentiles.

50. Michael Green, *Evangelism in the Early Church* (Grand Rapids: Eerdmans, 1970), p. 234. "From the Acts of the Apostles down to Gregory and Origen we find the same story repeated time and again. Discussion with Christians, arguments with them, annoyance at them, leads the inquirer to read these 'barbaric writings' for himself. And once men begin to read, the Scriptures exercise their own fascination and power. Many an interested inquirer like Justin and Tatian, Athenagoras and Theophilus, came to Christian belief through finding, as he read, that 'the Word of God is living and active and sharper than any two-edged sword,' and that 'the sacred Scriptures are able to instruct you for salvation through faith in Jesus Christ.' "

51. McGavran, *Understanding Church Growth,* pp. 136-37.

52. Samuel H. Moffett, "What Makes the Korean Church Grow," *The Presbyterian Layman,* October 1974, p. 4.

RESPONSE / Walter Frank

The test of each area of theology must always be, "Thus saith the Scriptures." Happily there is a dogmatic doctrine of the church but care must be taken not to judge one by his church growth theology.

I agree with Dr. Liefeld that there are *underlying biblical issues,* but as Roger Greenway has charged, "Most of church growth missiology's theological bases have been worked out after the methodological insights and mission principles were arrived at through field observation and experience." Let us continue in the admirable pursuit of church growth studies but not take the risk of structuring a *rigid theology* of church growth. This will allow us to pursue aggressively and creatively new approaches to church growth.

Aptly, one of Liefeld's major conclusions points out that the great commission as found in Matthew 28:19 does not in any way suggest the evangelization of "peoples" or "families" but all who are "outside the community of believers." He acknowledges that many times the gospel did penetrate families such as the households of Cornelius and the Philippian jailor. However, the words of our Lord come through loud and clear that a decision to follow Him must take priority over any family ties and will more likely than not divide families asunder (Mark 10:29-31; Luke 9:57-62).

One of the most beautiful evidences of God at work in Europe today is the present moving of the Spirit in the midst of the gypsies. In France alone that church boasts 30,000 members with 230 preachers. Here is a classic example (and perhaps the only one we can isolate in Europe) of multi-individual conversions (people movements) not only within family units but also within the larger cohesive sociological unit. Gypsy life can almost be considered a phenomenon in the midst of Western culture. All around these islands of gypsy communal life, however, are the vast oceans of individual Westerners out of which the Lord is calling the one who is willing "to leave brothers or sisters, father or mother or children or lands for my sake and the gospel."

The enigma of Europe remains as a challenge to all church growth missiologists. Indeed it continues to threaten the faith and endurance of even the most durable missionary church planters and churchmen with few exceptions.

Dr. Johnston states that "growth may be seen as *a normal function* of the church. Nongrowth represents a denial of her nature and role 'between the times.' " What does this say about the church in North Africa, Europe and Japan? Care must be taken not to indict every local church or every regional expression of the church where there is little evident growth. Some of the most godly men of all time have suffered through the pangs of decades of nongrowth or slow growth. Should we not rather relate this normal function of growth to the church universal?

It is clear from these two excellent papers that when we get beyond the message, the methods and means are up for grabs. This is evident both in the Scripture record and in history. Observe Whitefield preaching the gospel on the English hillside in defiance of all social and cultural norms. God was there to bless His word and this served as a launching pad for revival and awakening.

Back to the church of the first century! What of strategy? Michael Green observes, "It is doubtful if they had one." It is plain, however, that the Holy Spirit's plan is that after the initial evangelism local churches must be established to perpetuate the body of Christ and accomplish His program of world witness. Both Liefeld and Johnston agree here. When the church is not planted or where it is anemic and impotent, the rivers are dammed up slowing down evangelism and leaving whole areas without a witness. The Republic of Ireland will confirm this unalterable biblical procedure. The Protestant church in Eire is degenerating and dying. Noble evangelistic endeavors sow the seed and gain converts through literature distribution, open-air meetings, door-to-door witness, and home Bible study groups. But where is the church? Church planting is almost nonexistent. Consequently this land continues to be known by the title Stanley Mawhinney gave his book — "Darkest Ireland."

The early church was impoverished! She had no historical perspective — no seminars, no books, treatises, computers, graphs or seminary courses — but she knew the word of the Lord, "I will build my church," and she knew the command of the Lord, "Go into all the world and preach the gospel to everyone." The early church proceeded to demonstrate by life and by lip that their Lord's last command must be their first concern. *Let it also be ours.*

RESPONSE / Vergil Gerber

The subject which has just been presented to us lies at the very heart and center of this consultation. As Johannes Blauw says, "A theology of mission cannot be other than a theology of the church. . . . The people of God [are] called *out* of the world, placed *in* the world and sent *to* the world . . . ."[1] This is what church growth is all about.

Let me first lay down a basic premise: *The church is the biblical goal of evangelism.* If we don't agree on this, we have no starting point. In the twenty-seven nations where we have had evangelism-church growth workshops (and I have intentionally hyphenated the two words), again and again I have met missionary colleagues who consider the goal of evangelism to be "preaching the gospel." When that has been accomplished, they say their job is over and the Holy Spirit does the rest. Getting people "born again" is thus equated with "making a profession." What happens after that is considered "follow-up" and (though they may not realize it) consequently becomes something of lesser importance. Decisions rather than disciples become the end goal of the great commission.

Now I'm convinced that there is a New Testament theology of church growth that starts with Jesus' announcement of His missionary purpose (i.e., the church — Matt. 16:18), builds upon the great commission (Matt. 28:19, 20) and the first local church model in Jerusalem (Acts 2:41-47), and regards the development and multiplication of churches throughout the Book of Acts and the epistles as the biblical norm.

With that as a background, let me respond briefly to the two papers which treat the subject from very different perspectives.

Dr. Liefeld rightly points up the urgent imperative of building a theology of church growth on firm biblical foundations. While I am not really convinced, as Dr. Greenway (a specialist in urban church growth strategies) asserts, that "*most* of church growth missiology's theological bases have been worked out *after* the methodological insights and mission principles were arrived at through field observation and experience," I certainly do support Dr. Liefeld in his insistence on using the biblical data as the starting point, and from those data developing both the theology and principles of church growth.

I had hoped, however, that he would provide for us at least a skeleton outline of the biblical development of the subject which could later be fleshed out. Of course, I am not unaware of the comprehensive nature of this subject nor of the fact that a vast literature has already been written either challenging or defending church growth principles. But Liefeld has chosen to treat the subject selectively, picking out a few of the more controversial issues and supporting his stance in regard to them with his biblical insights. He treats only three of these issues. And he devotes a prolonged section to answering in some detail the arguments regarding the first of these issues, namely, multi-individual decisions. I wish that he had developed the other two issues with equal detail and biblical documentation for our consideration.

As one who is very much involved in church growth workshops around the world, I am grateful to Dr. Liefeld for sharing his critical insights and exegetical understanding of the passages cited. At the same time, I hope that our discussion groups will not get "hung up" on the controversial issues, and miss the main thrust of this consultation, that is, that church growth must lie at the heart of any biblical theology of mission.

Liefeld's final conclusion — the call for balance between exegetical bases and the practical outworking of the principles, rather than an exclusive choice between alternatives — is well stated.

Dr. Johnston has given us a biblical-historical perspective on the subject. His introductory paragraph sets the stage for our discussions.

It starts with the biblical mandate *to* the church and the expansion and extension *of* the church on earth as recorded in the Acts of the Apostles and makes the visible manifestation of the church and its numerical increase both in membership and in the number of churches upon the earth the central focus of the theology of mission, and therefore of the theology of church growth.

His paper rightly sees the historical development of planting local churches from biblical times to the present as the dynamic outworking of divine missionary purpose. He looks at church growth not as "a contemporary novelty or innovation, but a continuous, normal concern of mission leading to the 'great new fact' of our times — the autonomous church in all continents and in almost all countries of the world."

I would certainly agree with Dr. Johnston (and with Dr. Liefeld) that while there are a number of theological details and nuances on which evangelicals may differ, evangelicals in general are committed to the biblical concept of church growth and that as long as "the church growth movement retains its present biblical orientation, its contribution to the work of world evangelization may be even more significant in the future than it has been in the past."

I like the two foundations which he lays for church growth:

(1) The solid bedrock of a verbally inerrant Scripture as the basis of sound hermeneutics.

(2) The importance of the social, anthropological, psychological and communication sciences, and their continual subordination to the rigorous evaluations of Scripture.

As he says so eloquently: "These disciplines must be seen through the grid of Scripture, not Scripture through the grid of these disciplines."

FOOTNOTE

1. Johannes Blauw, *Missionary Nature of the Church: A Survey of the Biblical Theology of Missions* (New York: McGraw-Hill, 1962), p. 126.

RESPONSE / Victor L. Walter

My perspective is that of practical theology. That means that I'm one of those creatures of the seminary night which pop up occasionally from some unexplored valley where the common people reside and which lurk between the mighty ridges of learning constituted by academically respectable brethren. We practical theologians certainly join the common folk in gazing with awe and reverence at the lofty, unassailable crags of learning. How perpendicular, how eminent, how unapproachable the intertwined linguistic verbiage of their glacial slopes! May I point out that those of the valley also view such mighty slopes with a little apprehensive suspicion. More than one of our lush cows of devotion have turned into skeletons scarce fit for liturgical hamburger by being lost on that thin-grown tundra. More than one of our village churches lie in ruins under the avalanche of some wordy theological spasm from on high. More than one of our rustic, idealistic young preachers have been chilled out of their ardor by the inexorable march of ridge-top, frozen contexts.

To speak in a completely different framework: Have any of you ever wondered along about the thirteenth hour of one of these workshops if while Paul was out founding those churches in Acts, the Sanhedrin was not holding theology of church growth seminars back in that marble splendor, the temple of Jerusalem? Since God had served notice long since that His nostrils were tired of the smoke of sacrifices (somewhat akin to the prolonged odor of conference coffee), He didn't mind Titus' A.D. 70 misadventure too much. He cast His divine lot in with thorn-in-the-flesh Paul, weak-stomached Timothy, and that other Titus out among all those miserable Cretans. All of these remarks are preamble to (1) my five questions to the two papers from those twin scholarly peaks and (2) my own valley-grown observation.

FIVE QUESTIONS TO THE PEAKS

To borrow our New Testament scholar's imagery, the twin plowshares of Liefeld and Johnston have beautifully and ably broken up some "assumptive clods." Into this now fallow ground I drop five seeds of inquiry. The first three grains fall into Dr. Liefeld's field, and the last two are scattered into Dr. Johnston's plowing.

Grain one: Is it completely unwholesome that the Scripture has been used by those in the church growth movement instead of studied by them? While one must not minimize the need for careful exegetical study rather than prooftexts, is it not one of the glories of church growth that, already bloodied in the battle, its advocates cast an eye over the academic shoulder to find parallels in Scripture?

Corn two: Is the term *winnable peoples* one which we really wish to use? Does it not unwholesomely suggest that there are unwinnable people? Should we not rather speak of the largest number winnable or those most quickly to be won, for example, pre-evangelized groups? It seems to me that, if we must stay with this term, we should speak of winnable as over against "least winnable people." These least winnable people are the pre-evangelized who have stiffened the neck and rejected the gospel — such as Paul himself, bound for Damascus, kosher picnic basket over his pharisee arm.

Barley three: Why should we speak only of unity as the seen evidence of the Divine Unseen? Are there not just as many New Testament statements making love the evidence of the reality and the vitality of the redeemed community? May not this love be what crosses the anthropological cultural barriers to create unity in the first place?

Wheat four: Does not the statement that belief in an inerrant Scripture is necessary for church growth fly in the face of church history? Are there not some times of mighty expansion in the church when she certainly would not have defined her view of Scripture in our exacting terms? This is not in any way to challenge the necessity for or the claim of inerrancy; it is simply to assert that church growth probably can occur and has occurred in the absence of this dogma.

Seed five: In order to make my own valley-grown observation I return to the opening of Dr. Johnston's paper and his assumption that the apostle Paul was and is normative for "regulating evangelism, mission, and ecclesiology." If, as Dr. Johnston rightly points out in his conclusion, the work of the Holy Spirit through the Word in the hearer and His work within the proclaiming witness are necessary for continued church growth, we have, at least in part, two variables in twentieth-century hearer and modern proclaimer. Adding to these the variable of the cultural context, can we not question just how far Paul is normative, especially in ecclesiology?

THE VALLEY-GROWN OBSERVATION

Behind the legitimate statement that Paul's principles are normative in ecclesiology lurks the shadow of an unexpressed, but lovingly fondled, evangelical assumption that a particular church order is normative. I want to challenge this implicit assumption that there is one normative New Testament ecclesiology insofar as it applies to church order. To ask, "What is Pauline church order?" is to ask an illegitimate question. The proper and needful question is, "What purposes for church order are laid down in the New Testament, and, does the order of my freshly-planted church permit these purposes to be realized?" In the New Testament there seem to be at least nine purposes for church order:

(1) To permit the Holy Spirit to raise up and approve workers (Acts 13:1-4; I Tim. 3:1-13; Titus 1:5-9).

(2) To enforce apostolic discipline — this includes any challenge to apostolic doctrine (Matt. 18:15-20; I Cor. 5:1-5; II Cor. 2:6-11; I Tim. 5:19-22).

(3) To encourage the development and use of the gifts in all members of the body so that they are engaged in the ministry (this will include evangelism) (Rom. 12:3-8; I Cor. 12:1-30; I Thess. 5:11-15; I Peter 4:10, 11).

(4) To preserve the unity of the body (I Cor. 1:10-13; 12:24, 25; Eph. 4:1-6; II Thess. 3:6, 14, 15).

(5) To equip the saints personally so that they mature into Christlikeness (Eph. 4:11-16).

(6) To maintain orderly worship (Acts 6:2, 4; I Cor. 11:13-16; 14:18-40; I Tim. 2:11, 12).

(7) To protect the purity of the Lord's Table (I Cor. 5:7, 8; 10:14-22; 11:20-34; II Cor. 6:14-18).

(8) To support the ministry financially (I Cor. 9:1-14; Gal. 6:6; Phil. 4:10-19; II Thess. 3:8, 9; I Tim. 5:17, 18).

(9) To care for widows and the poor (Acts 6:1-6; I Cor. 16:1-3; I Tim. 5:9-16).

Church planting and rapid church expansion probably never have been dependent upon seeing Pauline ecclesiology as normative, but they certainly must take seriously the New Testament purposes for church structure.

Finally, my brethren, it was Swinburne who said, "I could stomach the Christ if He did not bring with Him His leprous bride the church." Swinburne missed the point. Now Christ is *sending* the bride. But let us evangelicals at least allow the bride her changes of raiment ecclesiastical until she is glorified by His coming into this weary world with her!

Well, so much for one valley stone lobbed toward those serene, cool, lofty heights where Johnston and Liefeld learnedly dwell. Along with my thrown pebble, I salute them and relish their brilliant work. My parting observation is that the valley will always be nourished by streams from the heights as long as the valley stays warm enough to melt any glaciers that are developed on the academic ridgetops.

REPLY / Walter L. Liefield

I greatly value the comments of Frank, Gerber and Walter, as well as those made in personal conversations. I find myself agreeing with Gerber's wish that I could have given a better proportioned outline of the entire subject. Although I began with the observation that my paper would be selective, I might well have abbreviated some of the points in order to enlarge other topics.

One such topic, unity, to which Gerber alludes indirectly, is mentioned under Walter's third "seed of inquiry." While the importance of unity in itself is indisputable, Walter is certainly correct in seeing love as the essential ingredient. This love is manifested by sacrifice for the good of others and by demonstration of the qualities celebrated in I Corinthians 13, but it is also manifested in mutual reconcilation. One is reminded of the observation in I John 4:20 that "anyone who does not love his brother, whom he has seen, cannot love God, whom he has not seen." One may ask on this basis how the world is expected to be convinced of the claim that we have been reconciled to the unseen God unless they see that we are indeed reconciled to each other. I recognize that people of similar background and interests do function better with one another than with those who are different. I was reminded by Dr. Buswell in conversation that in spite of the equalities mentioned in Galatians 3:28, the distinctives do, after all, remain (e.g., between male and female). He suggested that my word *blend* was too strong. I also realize that I lack firsthand awareness of non-Western cultures, and that my idealism needs to grapple with cultural realities.

If we acknowledge all this, it seems to me that we must strive (Eph. 4:3) to find ways in which our unity can be publicly affirmed. In the American urban and suburban situations various means have been attempted. One way is to meet for fellowship, prayer and study in small homogeneous (house church?) groups, but to come together for worship, teaching and the Lord's Supper. However it may be done at home or overseas, some way must be found which is realistic as to sociological factors and yet which demonstrates that the power and love of God can transcend these factors.

The topic of winnable peoples is graciously addressed by Walter. His thoughts here are certainly appealing, especially the example of Paul. Undoubtedly much further help can be found in both the precepts and examples of Scripture. One also must give full scope, as those deeply involved in church growth around the world seek to do, to the sovereign leading of the Holy Spirit.

In conclusion, I would like to stress again my sense of debt not only to those who offered sensitive critiques of my paper, but to all those who teach and apply biblical principles of church growth in their own ministries. May biblical theology and biblical evangelism be continually joined together in the service of our Lord.

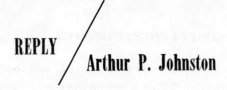

Victor Walter's crop analogy reminds us of the needs a particular field may have for fertilizer, weed control or pesticides!

Weed One: Church growth is methodological rather than primarily theological.

One essential purpose of this consultation is to show the interrelation between theology and missiology. "Theology," it may

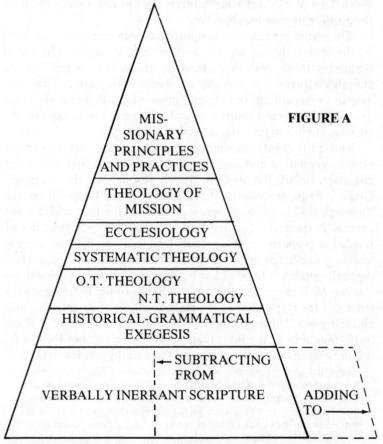

MIS-
SIONARY
PRINCIPLES
AND PRACTICES

FIGURE A

THEOLOGY OF
MISSION

ECCLESIOLOGY

SYSTEMATIC THEOLOGY

O.T. THEOLOGY
N.T. THEOLOGY

HISTORICAL-GRAMMATICAL
EXEGESIS

←SUBTRACTING
FROM

VERBALLY INERRANT SCRIPTURE

ADDING
TO →

By adding to the scriptural revelation or taking away from it (note dotted lines), *biblical* mission becomes distorted and defective.

be said, "bakes no bread." Yet T. J. Bach believed that "good theology makes good doxology." That is, sound theology produces right worship, satisfies the needs of the heart and generates an evangelistic dynamic. Dr. M. C. Tenney taught us as students that "it is difficult to be continually enthusiastic about nothing!" Good theology produces, maintains and sustains love for Jesus Christ, lost men and church growth (II Cor. 5:14-21).

Good missiology and church growth are built upon the solid bedrock of verbal inerrancy. Figure A illustrates how sound missionary theology and methodology are the result of careful exegesis and theological work.

Weed Two in "Wheat Four": Inerrancy has not historically been the position of growing churches.

The verbal inerrancy of Scripture has been universally accepted by the church throughout the postapostolic centuries. The use of Scriptures to support theological debate in the councils of the church confirms that the church accepted inerrancy. Dogmatic assertions regarding the divine' inspiration of Scripture were necessary in recent centuries in order to meet the attacks of the enemies of biblical infallibility (verbal inerrancy).

Vatican II (1961-1965) introduced a *new* tenor and wording, a view of revelation and inspiration *different* from that which was characteristic of the Roman church throughout the centuries. Gregory Baum records that "the authors of the Constitution, the Theological Commission, were conscious of the fact, and did not conceal it from the Council Fathers, that the understanding of revelation proposed by them would lead to a new theological epistemology and a new understanding of Christian truth."[1] Baum further calls attention to what has been omitted in the *Documents of Vatican II*. While it is noted that the books of the Bible were written under the inspiration of the Holy Spirit "in their entirety, with all their parts," there is nothing more about inspiration: it is the *truths* taught in all the Bible that are without error, *not the words*. It is *the church* that determines what these truths are. Baum notes:

> The third chapter announces the faith of the Church that Holy Scripture is inspired by the Spirit, that it has God as its author, and that it has been received as such by the Church. God works through men who freely use their own gifts and who thus must also be regarded as authors of the biblical books. Nothing more is said about inspiration . . . . Thanks to this inspiration, Scripture is the authentic and powerful message of God addressed to men. Catholic teaching speaks here of the inerrancy of the Bible . . . . In the final text of

the Constitution we read that the Bible teaches "the truth which God for our salvation wished to be contained in the sacred writings firmly, faithfully, and without error." The object of inerrancy is thus clearly narrowed to the saving truth contained in each and every part of Scripture. One may not understand this as if only certain parts of Scripture teach truth without error. According to the teaching of the Church, the entire Scripture is inspired in all its parts. It is the saving truth contained in all these parts that is communicated without error.[2]

The change from the doctrine of a verbally inerrant Bible, while only a seemingly minor one, actually represents a great crack in the foundations of the Roman Catholic theological system. This may account in part for the contemporary instability and theological pluralism in that church. This point was not noted in the studies of this consultation.

Prior to Vatican II the tradition of the Roman church had already distorted the biblical foundation. The old foundation of an inerrant Bible was further confused and shaken by the new view of inspiration advocated by Vatican II (see Figure B). Evangelicals must learn to look beneath the exposed iceberg tip of missiology and recognize the theological foundations that sustain or stifle mission. Good missiology grows out of good, biblical theology; bad missiology grows out of bad, extrabiblical theology. Sound and deep theology is essential for the true growth of the church. Viewing methodology or pragmatic theology (praxis) as the key to mission can ultimately result only in the demise already experienced by mainline churches.

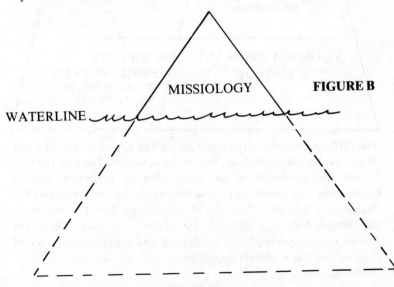

WATERLINE   MISSIOLOGY   **FIGURE B**

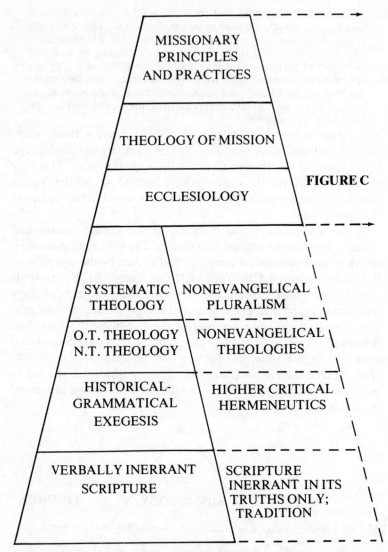

FIGURE C

The differences between the culture of the apostolic age and our own must be acknowledged, but we have ventured out on the thin ice of the evolution of an ecclesiological organism without recognizing that apostolic ecclesiology is normative for today. Ecclesiology is intimately linked with soteriology. In turn soteriology and ecclesiology are bedrock foundations of New Testament church growth principles. The identity and revealed character of the gospel in the world are imperiled.

Weed Three in "Seed Five": The normative nature of Scripture is unessential for church growth.

Vatican II has also led Baum to conclude that the normative nature of Scripture has been weakened. Inerrancy implies not only the infallibility of what God has said and done in the past, but also the *normative nature* of that which God revealed as His will for the church in the New Testament (II Tim 2:2). The principles and patterns of mission apply to us today. When verbal inerrancy and hence the historicity of the Bible are questioned, the teaching role and the normative nature of Scripture for missiology are also sacrificed.

Since divine revelation is no longer regarded as equivalent to divine teaching, it is possible to come to a broader understanding of scriptural inspiration and inerrancy and to a less literal concept of the historicity of the biblical books. The Scriptures do not mediate sentences containing truths closed in themselves; they are accounts that give witness to the wonderful things the Lord has done, and still does, for the salvation of His people. The truth of Scripture points to the person of Jesus Christ.[3]

If the conclusions of systematic theology are not normative for today — and they are not for many missiologists — ecclesiology, the theology of mission, and principles and practice are expanded to the limit of fertile imaginations (see Figure C). The inerrant Scriptures, and especially the New Testament, set a clear normative pattern for the effective growth of the church between the times of our Lord's ascension and the second coming.

FOOTNOTES

1. Gregory Baum, "Vatican II's Constitution on Revelation: History and Interpretation," *Theological Studies* 28, No. 1 (March 1962), p. 59.

2. Ibid., pp. 70, 71.

3. Ibid., p. 75.

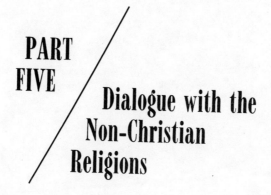

PART FIVE

Dialogue with the Non-Christian Religions

David J. Hesselgrave

INTERRELIGIOUS DIALOGUE— BIBLICAL AND CONTEMPORARY PERSPECTIVES

INTRODUCTION

However it might be characterized, the "brave new world" is still the world of the future. Two things can be said about the present world. First, it is not very brave. Second, in many ways it is not very new either.

It is an open question as to whether there is more brávery or more newness around, but when it comes to interreligious dialogue, at least, my vote is cast for *newness*. With the widening of the road of religion between West and East so as to accommodate two-way traffic, the past century has witnessed a remarkable upsurge in contact between adherents of the various faiths, and, to a certain extent, in interfaith dialogue as well.

As concerns *bravery*, about all one can lose in interreligious dialogue is *face* and *faith*. Because of their predominantly all-inclusive posture ecumenists have not risked much of either face or faith, so little bravery has been required on their part. Evangelicals, on the other hand, have felt that the risk of losing both face and faith is too great, and therefore have tended to avoid dialogue altogether. Their position has required no bravery whatsoever!

This paper constitutes a challenge to bravery on the part of both ecumenists and evangelicals in the belief that insofar as the world is new and dialogue is desirable there must be some old-fashioned daring.

INTERRELIGIOUS DIALOGUE AND ECUMENISTS

It is difficult if not impossible to do justice to the ecumenical understanding of dialogue in a few short paragraphs. Generalizations easily become *over*generalizations. References to the literature easily become selective and one-sided. If we fall into these traps in this attempt to analyze the ecumenical view on interfaith dialogue it is not due to lack of a conscious effort to avoid them.

Let us examine the ecumenical view of interreligious dialogue under three rubrics: its purposes, its presuppositions, and its prototypes.

The Purposes of Ecumenical Interreligious Dialogue

As one would expect, ecumenists do not speak univocally on the meaning and purpose of dialogue. Speaking from his background in the Christian-Hindu encounter, however, Eric J. Sharpe identifies four types of dialogue — each with its corresponding objective.

Discursive dialogue "involves meeting, listening and discussion on the level of mutual competent intellectual inquiry."[1] It is basically the activity which previously was called "dialectic" or "debate" and it is engaged in by those "who assume that the human reason is competent to lead individuals into an understanding of truth."[2]

Human dialogue can be explained in the following terms: "Doctrines divide; humanity unites. Put in its simplest form, this is the conviction (a rational conviction) that underlies the greater part of the activity that is today called interreligious dialogue. The 'I-Thou' relationship is all-important; what is said or done is less so."[3]

Secular dialogue "concentrates entirely on the situation of man in the world, aiming solely at the recognition of joint concern and the need for joint secular action, irrespective of divergencies in religious conviction."[4]

Interior dialogue eschews too much dependence on intellectualization, whether doctrinal or otherwise, and in the tradition of mystical, contemplative religion, is concerned with moving closer to the "divine mystery."[5]

Sharpe concludes that the goals of interreligious dialogue vary with the type or mode and that in only one case are the objectives fairly clear. That case is discursive dialogue in which the goal is "usually taken to be a better understanding of the other person's religious stance, possibly in order to facilitate the communication of the Christian message."[6]

The Presuppositions of Ecumenical Interreligious Dialogue

Sharpe is convinced that dialogue is a practical activity and as such is difficult to conceive of if utterly divorced from the discursive, intellectual element.[7] Nevertheless,

Dialogue does certainly involve first and foremost from the Christian side the rejection of the impatience and polemics and partisan controversies of the past — largely because the Christian theological foundations on which these once rested have now been widely revised. Once this point has been passed, and once it has been accepted that there is a common ground between believers, dialogue may turn in any one of a number of directions — intellectual, personal, secular or contemplative. Its advocates almost all assume, however, that the causes of past intolerance have to do with the doctrinal and other constructions that men have built around their central religious commitment, and seek for areas of common concern in which those constructions are transcended, penetrated or avoided.[8]

We have reviewed Sharpe's analysis at some length because he makes necessary distinctions while delineating the basic assumptions which have served the interests of ecumenical interreligious dialogue to this point.

In fairness, it should be noted that the phrase "almost all" in Sharpe's quotation implies that there are exceptions. Some who have been involved in ecumenical interreligious dialogue in one way or another have signaled that a re-examination of its basis is sorely needed. W. A. Visser 'tHooft,[9] Lesslie Newbigin[10] and Stephen Neill[11] (among others) have spoken pointedly to the effect that though dialogue may require the cultivation of a new attitude, it dare not demand the abandonment of truly Christian moorings. These warnings constitute *prima facie* evidence that all too often ecumenical interfaith dialogue has been built upon sub-Christian views of revelation, Christ, and man. Numerous proponents of — and participants in — such dialogues could be quoted to show that this is, in fact, so. But we turn, rather, to some actual dialogues which will illustrate what has been said.

Prototypes of Ecumenical Interreligious Dialogue

The first interreligious consultation called by the World Council of Churches was held in March of 1970 at Ajaltoun, Lebanon. Among the thirty-eight specially selected and erudite participants were three Hindus, four Buddhists and three Muslims.

In his introduction to the collection of documents presented at that consultation, S. J. Samartha writes that the consultation "was not an academic discussion *about* dialogue but an adventure into the experience of dialogue itself in a multilateral context."[12] He goes on to explain that the

> consultation was neither a group session of jelly fishes nor a battle between porcupines; it was a meeting between persons who were deeply committed to their respective faiths, who were aware of the perils and promises of dialogue, and who were yet willing to accept

that dialogue is not so much a problem to be solved as an experience to be shared in joy and expectation.[13]

An examination of the documents reveals the nature of this particular dialogue as well as of some interreligious dialogues which preceded it.

Klaus Klostermaier describes some Hindu-Christian dialogues in India in which he participated. The "promising pattern" which emerged in those meetings was "meditations on parallel Upanishadic and Biblical texts so as to receive the message of India to the church through her scriptures."[14] Klostermaier goes on to explain what this means.

> In order to be able to "listen to the voice of the Spirit" we have to free ourselves, as far as possible, from preconceived ideas and let the text —*Shruti,* the revealed voice of *Brahman!* — speak to us in its immediacy. This requires strict mental discipline, a kind of "epoche" (in the sense of Husserl, a "suspension of judgement") — ultimately a "*metanoia,*" a "*conversio,*" a re-thinking, an openness for God's Word . . . .
>
> We must read the Upanishads "*in conspectu Christi*" — to find Christ in them in a way analogous to that in which Christ found himself in the Old Testament. We have to discover the "*sensus plenior*" of the Upanishads — our Christian interpretation should not misread the meaning.[15]

Masatoshi Doi reports the gist of a speech by Dr. Nishitani, Professor of Otani University, at a 1969 meeting of Christian and Buddhist scholars in Japan. Nishitani said in essence:

> As far as religion is the state of being ultimately concerned with what is ultimately meaningful for a certain believing subject, to borrow Professor Tillich's concept, it is intrinsic to a religion to have a claim for absoluteness. Then, how could two absolute religions meet with each other in dialogical terms? If dialogical encounter is to be possible, each partner must have openness or emptiness within itself without losing the sense of absoluteness. Openness means the possibility to change, and emptiness means the ability to understand the other from within himself. Each religion must be unique and unchangeable in its fundamental position. But, in religion uniqueness implies universal validity, the unchangeable core of a religion embraces the infinite possibility of developing its meaning — contents. This openness or emptiness which is intrinsic to true religions is the basic presupposition for dialogical encounter between religions. Both parties must be ready to listen to the other and undergo changes through such encounters.[16]

Matatoshi Doi says that there was no radical opposition to Dr. Nishitani's position and adds, "It must be confessed that the present writer himself is groping in that direction."[17]

Lynn A. de Silva explains the Buddhist attitude toward dialogue in the following words:

> Although there is general agreement that theologically oriented and action oriented dialogue is most desirable in a situation of religious pluralism, for the purpose of mutual understanding and enrichment, for dispelling suspicions and prejudices, and for harnessing moral and spiritual values to eradicate social evils and promote and foster social justice, the Buddhists strongly feel that "evangelism" is most undesirable and incompatible with dialogue.[18]

Of signal importance are the reactions of the participants — especially the non-Christian participants — after the Ajaltoun experience in interfaith dialogue. The consultation requested four of its members (one from each religion represented) to write their personal reflections. These are anonymous in the record. One quotation seems to be more or less representative and is entered here:

> The dialogue, functioning as internal sign of hope, introduced most of us to a new spirituality, an interfaith spirituality, which I mostly felt in common prayer: who actually led the prayer or meditation, a Christian or a Muslim, or a Hindu, or a Buddhist, did not much matter, what actually was said during prayer was not all important, whether a Muslim would say "Amen" after a Christian prayer mentioning Sonship of Christ, was not the question; what we really became aware of was our common human situation before God and in God.
>
> We were thus led gradually into a new relation with God, with our own selves, and with others, and this new relation was perhaps to what entire human history was moving, a relationship that was not new in the sense that it differed from what it was in each religious tradition but in the sense that it was expressing itself in a universal convergent humanity. A new day was dawning not on a new earth, or in a new sky but on a new work of man, on man doing something new. This day is just begun. Our dialogue was therefore not an end but a beginning, only a step, there is a long way to go.[19]

Again, and in fairness to the more conservative proponents of interreligious dialogue in the conciliar movement, it must be recognized that not all instances of that dialogue completely delete notions of proclamation and conversion. The statement on dialogue coming out of an ecumenical consultation in Kandy, Ceylon in 1967 did say, "Dialogue may include proclamation, since it must always be undertaken in the spirit of those who have good news to share."[20] Objectivity compels us to add, however, that the very first *major* instance of ecumenical interreligious dialogue sponsored by the World Council of Churches lends little evidence to indicate that the proclamation of the good news of Christ was a significant feature of that dialogue. And there is little evidence to indicate that conversion was a consideration.

INTERRELIGIOUS DIALOGUE IN THE BIBLE

An evangelical understanding of dialogue must find its basic purposes, presuppositions and prototypes in the Scriptures. In considering them it would seem advantageous to change the order of the previous section of this paper and look first at examples of interreligious dialogue before proceeding to purposes and presuppositions.

New Testament Prototypes of Interreligious Dialogue

The word *dialogue*, of course, is derived from the Greek noun *dialogos* (the verb form is *dialegomai*) which, along with its cognates, was common in classical and Hellenistic Greek but was somewhat less common in the New Testament (in fact, the noun does not appear at all in the New Testament). In Greek philosophy the emphasis in *dialogos* was upon reaching truth by means of the dialectic inherent in discussion and debate. The New Testament usage of *dialegomai*, however, is quite different.

There is in the gospels no clear instance of the use of *dialegomai* in connection with interreligious communication. The cognate verb *dialogizomai* (which means "to converse or discuss with" but with perhaps somewhat greater stress on the discussion element) is used somewhat ambiguously in one instance of confrontation between the scribes and Pharisees and Jesus (Luke 5:21-24). The gospels do make it clear, however, that Jesus did not retreat from two-way conversation with His hearers whether they were friends or foes. We may take Jesus' encounters with the Jewish religious rulers and His conversations with Nicodemus and the Samaritan woman as examples of interfaith dialogue.

The most instructive instances of the use of the word *dialegomai* are to be found in the historical record of the ministry of the apostle Paul. He engaged in dialogue in the synagogues (Acts 17:2, 17; 18:4, 19), in the market place (Acts 17:17), in the school of Tyrannus (Acts 19:9), and in the church at Troas (Acts 20:7, 9). A relevant use of the word is also found in Acts 24:12 where Paul defends himself before Felix by insisting that his accusers from Jerusalem did not find him carrying on dialogues or causing riots in the temple, synagogues or the city itself. As in the case of the gospels, once it is clear what dialogue entailed in these instances, it is apparent that there are other cases where dialogue occurred even though the word is not used in reporting them.

An investigation of all of the relevant cases of dialogue in the Scriptures cannot be undertaken here. John Stott is undoubtedly correct when he points out that the God of the Bible Himself enters into dialogue with man, and that the Old Testament as well as the New Testament furnishes numerous examples of dialogue. As regards the latter, Stott reminds us that Jesus "seldom if ever spoke in a declamatory, take-it-or-leave-it-style. Instead, whether explicitly or implicitly, he was constantly addressing questions to his hearers' minds and consciences."[21] Stott, however, devotes most of his attention to the examples of dialogue in the ministry of Paul to which we have already drawn the reader's attention.

The Purposes of Interreligious Dialogue in the New Testament

What were the meaning and purposes of the prototypes of interreligious dialogue in the New Testament? It may be helpful to begin with a negative question: What did dialogue not mean in these instances and for what purposes was it not used?

First, it would seem clear that New Testament dialogue did not mean discussion with a view to the discovery of religious truth. As Gottlob Schrenk says:

> In the New Testament there is no instance of the classical use of *dialegomai* in the philosophical sense. In the sphere of revelation there is no question of reaching the idea through dialectic. What is at issue is the obedient and percipient acceptance of the Word spoken by God, which is not an idea, but the comprehensive declaration of the divine will which sets all life in the light of divine truth.[22]

Second, it also seems clear that more was involved than the delivering of sermons or lectures, though Schrenk himself is inclined toward that limitation. This is indicated, in the first place, by companion words in the same contexts such as *paratithēmi* (allege or prove) (Acts 17:3), *peithō* (persuade) (Acts 18:4; 19:8), and *parrēsiazomai* (speak boldly) (Acts 19:8). In the second place, the circumstances surrounding these instances of dialogue point to something beyond lecturing and preaching. In Athens the philosophers disputed with Paul and called him a babbler (Acts 17:18). In Corinth, members of the synagogue reacted to three months of Pauline ministry in a manner extreme enough to cause Paul to remove his disciples and to continue his mission in a school (Acts 19:8, 9). Paul's defense before Felix could be interpreted to mean either that he did not encounter those of other persuasions in such a way as to arouse their emotions, or (more likely) that at the time of his supposed troublemaking he was not engaged in this type of activity at all. In any event, the carrying out of his mission in Jerusalem and elsewhere was the occasion of a great deal of animosity on the part of some Jewish leaders.

On the positive side, then, what *was* the nature of dialogue in the New Testament? To what purposes *was* it used? All that we have said would seem to support Bauer, Arndt and Gingrich when they conclude that in some of the passages we have cited *dialegomai* meant to "discuss, conduct a discussion . . ." and that it was used "of lectures which were likely to end *in disputations*" (italics mine).[23] John Stott elaborates:

> Paul's dialogue was clearly a part of his proclamation and subordinate to his proclamation. Moreover, the subject of his dialogue with the world was one which he always chose himself, namely Jesus Christ, and its object was always conversion to Jesus Christ.[24]

The fact that Jesus and Paul were willing to listen as well as speak, and to answer questions of their hearers' devising as well as questions which their hearers should have asked but didn't, enhanced the faithful proclamation of the gospel and the likelihood of their hearers being attracted to it and converted. In no way can New Testament dialogue be construed as lacking in a concern for either truth or persons. In no way can it be construed as militating against proclamation and conversion. Dialogue was a method; proclamation was its nature; and conversion was its goal.

The Presuppositions of Interreligious Dialogue in the New Testament

The presuppositions of New Testament interreligious dialogue are too numerous to be fully explored here, but they include certain assumptions to which attention must be given if we are to faithfully carry out our Christian mission today.

Dialogue is *possible* because both the Christian missionary and the adherents of other religions have a common humanity which exhibits the imprint of the *imago Dei*, bears the marks of the fall, and shares in a general revelation.

Dialogue is *meaningful* because God has given a further (special) revelation in His Son and in the Bible which can be communicated by missionaries who have a knowledge of that revelation; it can be used by the Holy Spirit for the conversion of unbelievers.

Dialogue is *essential* because the missionary is obliged to engage in it by the very nature of his calling, and because his hearers are lost apart from repenting and believing the gospel which is at the heart of biblical dialogue.

Let us be clear here. Scriptural dialogue derives its characteristics from these presuppositions which are provided by biblical revelation. The presuppositions may or may not be made explicit in a particular case or dialogue, but they are always there to undergird and enforce it. Apart from them the prototypes of interreligious dialogue in the New Testament would have exhibited an entirely different character. And apart from them, interreligious dialogue today will exhibit an entirely different character from that of the New Testament prototypes.

THE EVANGELICAL AND
INTERRELIGIOUS DIALOGUE TODAY

Evangelicals are being challenged to demonstrate a new kind of bravery today. If the Christian messenger is to be taken seriously, he must demonstrate an interest in those great human concerns which are the topics of contemporary discussion. If the Christian messenger is to be heard, he must not be too timid to enter the forums of world opinion. If the Christian message is to be understood it must be framed with reference to the context of competing world views and faiths in which it is to be preached. If the Christian mission is to progress, its advocates must be prepared to advance in a new world of resurgent non-Christian religions.

Unless as evangelicals we are willing to risk locking ourselves up in a closet of monologue where we speak primarily to one another, the question for us is not, "Shall we engage in dialogue?" but, "In what kinds of dialogue shall we engage?" *Scriptural precedent clearly enjoins — and the Christian mission entails — interreligious dialogue that answers the questions and objections of unbelievers, proclaims the good news of Jesus Christ, and beseeches men to repent and believe.* Scriptural principle clearly precludes — and the Christian conscience condemns — any dialogue that compromises the gospel or countermands the great commission. Within these boundaries there are various types of dialogue which merit consideration by evangelicals.

Type 1: Dialogue on the nature of interreligious dialogue. It is to be deplored that the evangelical point of view has not been adequately represented in dialogues on dialogue. That lack of participation is due to several factors. First, for reasons of conscience evangelicals do not often hold membership in communions and organizations sponsoring such dialogues. Second, ecumenists are often predisposed not to include evangelicals in such dialogues lest predetermined purposes be jeopardized. Third, evangelicals are suspicious that little or no good can come from their participation. Fourth, because of lack of exposure to this kind of forum, evangelicals sometimes feel ill-prepared to engage in it. One could wish, therefore, that ecumenists would exhibit the same irenic spirit toward evangelicals that they do toward non-Christians. But one could also wish that, when the conditions are right, evangelicals thought it as important to faithfully expound their understanding of biblical teachings within the forums of Christendom as to faithfully proclaim those teachings in the contexts of heathendom.

Type 2: Interreligious dialogue that promotes freedom of worship and witness. There can be no question but that religious freedom is being challenged in one way or another among vast populations of people today. To accede quietly to totalitarian repression of religious faith, or to claim freedoms and privileges for one's own faith that are refused to others — such approaches are tacit denials of the most basic of men's inalienable rights. By what means will we implore the world's rulers and remind ourselves to respect those rights? The pursuit of that question may well merit interreligious conversation and even action.

Type 3: Interreligious dialogue concerned with meeting human need. This is similar to Sharpe's "secular dialogue," but it is not necessarily the same. In the first place, "secular dialogue" may not be the best nomenclature. Though definition of the term resolves some problems, it raises others. In the second place, from a Christian point of view it may be necessary that this dialogue stop short of complete cooperative action because it is incumbent upon the Christian that all he does in word and deed be done in the name of his Lord Christ (Col. 3:16). Nevertheless, discussion of ways and means may be invaluable in view of overwhelming and increasing human need.

Type 4: Interreligious dialogue designed to break down barriers of distrust and hatred in the religious world. If hatred is enjoined by any religion at all, it is certainly not enjoined by Christianity. Christians are admonished to love not only one another but all men. Canon Max Warren seems to imply that interreligious dialogue is basically of this type (or of Type 5, below).[25] It will be apparent that I have some difficulty with this understanding, but my disagreement is not with the idea that this kind of dialogue indeed can be profitable in breaking down barriers. There are excellent examples — too few, to be sure — that dialogue of this type can be used to dissolve distrust and break up log jams that have deterred the conversion of large groups of non-Christians.

Type 5: Interreligious dialogue that has as its objective the mutual comprehension of conflicting truth claims. This is close to Sharpe's "discursive dialogue" (especially as he has elaborated in one context),[26] but in contrast to discursive dialogue it is not committed to dialectic and the proposition that reason alone is a sufficient guide to truth. Its objective is to arrive at a common meaning, not necessarily a common faith. Evangelicals should give serious consideration to proposing and participating in this kind of dialogue because apart from it (in *some* form — so why not face-to-face?) real communication of the Christian faith becomes exceedingly difficult. It is apparent that our Lord and Paul understood the religious systems of their respondents and adapted to them. For altogether too long evangelical missionary communication has been monological because of lack of this understanding.

CONCLUSION

The Christian mission in the closing decades of the twentieth century challenges both the ecumenist and the evangelical to make a reappraisal of their attitudes toward, and participation in, interreligious dialogue.

Now is the time for ecumenists to review the direction that dialogue has taken and subject it to the standards of the revealed will of God in the Scriptures. Any form of dialogue that compromises the uniqueness of the Christian gospel and the necessity that the adherents of other faiths repent and believe it should be rejected and supplanted by forms of dialogue that enjoin conversion to Christ.

Now is the time for evangelicals to review their attitude of disinterest and nonparticipation in dialogue. To insist upon the uniqueness of the Christian gospel and the need of all men for salvation in Christ is not tantamount to engaging in biblical dialogue. Something new is needed. While it may be in the interest of the Christian mission to participate in those types of dialogue that have positive benefits and do not require abandonment or obfuscation of the Christian message, it definitely would be in the interest of the Christian mission to participate in those types of dialogue that enable evangelicals to enter the forums of the world with the understanding, commitment and courage that characterized the apostolic era.

In a world of religious pluralism evangelical witness, preaching, and teaching should become increasingly dialogical — answering those questions and objections raised by non-Christian respondents rather than simply answering questions of the evangelical's own devising. In the words of my colleague and friend, Carl F. H. Henry, "The only adequate alternative to dialogue that deletes the evangelical view is dialogue that expounds it. The late twentieth century is no time to shirk that dialogue."[27]

FOOTNOTES

1. Eric J. Sharpe, "The Goals of Inter-Religious Dialogue," in *Truth and Dialogue in World Religions: Conflicting Truth-Claims,* ed. John Hick (Philadelphia: The Westminster Press, 1974), p. 82.

2. Ibid.

3. Ibid., p. 83.

4. Ibid., p. 85.

5. Ibid., p. 87.

6. Ibid., p. 89.

7. Ibid., p. 90.

8. Ibid., pp. 91-92.

9. Cf. W. A. Visser 'tHooft, *No Other Name* (Philadelphia: The Westminster Press, 1963). In this book Visser 'tHooft identifies four waves of syncretism which have threatened the people of God and the uniqueness of the Judeo-Christian revelation. The fourth wave is the current one. Regarding this challenge he says that it is understandable that those who know little about Christian foundations interpret the missionary attitude of the church as evidence of arrogance and narrow-mindedness. But he maintains that serious students of religion and history would discover that the ground for the church's claim for Christ is not egocentricity but the New Testament: "It is not seriously possible to think of him as one of the prophets or founders of religion. A Christianity which should think of itself as one of the many diverse contributions to the religious life of mankind is a Christianity that has lost its foundation in the New Testament" (p. 117). For Visser 'tHooft this does not mean that there is no place for any form of interreligious dialogue. The presupposition of genuine dialogue is not the agreement of participants to relativize their convictions but rather to accept one another as persons. "The dialogue will be all the richer, if both of us give ourselves as we are. For the Christian that giving must include witness" (p. 118).

10. Cf. Lesslie Newbigin, *Trinitarian Faith and Today's Mission* (Richmond: John Knox Press, 1964). In this work the author encourages interfaith dialogue as espoused by the ecumenical movement: "We have indeed to enter into real conversation with men of other religions if they are to apprehend Jesus Christ as Savior and if we are to learn all the manifold wisdom of God which he set forth in Jesus"

(p. 17). At the same time he recognizes certain dangers in reopening "a living dialogue through which the Gospel can be commended to men of other faiths and no faith" (p. 27). "For the churches of the East the danger is 'ghettoism' — a practical withdrawal into the position of a tolerated and static minority." For the churches of the West the danger is syncretism: "There seem to be many who think it only natural that the usual list of religious allegiances — Roman Catholic, Protestant and Jewish — should be extended as the occasion arises to include Hindus, Muslims and Buddhists also."

11. Cf. Stephen Neill, *Creative Tension* (London: Edinburgh House Press, 1959), pp. 9-29. In these pages the author elucidates the various attitudes vis-à-vis non-Christian religions and their adherents taken by Bartholomew Zicgenbalg, William Carey, William Ward, Arnold Toynbee, W. E. Hocking, Hendrik Kraemer, H. H. Farmer and Kenneth Cragg. He notes that Ziegenbalg, for example, entertained no doubt as to the uniqueness of Christ and the necessity of His salvation but was motivated "to understand the mind and heart of his non-Christian neighbors" (p. 10). As the comparative study of religions has progressed, however, there has been a tendency to agree with non-Christian religions at the points of their highest development, and then show that they are still imperfect and need Christ. Neill asks if it would not be better to proceed in just the opposite way, namely, to "recognize quite frankly that the Nay comes first, that Christ is the Destroyer before he can be the Savior?" (p. 29). In the same author's later work *Call to Mission* (Philadelphia: Fortress Press, 1970), he asks how the claim that one religion is true can be reconciled with the principles of tolerance and pluralism, and how that claim can be made without offending adherents of another religion. His answer is unequivocal: "Whereas there should hardly be any limits to our tolerance of people as people, the moment we raise the question of truth, we are faced by the painful issue of the intolerance of truth. In this strange world of ours, if one statement is true, any other statement inconsistent with it is necessarily untrue, or at least wide of the truth" (p. 9).

12. S. J. Samartha, ed., *Dialogue Between Men of Living Faiths* (Geneva: World Council of Churches, 1971), p. 8.

13. Ibid., p. 9.

14. Klaus Klostermaier, "Hindu-Christian Dialogue," in *Dialogue*, ed. S. J. Samartha, p. 12.

15. Ibid.

16. Masatoshi Doi, "Dialogue Between Living Faiths in Japan: A Beginner's Report," in *Dialogue*, ed. S. J. Samartha, p. 34.

17. Ibid.

18. Lynn A. de Silva, "Some Issues in the Buddhist-Christian Dialogue," in *Dialogue,* ed. S. J. Samartha, p. 55.

19. "Dialogue Between Men of Living Faiths, The Ajatoun Memorandum," in *Dialogue;* ed: S. J. Samartha, p. 114.

20. The text of the statement drawn up by the Protestant-Orthodox-Catholic consultation convened by the World Council of Churches at Kandy from February 27 to March 5, 1967, is given in *Study Encounter* 3 (1967), 52-56. The quotation is from the section entitled "Dialogue and Proclamation" (p. 55). It is included here to show that ecumenical dialogue certainly does not preclude proclamation. It is still true, however, that proclamation is not central to that dialogue. Furthermore, the Kandy statement itself casts a shadow over the meaning and significance of proclamation in this context. It says, "For the Christian, a deep sense of community

is given by his belief that all men are created in the image of God, by his realization that Christ died for every man, and by the expectation of His coming Kingdom. Here is the foundation of the Christian's approach to any human being. And since he must take seriously the personalities of his neighbours, he must of course respect their particular religious faith as an integral aspect of their culture and humanity. As our dialogue with men of other faiths develops, we gain light regarding the place held by other religious traditions in God's purposes for them and for us; this is a question which cannot be answered a priori or academically, but must continue to engage our earnest study and reflection" (p. 53).

21. John R. W. Stott, *Christian Mission in the Modern World* (London: Falcon, 1975), p. 61.

22. Gottlob Schrenk in *Theological Dictionary of the New Testament,* 9 vols., ed. Gerhard Kittel, trans. and ed. Geoffrey W. Bromiley (Grand Rapids: Eerdmans, 1964), vol. 2, p. 94.

23. Walter Bauer, *A Greek-English Lexicon of the New Testament and Other Early Christian Literature,* fourth revised edition, trans. and ed. William F. Arndt and F. Wilbur Gingrich (Chicago: University of Chicago Press, 1957), p. 184.

24. Stott, *Christian Mission,* p. 63.

25. Cf. Max Warren, "Pre-Evangelism and Evangelism," *Milligan Missiogram* II, No. 3, 3 (Fall 1975), 1. Warren says, "Dialogue . . . insofar as it is a genuine, humble, receptive listening to the other man's testimony to his own religious experience, and a courteous answering to ours, is certainly a form of Pre-Evangelism. It must not be confused with Evangelism."

26. Sharpe, "The Goals of Inter-Religious Dialogue," pp. 89-90. After discussing the various types of dialogue, Sharpe says, "In only one case is there a fair measure of clarity. The goal of discursive dialogue is usually taken to be a better understanding of the other person's religious stance, possibly in order to facilitate the communication of the Christian message. It has been repeatedly pointed out this century that it is useless for the Christian missionary to embark upon a programme of evangelization without a thorough prior knowledge of the people to whom his message is addressed — their language, their culture, their modes of thought, religious and secular, and so on. And for those whose Christian faith involves an imperative missionary dimension, and who are still prepared to make use of the terminology of dialogue, the attempt to enter into a sympathetic understanding of the non-Christian must take some such form as that which I have called discursive dialogue."

27. Carl F. H. Henry, "Confronting Other Religions," *Christianity Today* XIII, No. 22 (August 1, 1969), 31.

Norman L. Geisler

SOME PHILOSOPHICAL PERSPECTIVES ON MISSIONARY DIALOGUE

INTRODUCTION

The Christian accepts as axiomatic that his task is to communicate Christ to the world. That sounds simple enough, but in fact it is very complex. It is complex for at least three reasons: first, there are many views of "Christ"; second, there are many ways to "communicate"; and third, there are many "worlds" to which Christ must be communicated. It is our purpose in this essay to focus on several philosophical, theological and apologetical problems surrounding the last two of these areas. It will be taken for granted that it is the "Christ" of historical-biblical Christianity who is to be communicated and not the mythical "Christ" of liberal or existential theology. It will be understood, then, that the Christ we are commissioned to communicate is Jesus of Nazareth, the incarnate Son of God who died on Calvary's Cross and rose bodily from Joseph's tomb. Having decided which "Christ" is to be preached, the evangelical missionary must ask two further questions: first, to which "world" will he be communicating and, second, what is the most effective way to communicate with it? There are many aspects to these problems — cultural, linguistic, religious, and so forth. Our intention is to zero in on the philosophical dimension. Let us begin with the problem of the "world" to which the missionary communicates.

The first problem confronting us is that there are *many* "worlds" to which the Christian is commissioned with the gospel of Christ.[1] The one physical world in which we live may be divided geographically into "Eastern world" and "Western world," and there are many differences that make communication between the Eastern mind and the Western mind a real problem. Moreover, *culturally* there are many different "worlds." Further, there are many miniworlds or subcultural groupings that add to the difficulty of the communication process. Also, there are many different "worlds" *religiously*. The rituals, rites, and spiritual practices among men show great diversity which makes communication extremely difficult. But perhaps the most fundamental differences among the "worlds" with which the Christian communicates are the differences among the *philosophical* "worlds."

DEFINITION AND CATEGORIZATION
OF WORLD VIEWS

Definition of a World View

There are many different world views or overall frameworks of meaning through which men view the totality of their environs. These *Weltanschauungs* or world-and-life views are the tinted "glasses" through which every fact is seen. They are "grids" through which everything in life is screened in a particular way.[2] A world view is a conceptual framework or "system" of thought through which everything is given meaning and context. It is a structure by which all the "stuff" of experience is given meaning and coherence. Without an overall world view the facts of life are like unconnected dots on a page. Even the philosophical positions which say that there is no way to connect the dots into a coherent picture or that each person connects the dots in his own way by doing his own "thing" are themselves ways of viewing the world. These positions claim that there is no objective meaning in the world but rather all meaning is entirely subjective.

Everyone views the world in some way; each person "pictures" the world in some general or vague way. Each rational person has some overall idea in mind as to how all the "pieces" of life fit together, or at least an idea of *whether* they fit together. It is self-defeating to contend that one can know the bare facts of the world without using some framework of meaning through which he understands these so-called bare facts.[3] The assertion that "facts can be known apart from meaning" is itself a meaningful statement about facts. In the very attempt to claim that facts can be known apart from frameworks of meaning, the statement gives a meaning to the facts. Actually, fact without meaning is a fiction. All the "stuff" in life must be given some structure or else it is unintelligible. It is the function of a world view to provide the structure of meaning by which a man views all that he experiences.[4]

Categorization of World Views

There are many ways to view the facts of the world, that is, there are many world views. Lines may be drawn many different ways between the same dots. The same letters may be used in spelling many different words, and the same words take on many different meanings in different contexts. The same fossil record is capable of both evolutionary and creationary frameworks. Historical data can be viewed via a chaotic, cyclical or linear philosophical theory. Likewise, there are many different ways to understand the experiences of mankind. The "worlds" in which men live, or world views by which they live, may be categorized in many different ways. For the purpose of clarification, comparison and contrast, a philosophical typology will serve best. Comparing the relation of God, man and the world, the following main world views emerge: polytheism, atheism (naturalism), theism, deism, pantheism, and pan-en-theism.[5] Polytheism believes there are many finite gods beyond the world. Atheism holds that there is no God (or gods) either finite or infinite. Theism claims there is an infinite God beyond the world who is causally operative in it both naturally and supernaturally. Deism is theism minus the supernatural — God is transcendent over the world but not supernaturally immanent or active in it. Pantheism identifies God and the universe; God is the world. Finally, pan-èn-theism is a kind of cross between theism and pantheism, holding that there is a finite god whose body is the actual changing world but who also has an unchanging infinite potential beyond the world. Of course some men desire to suspend judgment about the whole question of world view, but this is itself a kind of world view called skepticism. Others claim that one cannot (or, does not) know enough about reality to formulate a position; this view is called agnosticism.

For the purposes of narrowing our discussion we will discuss the principal world views encountered in the missionary enterprise — polytheism, pantheism, and atheism (naturalism).

COMMUNICATION AMONG DIFFERENT WORLD VIEWS

It is taken as axiomatic that effective communication from a person in one world view to someone in another will necessitate understanding of both world views. One may *speak* from one world view to (at?) persons in another world view without understanding their world view, but if he desires to *communicate* with the other persons, then understanding is a *sine qua non*. Speaking *to* does not necessitate mutual understanding but communicating *with* does.

The Problem of Communication

This is precisely where the philosophical problem begins for the

Christian missionary in the context of a non-Christian world view. How can a naturalist, for example, understand the New Testament gospel? The Christian claims that Jesus is the Son of God and that the Bible is the Word of God. But can this make any sense to a man who does not believe that there is a God? Surely if there is no God, then it follows that there is no Son of God or Word of God! But could not the Christian offer evidence to the atheist by way of the resurrection of Christ that Christ is the Son of God and the gospel is the good news from God? The answer to this is crystal clear: on the naturalistic assumption that there is no God, the resurrection would never be accepted as evidence, because it makes no sense whatsoever to speak of an act of God (i.e., miracle). How can a God who does not exist perform any acts?[6]

Within the naturalistic world view, acts of God do not occur, since there is no God who can act. Even if it were proved that the corpse of Jesus of Nazareth resuscitated after three days of being medically dead, this would prove only that a very unusual natural event had occurred for which the scientists must continue to seek a natural explanation.

Within a natural world, every event has a natural explanation whether or not that explanation is known. To speak of God, His Son, His Word and His acts, is to assume gratuitously what the naturalistic "grid" denies. The world must be seen through the "glasses" of a naturalistic world view. To continue to preach the gospel to a naturalist is vain. No communication is occurring, that is, no communication of the Christian message is occurring. Words with Christian meaning are being spoken to a mind that filters them through its naturalistic world view, thereby robbing them of their true supernatural significance.[7]

The same problem occurs when a Christian preaches to a pantheist. In his view, the world is God and God is the world. In such an arrangement, it is neither unusual nor miraculous that someone should claim to be the Son of God. All men are manifestations of God in one degree or another. For Christ to claim to be God in a pantheistic setting, say, in Bombay, India, would not draw stones from the crowd as it did in the monotheistic context of first-century Jerusalem. Pantheism robs the Christian message of its uniqueness and theistic meaning. Pantheism operates like a gigantic suction pump, absorbing all views into its monistic whole. Instead of Christ being the unique Son of God incarnate, He becomes merely one of an endless series of incarnate deities.

The Christian missionary can "preach" Christ endlessly

without ever really communicating Christ to this pantheistic "world." The pantheistic filter screens out the uniqueness of Christianity and simply absorbs it into a syncretistic whole. It is in this regard that some neo-pantheists have even claimed that pantheism alone is capable of being a truly universal religion. This claim is obviously disputable. Nevertheless, the problem is real — unless the pantheistic "filtering" can be avoided, no real communication of Christ can occur. And it is clear that if there is no real Christian communication, then there will be no true Christian conversion. Hence, the whole missionary enterprise is dependent on a resolution of this important problem of communication from within one world view to another.

Some Possible Solutions to the Communication Problem

There are three basic ways communication can occur despite the differences in opposing world views. First, the Christian may ask the non-Christian to leave his world view and adopt a theistic way of looking at things so that he can at least understand the Christian message. This approach has two basic problems, an existential one and a philosophical one. As to the first problem, how likely is it that anyone who is satisfied with his world view will waste the time trying to understand another? Allegedly, scholars of comparative religions attempt to understand other world views, but few others have the time or inclination to do so. Hence, it is not likely that this will be a fruitful approach for reaching the whole world with the message of Christ. Further, even if we grant that some may be interested enough to come across the line and adopt another world view for the sake of understanding, there still remains the fundamental philosophical problem of how a world view can even be understood if it is being filtered through the meaning structure of another. If every fact of the world is understood in terms of one's own world view — and it must be or else it would not be a *world* view — then how can anything viewed one way by one world view aid in understanding a diverse meaning seen from the perspective of another world view? Through red glasses, *everything* looks rosy, and through pantheistic eyes, even theism will look pantheistic.

On the face of it, the second approach looks more fruitful. The Christian could adopt the non-Christian world view for the sake of understanding. He could literally "become all things to all men" in an intellectual way. This would overcome the practical improbability of getting non-Christians to come over to the Christian side in order to understand the gospel. But even here, the same philosophical problem remains. How can we really understand the non-Christian view any better than non-Christians understand ours? If we filter our understanding of a pantheistic world view through the grid of our theistic understanding, can we really understand the pantheistic view in anything other than theistic terms? The most our efforts at understanding can accomplish is a transition of ourselves to a standpoint within the framework of their world view. Once we are on their shore, how will we ever entice them to leave? And even assuming we could allure them to venture out to sea with us, how would we ever explain our position to them when they arrived at the shores of the new "world"? There still remains the whole problem that they see everything through the lenses of their world view. We must not forget that everything within our theistic world view has a different meaning to us than it does to a nontheist. Every fact has a different significance. Even taking our nonbelieving friends on a tour of Jesus' empty tomb will not help them believe in the resurrection as long as they look at the event through the colored glasses of a naturalistic or pantheistic world view.

There is a third possible solution to this communication problem. Perhaps neither party need go to the other side of the communication gulf in order to have a meeting of the minds. Could not a bridge be constructed from each end until at last they join in the center? Maybe we can meet in the middle of this bridge. Laying aside for the moment the practical or existential difficulties of getting people who are satisfied with their own "world" to want to build a bridge to another that they neither want nor understand, let us grant that the bridge *can be built* from both ends. In that case, we are faced with the question: Can such a bridge ever *meet* in the middle? The answer seems evident: "East is East and West is West and never the twain shall meet!" How can two entirely different world views, each of which interprets *everything* in the world in a different light and context, ever meaningfully overlap? In order to have a meaningful overlap, there must be an overlap in meaning. But in two totally diverse structures of meaning, there is no common meaning. Therefore, since there is nothing in common, there would be no way to connect the bridges built from both ends. The Russian and American spaceships could link in outer space only because they shared common mechanical and scientific systems. But communism and capitalism as such cannot be linked because they are mutually exclusive economic systems. The same holds true for world views.

At this point, the inventive person may offer another alternative. Perhaps the two worlds could simply agree to leave their shores behind and meet on an "island" in the middle. If the bridges of their diverse world structures will not meet, then maybe their worlds will at least allow for communication-seeking vessels to sail out into the sea of meaninglessness that separates them, in order to seek out a common ground or island in the middle! But here again, we are faced with the same problems. First, why even set sail unless one is among the venturesome few or among the dissatisfied minority? Further, once the few arrive from East and West at the "common ground," how are they going to understand each other when they get there? Here the whole problem begins all over again as to who is going to step over into whose position and, once he does, how he is going to describe his theistic world in pantheistic terms or vice versa? Can a man describe a blue world to a person who sees everything through red-tinted glasses?

The illustration seems to point to the following conclusion. Either no communication is ever possible from within one world view to another, or else it must be possible for one to take off his colored glasses and view things as the other sees them. But again, why should anyone even want to take off his glasses? (If this is the only way he has ever seen things, then why see them any other way?) Or, more fundamentally, how can one even know that they are glasses and not rather eyes which are indispensable if he wishes to see the world? We must conclude, then, that a world view must be more like a pair of glasses than a pair of eyes. For one cannot take out his eyes and see the world without them. Nor can one who is color-blind see things in anything but shades of gray. If world views were part of man's very nature, then it would be impossible to dispense with them and to see the world in any other way.

The Christian might be tempted at this point to invoke the supernatural. Perhaps God must create a new pair of eyes before one can change a world view. Maybe a miraculous conversion is the only solution. However, before we yield to this tempting possibility of resolving the difficulty, we must remind ourselves of one basic fact, namely, not all conversions from one world view to another are Christian conversions. Some confessed Christians have adopted pantheistic world views; some pantheists have become atheists, and so forth. Surely, we are not willing to say that these are all supernatural conversions. But if natural conversions are possible, world views must be more like a pair of glasses than a pair of eyes. For if a person were not able to "put on" and "take off" his world view or at least "see around" it at times, he would have no means of ever seeing things another way.[8] He would have no way to know there is another way to view things and surely he would see no reason why he should ever look for another pair of "glasses" through which to view the world. Unless there is some broader knowledge of some dimension that transcends the glasses one wears, for what purpose and on what basis would anyone ever choose to look through another set?

Another solution to this problem offers itself at this juncture. Maybe we are to suppose that the choices for changing world views are entirely subjective and personal, and that there are no objective criteria on which one can decide. Existentially speaking, maybe only a "leap-of-faith" can make the transition. Is voluntaristic fideism the only solution? The answer to this is clearly negative.[9] The Christian's claim is more than subjective; he lays claim to objective truth. The Christian does not claim that his world view is true only subjectively for him but that it is objectively true for everyone. But if it is objectively true for everyone, then there must be some objective way for everyone to test it. This is surely in accord with the constant injunction of Scripture to "test the spirits" (I John 4:1), to "beware of false prophets" (Matt. 7:15), and to avoid vain philosophies (Col. 2:8). Indeed, it must be the case that there is some way common to all men to test the truth of a world view, that is, some way for all men to see "around the glasses" of their world view. If this were not possible, then no communication would ever occur between people of different world views, and no one would ever be able to change world views. But communication does occur and conversion does happen. Furthermore, it is self-defeating to argue for the fideistic position. If one offers reasons for accepting fideism, then he is really not a fideist. But if he does not offer evidence for belief, then he has no rightful claim to truth.

JUSTIFICATION OF A WORLD VIEW

This raises the important question of just what it is that the Christian and non-Christian have in common that enables communication and conversion to occur. How is dialogue possible and how can it lead to a change in *Weltanschauung?*

The Meaning of Dialogue

Without a common basis for understanding, no true dialogue

can occur. Persons may speak *to* (at?) each other without common ground, but they do not speak *with* each other. But despite the fact that dialogue presupposes common ground for meaning, it does not presuppose that one view must accept the truth of the other before dialogue is possible. For not more than one world view can be true; the others *as systems of truth* are wrong. Therefore, only *one* system can provide a ground for truth; all other systems can have meaning but as systems they must be false. What this means is that communication is possible because there is a common basis for meaning between the views. Further, truth is possible because one system is true. But since meaning presupposes truth, the system that is true is actually providing the basis for the meaning in the dialogue.

Of course, the dialogue may occur with both participants *believing* that it is their system that makes the meaningful dialogue possible, but how this belief is *justified* in the face of a contrary belief is another matter. Neither view, however, need give up its belief in the truth of its system in order to enter the dialogue. Dialogue depends only on common meaning, and meaning depends only on the *possibility* of truth. It may be that both systems are wrong and that it is the truth of a third system that makes their meaningful dialogue possible. But somewhere there must be some system or world view that is true or else there would be no meaningful communication occurring.

The fact that translation from one language system to another and transformation from one view to another occur proves that communication does occur. Therefore, true dialogue is possible between world systems because there is at least one system of truth by which meaningful dialogue with other systems is made possible. This leads us to the need for an *apologia* or defense of the faith.

The Meaning of *Apologia*

In the New Testament, the Christian was commissioned to bear a message. As long as he spoke to men of the same world view (i.e., to monotheistic Jews), he could offer his *kerygma* (i.e., proclamation) without any justification for accepting that world view. When, however, his world view was challenged or not accepted by the audience, the evangelist was called upon for an *apologia* (I Peter 3:15) or defense of his belief. How the apostles went about justifying their claims to having truth is instructive for the Christian as he confronts other world views.

Preaching to Polytheistic World Views

Before the gospel can even penetrate the understanding of the polytheist, there must be some pre-evangelism.[10] Since some 40 percent of the world believe in many gods,[11] it must be made clear that the Christian is not proclaiming a message about any of them. The polytheists at Lystra were told to "turn from these vain things to a living God who made the heaven and the earth and the sea and all that is in them" (Acts 14:15). The Gentiles at Thessalonica were reminded how they had "turned to God from idols, to serve a living and true God" (I Thess. 1:9). The Old Testament prophets often elaborated the negative side of this pre-evangelistic activity by stressing the ridiculousness of worshiping idols. Isaiah said, "They bow down to the work of their hands, to what their own fingers have made" (Isa. 2:8). The idolater "cuts down cedars . . . . he takes a part of it and warms himself . . . . and the rest of it he makes into a god, his idol; and falls down to it and worships it; he prays to it and says, 'Deliver me, for thou art my god!' " (Isa. 44:14-17).

But tearing down idol gods is not a sufficient pre-evangelistic technique; there must also be a positive side. In this regard, the prophets and apostles pointed to the "true and living God who made heaven and earth." Jonah's testimony to the pagans aboard the ship to Tarshish was, "I fear the Lord, the God of heaven, who made the sea and the dry land" (Jonah 1:9). Paul gave a similar description of God to the heathen at Lystra, calling Him the "living God who made the heaven and the earth and the sea and all that is in them" (Acts 14:15). As positive evidence of this God, Paul appealed to the witness of creation. God did not "leave himself without witness, for he did good and gave you from heaven rains and fruitful seasons, satisfying your hearts with food and gladness" (Acts 14:17). On Mars Hill, Paul added a further evidence of this one Creator God by quoting the Greek poet Aratus that "we are indeed his [God's] offspring." If we are God's offspring, argued Paul, then "we ought not to think that the Deity is like gold, or silver, or stone, a representation by art and imagination of man" (Acts 17:28, 29).

Summarizing apostolic pre-evangelism to polytheists, we may conclude that the apostles both criticized the belief in many gods and appealed as well to the evidence that there is a Creator God who made heaven and earth. Since preliterate polytheists invariably have a concept of a "High God" or "sky God," it is not difficult to identify the God of whom they speak with the distant One from whom the pagan finds himself separated by his sins (cf. Isa. 59:2). Sometimes the identification must be with the God who is not known at all but who is believed to be there somehow. When Paul found on Mars Hill the inscription "to an unknown god," he declared, "What therefore you worship as unknown, this I proclaim to you" (Acts 17:23, 24). Whatever concept of a High, Supreme, Unknown Maker polytheists possess may be used as the positive pre-evangelistic common ground for communicating a theistic world view to them.

Preaching to an Atheistic World View

Atheism was not widespread among the people of biblical times and, hence, the Scriptures offer little direct information on how to approach atheists. Today, however, with the widespread influence of Marxism, naturalism and humanism, the situation is different. Fortunately, there is enough material that can be gleaned from various contexts to construct an approach. First, it must be remembered that atheism begins in the "heart" and not in the "head." The psalmist wrote, "The fool says in his *heart*, 'There is no God' " (Ps. 14:1). We may infer from this that atheism is an existential choice made on moral or spiritual grounds that begins in the "heart" and spreads to the "head." Rational arguments in defense of atheism, then, are usually after the fact. We must begin, however, where men are. Hence, the first move is negative. We must, as Paul urged, "destroy arguments and every proud obstacle to the knowledge of God" (II Cor. 10:5). An illustration or two will point out the procedure we should follow. First, some atheists claim there cannot be a God because there is injustice in the world. But this argument is clearly self-defeating. In order to know that there is some ultimate injustice in the world, one must know what is ultimately just. One cannot know what is unjust unless he knows what is just. But if one must posit an Ultimate Justice beyond the world (i.e., God) by which he knows that some things in the world are ultimately unjust, then he is really positing God in order to disprove God.[12]

A second illustration of the circular or self-defeating nature of atheistic arguments will speak to the same point. There is a more sophisticated form of linguistic or semantic atheism which claims in effect that the word *God* is dead.[13] Some claim that there may *be* a God but that it is meaningless to *speak* of Him. All talk of God is mystical or parabolical, and purely mythical or symbolical. But this view is also self-defeating, for it claims that "it is not possible to make cognitively meaningful statements about God" when that very statement is offered as a cognitively meaningful statement about God. If there is no known meaning for the word *God*, then one cannot make a meaningful statement denying that God can be known. One cannot deny that the term *God* has meaning unless he already has a meaning for the term.[14]

Destroying the arguments for atheism and showing the meaningfulness of talking about God are usually not sufficient groundwork for evangelizing atheists. Atheists will often admit the sheer *possibility* there is a God; what they desire is something to support the plausibility for believing in God. It is here that the *apologia* must be invoked. The Christian must give a "reason" for the hope that is in him (I Peter 3:15).

The Bible sketches several "reasons" that can serve as common ground with the atheists. Whether the atheist admits it or not, he lives in God's world and is surrounded by evidence that God exists. Paul appeals to the *cosmological* evidence in Romans 1:19, 20:

> What can be known about God is plain to them, because God has shown it to them. Ever since the creation of the world his invisible nature, namely, his eternal power and deity, has been clearly perceived in the things that have been made. So they are without excuse.

According to this passage, God is not only knowable but is *clearly known* by the unbeliever. There are times he has looked at the world without his naturalistic or atheistic "glasses" and he knows it. To be sure, men "by their wickedness suppress the truth," but they must possess it or else they could not repress it. No doubt ardent atheists do not have God in view. Paul says that though they knew God "they did not honor Him as God or give thanks to him, but they became futile in their thinking and their senseless minds were darkened" (v. 21). Nonetheless, even in the darkness of unbelief, there are flashes of divine lightning by which the outline of the landscape is seen clearly, albeit only briefly. It is part of the task of the pre-evangelistic *apologia* to provide philosophical argumentation by which theistic light is shed on the landscape of our common world.

The New Testament offers supportive evidence for God's existence in the *moral* dimension. God has not only an external witness (in nature) but an internal moral witness within man's heart. The moral law is written on the heart of man and from this he should conclude that there is a Moral Lawgiver. For "when Gentiles who have not the law do by nature what the law requires, they are a law to themselves, even though they do not have the law. They show that what the law requires is written on their hearts" (Rom. 2:14, 15).

A third area of evidence in our common world to which those in the atheistic world view should be pointed is the *teleological* evidence. God's fingerprints are on His creation. The wonderful design of the world implies a Designer beyond the world. As the psalmist put it, "The heavens are telling the glory of God; and the firmament proclaims His handiwork" (Ps. 19:1). Even the agnostic philosopher Immanuel Kant, who denied the validity of rational arguments for God, wrote: "Two things fill the mind with ever new and increasing admiration and awe, the oftener and more steadily we reflect on them: the starry heavens above me and the moral law within me."[15]

Adding the positive evidence for theism, we may conclude from the cosmological argument that there is an all-powerful Creator of the world. And from the moral and teleological evidence we can see that this Creator is both *moral* and *intelligent*. Such is the positive side of the Christian *apologia* for those within an atheistic world view. Once it is evident to the nonbeliever that this is a theistic world, then it makes sense to proclaim the gospel to him. Once it is known that there is a God, then the claims of Christ the Son of God will become meaningful and the gospel as the power of God can become effective.

Preaching Christ to a Pantheistic World

It seems to this writer that the most significant failure of the Christian missionary is the failure to communicate Christ effectively in the context of a pantheistic world view. The flood of Eastern thinking into the West has accented this problem in Western countries. The naive and all too widespread assumption that all we need to do is preach the "gospel" to Hindus and Buddhists has proved to be a colossal failure. There is a world of difference between a pantheistic world view and a theistic world view.[16] It must be remembered that when a Hindu or Buddhist views what the Christian theist shows him, he views it through the tint of his pantheistic "glasses." It is necessary, then, to appeal to the vision "around" the glasses. Everything the pantheist sees in his line of focus will be viewed pantheistically. The theist must appeal to what the pantheist sees, as it were, "out of the corner of his eye." Since the New Testament provides little direct confrontation with a pantheistic system, we are left — with general biblical guidance — to devise our own *apologia*. Space here permits only two suggestions in this regard.

First, before meaningful dialogue can occur with pantheists, we must establish the "thinkability" of ultimate reality. It is characteristic of pantheists to deny that one can have any cognitive or noncontradictory knowledge of God, the Absolute, Brahman, the One, Nirvana, Ultimate Reality, or whatever it may be called. Basic to this way of thinking is the contention that the Ultimate is unthinkable, that is, that the laws of thought do not apply to ultimate reality. It is believed that contradictions in thought are not necessarily undesirable; indeed, they are essential at the highest level.

Before the Christian can ever begin to communicate with those holding this position, he will have to establish some common ground or meaning. But since all meaning is dependent on the law of noncontradiction, it will be necessary to defend the law of noncontradiction. For if the law of noncontradiction does not hold, then no meaningful statements can be made. And if a statement is not at least meaningful, then it follows that it cannot be either true or false. Hence, if the pantheist wishes to make a truth claim about ultimate reality, then he must bow to the law of noncontradiction. No position has the right to claim universal truth, as a world view does, unless it has some universal test for truth. If the law of noncontradiction is not universally valid, then neither is truth objectively and universally valid. Truth and noncontradiction are coextensive.[17]

What is more, there is really no way to deny the law of noncontradiction of ultimate reality. For the very statement "the law of noncontradiction does not apply to ultimate reality" is itself a noncontradictory statement about ultimate reality. Thus the very attempt to deny logic of reality affirms logic of reality. The denial of the intelligibility of reality is an intelligible affirmation about reality. The pantheistic position is thus self-destructive.

There remains one more extremely important difference between a pantheistic and a theistic view. The pantheist claims that God and the world are one, whereas the theist holds that they are different. This means that for the pantheist all limitations, change and evil in the world are ultimately not real. There are many ways one might attempt to convince the pantheists that the finite, changing and evil world is real. The theist might insist, for example, that it is the pantheistic position, not the world, that is an illusion. He might use a Freudian kind of argument to the effect that "it would be nice if there were no pain and evil, but the very fact that one wishes it to be that way makes the pantheistic belief that the evil in the world is unreal highly suspect." Wishing a pot of gold at the end of the rainbow doesn't make it so. Or, the theist may ask what difference there is between the so-called "illusion" of evil in the "illusory" world and "real" evil in the "real" world. What makes the illusion *seem* so real? If it is not real, then why is it that when I sit upon a pin and it punctures my skin I dislike what I fancy I feel?

Whatever effectiveness the foregoing psychological tactics may have, there is a philosophical route which is more useful in dealing with pantheism. Simply put, pantheism is self-defeating because the pantheist affirms his own reality in the very process of denying it. The pantheist says in effect, "Ultimately God is and I am not." But there is no way to deny oneself without affirming oneself. Every affirmation has an affirmer. And it simply begs the whole question for the pantheist to claim "*I* am not affirming that statement but *God* is affirming it through me." Even in this second affirmation, there is the finite "I" who is claiming that there is not a finite "I" making the affirmation.

In like manner, the pantheistic position cannot avoid self-destruction by denying the reality of change in the world. God, they admit, is infinite and unchanging, while the "world" is finite and changing. But the "world," the pantheist says, is ultimately not real. Hence, all that is necessary to refute the pantheistic claim is to show the reality of change. In this regard, no one need refute the pantheistic claim, for it is self-refuting. Every pantheist who claims that he has come to believe that he does not change in his knowledge or that he has arrived at the conclusion that he is identical with God is involved in a self-destructive enterprise. The very concept of "come to believe" or "arrived at" necessarily involves a change in knowledge. In brief, there was a time when the pantheist did not believe that he is identical with God and a time after which he concluded that indeed he is. The very fact that he went through a process of change to arrive at the conclusion that change is not real refutes the pantheist's position.

Space will not permit further elaboration of this apologetic method for establishing the truth of a theistic world view in which alone the gospel makes sense. It will suffice here to point out that this approach is built on the principle that self-stultification is a test for truth. Whatever is actually unaffirmable is false. Those world views that are contrary to theism can in some way be shown to entail essential premises that are actually unaffirmable. In addition to this negative approach, the Christian may supply positive arguments for theism so that the missionary task can be fulfilled. For the gospel cannot be communicated *through* another world view. It can, however, be communicated *to* persons within another world view, providing we can get them to look *around* that world view. If they do not look around the "glasses" of their non-Christian world view, their eyes will never be opened to the light of the glorious gospel of Jesus Christ. To change the illustration, if the missionary message is always filtered through the earphones of another system, the gospel will never be truly "heard." In this respect, we may paraphrase the apostle and ask, "How shall they hear without a preacher and how shall they preach unless the hearer can hear the truth of God being preached on theistic earphones?" Indeed, unless the missionary is alert to the pre-evangelistic need to provide theistic earphones, the audience will not truly "hear" the gospel. His voice will be no more than a "sounding brass or tinkling cymbal." Let us then make sure that the missionary trumpet does not make an "uncertain sound."

FOOTNOTES

N. B. Bible quotations are from the Revised Standard Version unless otherwise noted.

1. A helpful recent catalog of world views is presented by James Sire in *The Universe Next Door* (Downers Grove, IL: Inter-Varsity Press, 1975).

2. Some thinkers, for example, Paul Feyerabend, contend that a world view determines not only *how* we view things but *what* we actually see.

3. On self-stultification as a test for truth, see my *Christian Apologetics* (Grand Rapids: Baker, 1976), ch. 8.

4. Ibid., chs. 4-5.

5. Ibid., chs. 9-13 contain a fuller elaboration of each of these world views.

6. Ibid., ch. 5.

7. This point has been made by presuppositionalists like Cornelius Van Til. See his *Defense of the Faith* (Nutley, NJ: Presbyterian and Reformed Publishing Co., 1965), pp. 116-22.

8. We, therefore, differ with Van Til who argues that the glasses are "cemented to one's face." See his statement in *Jerusalem and Athens,* ed. E. R. Geehan (Grand Rapids: Baker, 1971), p. 381.

9. See my *Christian Apologetics,* ch. 3.

10. Polytheism has received a literate defense by David L. Miller in *The New Polytheism* (New York: Harper & Row, 1975).

11. See S. Neil, *The Christian Faith and Other Faiths* (London: Oxford University Press, 1970), p. 125.

12. C. S. Lewis makes this telling point in *Mere Christianity* (New York: Macmillan, 1960), pp. 45-46.

13. See Paul van Buren, *The Secular Meaning of the Gospel* (New York: Macmillan, 1963).

14. For further discussion of the meaningfulness of talk about God, see my *Philosophy of Religion* (Grand Rapids: Zondervan, 1974), chs. 10-13.

15. Immanuel Kant, *Critique of Practical Reason,* trans. Lewis W. Beck (Indianapolis: The Bobbs-Merrill Company, Inc., 1956), p. 166.

16. See my *Christian Apologetics*, ch. 10, for an elaboration and critique of pantheism.

17. Ibid., chs. 2, 8.

RESPONSE / Warren Webster

Eugene Nida in *Customs and Cultures* observes that "wherever missionary work has been singularly unsuccessful, unfruitful, unproductive, one will always find a failure to resolve the missionary's two great problems: identification and communication."[1] The contemporary emphasis on dialogue in mission is one attempt to solve a common failure to get inside a religious culture for understanding and Christian communication.

Dialogue, in its classical Greek sense of "reaching truth by means of the dialectic inherent in discussion and debate" is unknown to the New Testament, as Dr. Hesselgrave points out. The Greek verb *dialegomai* is used nine times in the Book of Acts to describe the preaching of Paul who not only "proclaimed," but "reasoned," "persuaded," and "proved." But, as John Stott has observed, this was "not the sort of dialogue which people envisage today, for Paul's dialogue was part of his Christ-centered proclamation" and its object was always repentance and conversion.[2]

Dr. Geisler gives some insight into one reason the apostle Paul was free to concentrate on proclamation almost everywhere he went: "As long as he spoke to men of the same world view (i.e., to monotheistic Jews), he could offer his *kerygma* (i.e., proclamation) without any justification for accepting that world view." Even when he addressed non-Jews it was in a religious and cultural setting in which the Jewish world view was already somewhat known. Moreover, being both bilingual (or, trilingual) and bicultural by virtue of his birth and education, when Paul preached to Greeks and Romans he did not have to search vaguely for some common ground inasmuch as he was already well conversant with their literature and thought patterns over a lifetime of close contact. In essence, Paul was a "home missionary" traveling evangelist within the Roman Empire whose ministry was essentially directed to peer evangelism among fellow Jews (E_1) or evangelization of slightly different peoples near at hand (E_2). Had Paul subsequently been directed to the people of India, China or Japan, where he would have had neither a linguistic or cultural foothold to begin with, it is very possible he would initially have turned to some type of dialogue with the adherents of Oriental religions to gain understanding and identification as a basis for further communication and proclamation of the gospel. At this point we may thoroughly agree with Dr. Geisler's axiom that "effective communication from a person in one world view to someone in another will necessitate understanding of both world views."

In pointing up the seriousness of our failure to understand other thought worlds, Dr. Geisler states his conviction "that the most significant failure of the Christian missionary is the failure to communicate Christ effectively in the context of a pantheistic world view." Christians seem to be providing answers to questions the Buddhist or Hindu is not initially asking. We invite him to be "born again" when he is trying desperately to escape the ceaseless cycle of rebirths in his religion. We promise him a life that never ends when the highest good in his world view is the cessation of individual existence through absorption into the "world soul" like a drop of rain losing itself in the ocean. It is little wonder then that in almost no major region of the Hindu-Buddhist world "apart from aboriginal areas has Protestant missionary work gained more than one percent of the population."[3]

James Engel and Wilbert Norton imply that one problem in many situations is that missionaries have been "program oriented" rather than "audience oriented."[4] Jesus knew His audience. He completely understood the nature of man. He "knew what was in man" (John 2:25). So must we.

In a world of religious pluralism some type of evangelical dialogue with the followers of non-Christian religions is essential to understanding their needs and aspirations as a basis for meaningful Christian communication. The Lausanne Covenant states, "That kind of dialogue whose purpose is to listen sensitively in order to understand . . . is indispensable to evangelism" (Article 4).[5]

Over against the ecumenical call to dialogue which tends to minimize the uniqueness of Christ and His gospel there is a valid and necessary role for an "evangelical dialogue" with non-Christian faiths. But we must insist that dialogue is not synonymous with evangelism nor a substitute for it. It may, however, be an indispensable aspect of pre-evangelism:

(1) Dialogue aims at understanding (through Christian presence),

(2) Understanding aims at communication (through Christian proclamation),

(3) Communication aims at transformation (through Christian persuasion).

That, according to Dr. Hesselgrave, is how it was in the first century: "Dialogue was a method; proclamation was its nature; and conversion was its goal." So should it be today.

Christianity, like electricity, flows best where there is good contact. Evangelical dialogue should be one of the points of contact.

FOOTNOTES

1. Eugene A. Nida, *Customs and Cultures, Anthropology for Christian Missions* (New York: Harper and Row, 1954), pp. 250-51.

2. John R. W. Stott, "The Biblical Basis of Evangelism," in *Let the Earth Hear His Voice,* ed. J. D. Douglas (Minneapolis: World Wide Publications, 1975), p. 71.

3. Eugene A. Nida and William A. Smalley, *Introducing Animism* (New York: Friendship Press, 1959), p. 59.

4. James F. Engel and H. Wilbert Norton, *What's Gone Wrong with the Harvest? A Communication Strategy for the Church and World Evangelism* (Grand Rapids: Zondervan, 1975), ch. 3.

5. Cited in *Let the Earth Hear His Voice*, p. 4.

RESPONSE / Wesley L. Duewel

The splendid but too brief central section of Dr. Hesselgrave's paper confirms dialogue as a biblical ministry. Is too much space given in the rest of the paper to analyzing and reacting to the ecumenical view of dialogue and to deploring inadequate evangelical participation in dialogue?

As a method, dialogue is face-to-face interaction with a view to communication of truth and the other person's understanding of and surrender to that truth. Jesus used this method (Matt. 19:16-22; Luke 7:39-50; 10:25-37; 20:16). *As an approach,* it may also be used in proclamation where mutual discussion is not possible (e.g., in mass evangelism, literature evangelism, radio, television, and film evangelism). It involves the honest facing of questions arising from the context of the hearers' divergent backgrounds, understandings, and previous religious convictions and prejudices. Jesus, "knowing the thoughts" of His hearers, used this approach (Matt. 12:25; Mark 12:15; Luke 11:17; John 6:61, 64, 65; 16:19).

Dr. Geisler has carefully established the inescapability and role of a world view, and the diversity of man's basic world views in regard to God. He has perhaps overdramatized the difficulty for the Christian in communicating with a person of another religious world view. More recognition could be given, not to "the dissatisfied minority," but to the basic longing of each human soul and the inability of other world views to answer man's deepest questions. Man is created for God.

In the second half of his paper, Geisler confirms that dialogue is possible and rapidly sketches basic apologetic approaches to polytheists, atheists, and pantheists. He concludes with a brief mention of the need for theistic pre-evangelism.

A full recognition of the problem is essential in order to motivate the evangelical to adequate preparation for dialogue by the study of other religious world views, but I am somewhat disappointed in what seems to be a lack of emphasis upon positive factors in Christian dialogue. I also would have appreciated a more positive conclusion, stating faith in the potential effectiveness of such communication and dialogue.

Dialogue is evangelical when:

(1) It is motivated by biblical concern.

(2) It is true to biblical revelation.

(3) Its objective is biblical understanding and conversion.

(4) It depends throughout on the ministry of the Holy Spirit.

As Christ came a greater distance to reach man than man comes to meet God, so the Christian imperative poses a greater responsibility on the Christian communicator in the process of dialogue than may be expected of the non-Christian with whom dialogue is sought.

The Holy Spirit works in both participants in the process of biblical dialogue. In the person with whom communication-dialogue is sought we note:

(1) *Creation in the image of God.* This provides the possibility of dialogue. The human soul is predisposed to serious dialogue by the emptiness and restlessness it feels apart from Christ.

(2) *The work of prevenient grace.*

(3) *The illumination and conviction of the Spirit.*

The evangelical's participation in dialogue is facilitated by his faith in:

(1) *The biblical view of man.* This fosters a genuine interest in everyone as a person, and an acceptance of the inestimable worth of the person and his potential through grace for God's kingdom.

(2) *Christ.* As the Wisdom of God, Christ is the ultimate answer to man's deepest questions. As Savior He is the answer to man's deepest needs.

(3) *Scripture.* Scripture is the sword of the Spirit and its good news the power of God unto salvation.

(4) *The Holy Spirit as the Spirit of identification.* Through the Holy Spirit, the Son of God became incarnate; through His working, the believer is enabled to identify with those to whom he is sent.

(5) *The Holy Spirit as the Spirit of communication.* He who spoke to and through prophet, apostle, and evangelist, and who inspired and illuminates the Word is able to bridge the gap between the world views of the Christian and the non-Christian.

(6) *The Holy Spirit as the Spirit of love.* He fills the believer with God's love, thus enabling attitudes and actions which illustrate, confirm, and give context to the verbal communication in dialogue.

(7) *The Holy Spirit as the sovereign bestower of gifts.* He equips with abilities and gifts for the ministry of dialogue.

(8) *The Holy Spirit as guide.* The Spirit guides, counsels, and helps in the dialogue He enables.

Apart from the Holy Spirit, the problem of communication as outlined by Geisler and as experienced by every missionary with evangelistic concern would be insurmountable. Because of the Spirit, we can enter dialogue with faith.

RESPONSE / E. Eugene Williams

Seneca, Spanish-born Roman statesman and tutor of Emperor Nero, in his philosophic treatise, *De Beneficiis*, wisely counseled, "Let the man who would be grateful think of repaying a kindness, even while receiving it."[1] I wish to do this as I express thanks to Norman Geisler and David Hesselgrave for inspiration and instruction received from their papers. As I make brief critical assessments of what both men have written, I hope that my response to Seneca's advice will improve upon Nero's to the Christian brethren.

Initially, my comments are directed toward Dr. Geisler's paper. There is no disagreement with his observation that the task of communicating Christ to the world is complex, nor with his premise that there are many "worlds" to which the Christian is commissioned with the gospel of Christ. Dr. Geisler's paper would have been strengthened if more attention had been given to positive rather than negative concerns.

In the midst of his presentation on the process of communication Geisler stumbled into two traps. The references in question occurred in tandem. He stated: "To continue to preach the gospel to a naturalist is vain. No communication is occurring . . . . Words with Christian meaning are being spoken to a mind that filters them through its naturalistic world view, thereby robbing them of their true supernatural significance."

Communication theorists concur with Paul Watzlawick that "one cannot not communicate."[2] Silence and inactivity are no exceptions. It is not possible to conceive of nonbehavior for living persons. The concept that "one cannot not communicate" requires but one condition: that the behavior, verbal or nonverbal, is being interpreted by someone. The communication in Geisler's reference does meet that condition. The fact of the matter is that the communication *desired* by the person speaking is not occurring.

The second issue concerns "words with Christian meaning."

Meaning is not inherent in words. Meanings are within people. As Julius Laffal affirms, "the locus of meaning is inescapably within the individual user of language."[3] Meaning is the experience an individual perceives as he responds to symbols, including word symbols. Meanings, then, occur inside people — in their ideas, their feelings, their attitudes. People give meanings to words. The fact that Dr. Geisler does express the idea that meanings are crucial, that it is readily apparent when essential differences of meaning exist, and that these differences of meaning can affect the communication process, often adversely, is significant.

If I were to be critical at any other point it would be a desire to see greater emphasis placed upon the supernatural power of the Holy Spirit to bring about mutual understanding from one *Weltanschauung* to another. The primary outreach of God to men is through His Spirit, and in concert with His sovereign will. If we purpose to change lives according to God's plans, we cannot risk putting our primary dependence upon natural means. Geisler is aware of this truth. I wish that his paper had placed more emphasis upon it.

Regarding Dr. Hesselgrave's paper, I appreciated the call to courageous biblical dialogue in interfaith arenas. The historic tendency toward polarization is both tragic and tension-producing.

Dialogue essentially involves two things: relationship and content. Generally, the former determines the latter. Entering into meaningful dialogue demands the calculated risk of personal involvement.

Dialogue aims directly at differences and similarities. Generally, when two persons come together to interact they are making a symbolic commitment to one another to respect the role each chooses to adopt. Basic to most situations in interfaith dialogue is the role of being a human person, worthy of consideration and respect. This stance can lead to an appreciation of common human qualities despite cultural differences which tend to polarize.

Dr. Hesselgrave made it clear that biblical dialogue is not professional spiritual promotion. I wish that he would have spent more time presenting strong arguments to support his conclusion that "all too often ecumenical interfaith dialogue has been built upon sub-Christian views of revelation, Christ, and man." Moreover, I would have appreciated greater distinctions between pre-evangelistic and evangelistic intercultural dialogue patterns.

Both Geisler and Hesselgrave have pointed out the importance of dialogue between Christians and non-Christians. For their cogent comments I express my gratitude as a means of "repaying a kindness, even while receiving it."

FOOTNOTES

1. Cf. Moses Hadas, *A History of Latin Literature* (New York: Columbia University Press, 1952), pp. 255-56.

2. Paul Watzlawick, J. Beavin, and D. D. Jackson, *Pragmatics of Human Communication* (New York: Norton, 1967), p. 49.

3. Julius Laffal, *Pathological and Normal Language* (New York: Atherton Press, 1965), pp. 1-2.

REPLY / David J. Hesselgrave

The bit of homespun wisdom which says that one's best friends are his critics may not always be true, but in this case it is. I am helped by, and indebted to, my respondents. I may well be guilty of: (1) devoting too much space to an analysis of ecumenical interreligious dialogue (although Dr. Williams' call for still more arguments supporting my conclusion on ecumenical dialogue seems to point up the need for this); (2) devoting too little attention to examples of dialogue in the New Testament; and (3) devoting too little attention to distinguishing pre-evangelistic and evangelistic dialogue. To explain the rationale for the imbalance pointed out by these criticisms does not correct that imbalance, but it will serve to direct attention to the intended thrust of my paper.

The intent of what I have written is twofold: (1) to encourage ecumenists to re-examine in the light of biblical perspectives the direction their interreligious dialogues have taken; and (2) (primarily) to challenge fellow evangelicals to rethink their apparent position of disinterest in and distrust of interfaith dialogue in the face of the new world situation.

With the foregoing in mind it was my hope to demonstrate to those in the conciliar movement that the directions of dialogue in apostolic Christianity and contemporary ecumenism are so diverse as to assure that they will never intersect without a studied incourse correction. At the same time it seemed necessary to assure evangelicals of my awareness of the dangers inherent in the types of interfaith dialogue proposed in the last section of the paper.

Insofar as the respondents and other participants in the consultation are representative of evangelicals, one fact seems to be apparent as a result of our interaction. For whatever reasons, evangelicals are not really ready for any of the five types of interreligious dialogue proposed in my paper. That there must be a pre-evangelistic preparation which will enable us to communicate the gospel effectively to adherents of other religions — on this we are agreed. Many evangelicals will agree with Dr. Geisler when he states that the philosophical starting point for this preparation must be the attempt to understand alternative world views. That I take this position will be apparent from what I have written elsewhere.[1] But when it comes to interreligious dialogue on: (1) the nature of dialogue, (2) the preservation of religious freedom, (3) the meeting of human need, (4) the breaking down of barriers of distrust and hatred, and (5) the comprehension of competing truth claims, the time for evangelical participation has not yet come. I deduce this from the almost total lack of response from my colleagues to this section of my paper. To me, that seems to be the way the matter stands. Perhaps it is also the way it *should* stand. Certainly, until such time as the position of evangelicals entering such dialogue is clearly understood by both nonevangelical participants and a wider evangelical constituency, the cause of biblical Christianity at least is better off without their participation.

FOOTNOTE

1. David J. Hesselgrave, "Dimensions of Cross-Cultural Communication," *Practical Anthropology*, 19, No. 1 (Jan.-Feb. 1972) 1-12.

REPLY / Norman L. Geisler

Since Webster's comments were in substantial agreement with mine, I will confine my reply to Dr. Williams' remarks.

My first observation is that he seems to confuse communication and speaking. Watzlawick's statement that "one cannot not communicate" because nonbehavior is inconceivable for humans misses the point. Of course, men will be *speaking* verbally or nonverbally and others will be *interpreting* this in some way. However, the question still remains as to whether they will be correctly *understanding* what is spoken. If not, *communicating* has not occurred. So, our point is that as long as one has on the "glasses" of a nontheistic world view, we have not really communicated the gospel.

Second, we wish to take exception to the statement, "Meaning is not inherent in words." It seems to us that this is precisely where meaning is found. True, words do not carry intrinsic meaning. But meaning that emanates from minds certainly resides in words, which are the vehicle for conveying meaning. How can anyone who believes in the verbal inspiration of the Scriptures hold that there is no meaning within the words of Scripture but only within the minds and ideas of the authors?

A third response relates to the "desire to see greater emphasis placed upon the supernatural power of the Holy Spirit." We would point out here that the topic was not "Some *Theological* Perspectives on Missionary Dialogue." Rather, it was "Some *Philosophical* Perspectives on Missionary Dialogue." This delimitation of topic should in no way imply a lack of belief in or concern for the absolute dependence on the ministry of the Holy Spirit in Christian conversion. Further, it seems to us that an important distinction must be made between belief *in* and belief *that*. Philosophical arguments may help someone to believe *that* this is a theistic world, but only the Holy Spirit can lead a man to believe *in* Christ. It is unlikely that one can believe *in* someone (say, a wife) without evidence or reason to believe *that* that person exists. In this regard, pre-evangelistic dialogue seems essential to evangelization. Is it not circular reasoning to assume that the supernatural can be understood even by someone who filters everything through his naturalistic "glasses"? The naturalists in John 12:28, 29 heard the voice of God as "thunder." Hence, the hearer must be fitted with new earphones before he can ever understand the gospel. This essential role of pre-evangelism is a neglected function of many missionary efforts, and it is no doubt one of the significant reasons for the pathetically low results among nontheistic peoples.

PART
SIX

Mission Strategy
and Changing
Political Situations

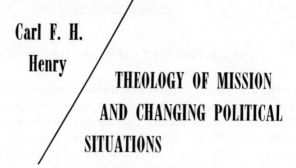

Carl F. H. Henry

THEOLOGY OF MISSION AND CHANGING POLITICAL SITUATIONS

INTRODUCTION

The Bible depicts Yahweh's covenant with the Hebrews from Abraham onward as a source of incomparable blessing to mankind: "I will make of thee a great nation . . . and in thee shall all families of the earth be blessed" (Gen. 12:2, 3, KJV; the RSV reads "will bless themselves," assuming the ongoing particularity of the nations). "Abraham shall surely become a great and mighty nation, and all the nations of the earth shall be blessed in him" (Gen. 18:18). "And in thy seed shall all the nations of the earth be blessed; because thou hast obeyed my voice" (Gen. 22:18). Where the New Testament quotes such passages it identifies the instrument for this world-wide blessing as the divine covenant mediated through Abraham and his seed to all those who with them will inherit the world through righteousness which is by faith (Rom. 4).

The outward political conditions under which this biblical blessing for the world was mediated, ratified and implemented were remarkably diverse. They ranged from nomadic existence in the desert, oppression by Egyptian pharaohs, post-Exodus wanderings and life in the Hebrew theocracy, and Jewish exile in Babylon and resettlement under Roman rule, to the multinational outreach of the Christian apostles intent upon dispatching the gospel to all nations.

Although Scripture does not systematically detail how mission theology is to be related to changing political conditions, it does imply some distinct principles we can use. The practical application of these principles as exemplified in biblical terms is illuminating. The purpose of this paper is not so much to portray the changing political conditions which prevailed in biblical times — a task more appropriate to an ancient historian — but to set forth major theological perspectives that controlled the implementation of the Judeo-Christian mission.

A DISTINCTIVE VIEW OF THE COSMOS

Hermann Sasse remarks that no more incisive event occurred in the history of the Greek word *kosmos* than its Septuagint adoption, which imparted distinctive biblical features while preserving certain Greek conceptions.[1] The Old Testament "has no word for the universe," writes Sasse, but speaks rather "of heaven and earth, or occasionally of the 'all.' " Although in New Testament usage *kosmos* "denotes the world in the spatial sense and replaces the older 'heaven and earth,' " Jesus regularly employs the Old Testament phrasing, and the synoptists rarely use *kosmos*. In the New Testament the *kosmos* is always viewed as created and transitory, and as standing under judgment and in need of redemption. More narrowly, the term is used for the earthly theatre of human life and history, that is, for the "inhabited world." The New Testament depicts a special understanding of the *kosmos*, Sasse adds, "as the theatre of salvation history, as the *locus* of revelation in Christ."[2] Speaking of "God's promise to give the whole *kosmos* to Abraham and his descendants," Romans 4:13 merges the sense of the inhabited world into that of the nations of the world. Romans 11:12 and 15 employ *kosmos* as synonymous with *ethnē* to designate the nations outside Israel ("the nations of the world"). But Romans 3:19 would expressly include Israel in the whole world guilty before God; only the true people of God are differentiated from the *kosmos* that is doomed to judgment and condemnation. In Sasse's words, "when the *kosmos* is redeemed, it ceases to be the *kosmos*."[3] At the same time, to inherit the *kosmos* means also sharing in the fulfilment of the prophetic promises that center in the Messiah and His universal kingdom (cf. the Sermon on the Mount, where Jesus speaks spiritually of world inheritance: "The meek . . . shall inherit the earth," Matt. 5:5).

Thus there emerges in the Bible from the time of the patriarchal covenant, and through the prophetic emphasis on Yahweh as Lord and Judge of all nations, and through the distinctive New Testament conception of Christ and the cosmos, a global view that is both earlier and more comprehensive and profound than that of the Pax Romana. However global may have been later totalitarian visions of political aggrandizement as reflected in Hitler's infatuation with *Deutschland über Alles* and in Marxist proposals for world revolution, and even in League of Nations or United Nations concepts of an international forum and perhaps ultimately of a possible world government, all such projections are dwarfed by the world view of the Bible. In the biblical outlook, the cosmos is nothing less than the divine creation shattered by the fall and standing under divine judgment, the arena into which Jesus Christ appears as Redeemer. This biblical view is essentially messianic and universal ("For unto us a child is born, unto us a son is given; and the government shall be upon his shoulder: and his name shall be called . . . The Prince of Peace. Of the increase of his government and peace there shall be no end . . . ," Isa. 9:6ff.). This entire perspective the New Testament comprehends in Jesus Christ, the light of revelation to the nations (Luke 2:32) and the harbinger of peace on earth (Matt. 21:5; cf. Zech. 9:9f.).

AN URGENT MISSION TO THE NATIONS

Mentioning more than seventy ethnic groups that comprise all mankind, the table of nations in Genesis 10 reflects an interest in the nations of the world unparalleled in ancient literature. It manifests the conviction that all history is an arena of Yahweh's revelation and all nations objects of a divine purpose and final judgment. Underway already in patriarchal times, this division of mankind into nations was part of God's intention (Deut. 32:8). It is simply the multiplication of the human race and the rise of different clans, languages, customs and external conditions. In the eschatological future the throne of the Lamb will be surrounded by "a great multitude which no man could number, from every nation, from all tribes and peoples and tongues" (Rev. 7:9, RSV).

Israel knew her origin was as a people set apart by God's covenant. Yet the Old Testament affirms that Yahweh is King of all peoples (Jer. 10:7; cf. Rev. 15:3). Because of their prideful deviation from the service of the living God, and, because of their perverted mission, the nations invite God's wrath and condemnation upon themselves and execute it on each other. Cyrus, for example, when he serves the cause of justice in behalf of the Hebrews, is dignified as "God's anointed" (Isa. 45:1, LB).

The multiple world kingdoms at odds with each other constitute a stark contrast to the coming kingdom of God that centers in the messianic ruler. In their hymns the Hebrews exhorted the "kings of the earth" to praise Yahweh's name (Ps. 148:11). But Hebrew preoccupation with the theocracy dulled interest in other nations except as international allies for political or commercial reasons or as candidates for divine wrath. Prophetic passages, of course, accord other nations a place in God's eschatological future no less than Israel (Isa. 2:2ff; 25:6f.; Mic. 4:1ff., etc.). They speak of the waiting nations (Isa. 42:1ff.; 51:4f.) that shall, in fact, look to Israel for light and life (Isa. 42:7; 45:22; 49:9; 61:1). "Blessed is the nation whose God is the Lord" (Ps. 33:12) occurs in a context contrasting the chosen people with the nations whose counsel Yahweh brings to naught. The Book of Jonah indicates how abhorrent had become the very thought of salvation for the Gentiles, although Jonah's reluctance may have been due to the fact that the Assyrians were great oppressors.

For all the Old Testament emphasis that God is the Creator and Preserver of the universe who exercises inviolable sovereign authority over even the heathen and does so in a world-embracing dominion that contemplates a universal purpose through His rule over Israel, there is lacking, says Walter Eichrodt, "any real application of the idea of God's salvation to the heathen world . . . . We find only vague indications which never reach the stage of clear and definite assertions that the full salvation enjoyed by Israel is promised to all peoples."[4]

While the New Testament uses the expression "all nations" without apparent distinction between any of them (e.g., Matt. 24:9, 14; 25:32; 28:19; Rom. 15:11; Gal. 3:8), Karl Ludwig Schmidt thinks that a contrast with Israel may be implicit, inasmuch as Israel already has in principle what some of these texts now promise to all nations. Yet John the Baptist commences New Testament proclamation by rebuking Jewish nationalists; the sons of Israel are not limited to Israel on the basis of flesh (Matt. 3:9).

In most instances the New Testament by *ethnē* means Gentiles as distinct from Jews or Christians (cf. Matt. 6:32; 10:5; 20:19; Acts 14:16), Christians being viewed as true Israelites (e.g., I Cor. 5:1).[5] The Gospel of John in particular uses *ethnē* of unbelieving Jews who are linked with the rebellious world by their obduracy.

Concern lest Jesus' multiplied followers seem to Roman authorities to signal an impending insurrection led Caiaphas to condition the security of both the Hebrew people and their nation on the destruction of the Nazarene (John 11:50); thus, as the apostle John comments, Caiaphas unwittingly prophesied "that Jesus should die . . . not for that [Jewish] nation only but that also he should gather together in one the children of God that were scattered abroad" (vv. 51, 52). Christ indeed died for the people, but the people perished nonetheless not only politically but also individually except for those who received eternal life (John 3:16). Israel shares finally in the curse of the nations. As she was scattered first in the exile so is she scattered again in the Christian era, until at the eschatological end time she will finally be regathered from the nations of the world. Jesus declared that in the last judgment the other nations would themselves condemn Israel for hardness of heart (Matt. 12:41f.). In Peter's Pentecost appeal to the Jews to fulfill their intended mission to the nations (Acts 3:25f.) he recalled the promise to Abraham (Gen. 12:3), and Paul quotes Isaiah 49:6 in anticipative judgment upon their failure to fulfill that mission (Acts 13:47).

The Bible not only espouses a comprehensive world-and-life view that embraces all mankind and all nations and that differs notably from rival perspectives by its grounding in intelligible divine revelation, but it also centrally proffers good news of the divine Messiah to be imperatively shared with every last member of the human race as a redemptive opportunity. The early Christians knew they were mandated to proclaim the gospel to the nations world-wide: "Go ye therefore, and teach all nations, baptizing them in the name of the Father, and of the Son, and of the Holy Ghost: Teaching them to observe all things whatsoever I have commanded you" (Matt. 28:19f.). The purpose of Christ's death, as Paul puts it, is that "in Christ Jesus the blessing of Abraham might come upon the nations" (Gal. 3:14; the RSV reads "Gentiles"). It was imperative that these tidings be proclaimed to the ends of the earth and without deference of any kind to nations and rulers.

A WORLD MANDATE FROM THE RISEN LORD

From the very first the Christian witness stemmed from apostolic eyewitnesses of the risen Jesus who had given them the missionary mandate.

If His supreme injunction was to *go*, His conditional instruction was to *wait*. Today the church's global mission so burdens the Christian community that in implementing it we often overlook all gearshift positions except "overdrive." To be sure, a "park" or "stop" position that yields the right of way to others, or like Old Testament Jewry merely waits for traffic to move from the world to the temple, is precluded by Christ's redemptive triumph over sin and death and Satan and the condemning power of the law. But the early church knew what modern Christians often forget, namely, that fulfilling the mission to the nations is a Spirit-directed effort in which the risen Lord remains sovereign over evangelical witness and momentum. "Neutral" and "low" are not therefore always to be demeaned as mere idling, nor are "high" and "overdrive" always to be commended as exemplary.

In the course of their earthly mission an inseparable link between the early Christians and their risen Lord is evident from the very outset. Jesus' followers returned from the ascension to participate in the very first Christian prayer meeting at which Jesus was no longer visibly present, but they were nonetheless still positioned at the gates of heaven through which He had so recently passed. This first postascension gathering of witnesses was not for planning and projection, but for waiting — waiting together for what none had ever seen or heard, that is, the promised manifestation in power of their risen and ascended Lord. They were united in recognizing Christ as their living Head; they were one in their resolve to know and do His heavenly will. Their waiting time was an awesome silence in the presence of Christ's omnipotent actuality. In the Book of Revelation we read of "silence in heaven, for the space of half an hour" between the breaking of the seals and the appearance of the angels. But here ten days of waiting in prayer follow Christ's completed work on earth and precede the uncommenced work of the Holy Spirit in the life of the church. But this was as spectacular as the events in any other chapter of the Book of Acts because it displayed the missionary church in the act of obedience.

Assuredly the Day of Pentecost is past as a once-for-all event in the history of Christianity; no longer has the company of believers a pre-Pentecostal character. The Spirit is outpoured; in the ongoing life of the church the Spirit's fulness is our daily and momentary prerogative. But the early Christians' time of waiting before Pentecost is a paradigmatic reminder that no ambassador of Jesus Christ sets out properly on his mission unless he is empowered from on high, and puts time and space between himself and wordly preoccupations. In this post-Pentecostal era ten days may seem to many of us an almost inexcusable waiting period. But that does not cancel waiting as an indispensable aspect of mission, incongruous as that may seem to a computerized, perpetual motion generation. They waited for fulfilment of the promise, for divine empowerment of their ranks. If perchance some restless witnesses were impatient to carry news of the resurrection to distant cities, God was already at work in His own way readying some from "every nation under heaven" (Acts 2:5) to hear the witness at Pentecost. All of God's promises require us to wait for His proper timing. Without it our service becomes presumptuous and subordinates unity, vision and power to activism.

The ability to wait, to wait on God, to recognize His divine providence in apparently closed doors as well as in obviously open doors, was therefore a distinguishing mark of the postresurrection church. It did not consider the great commission a requirement to be always vocal in all places and circumstances but rather to be always and everywhere obedient to God's appointment where and how He leads. The fact of some tightly closed doors neither collapsed their faith nor signaled a return to the nets to "go fishing." By twentieth-century standards a waiting period often seems a crushing burden for evangelicals. Rather than focusing on the constant divine source of power and wisdom, someone must appear regularly to chime out the time clock's latest population figures, exhibit the newest breakthrough possibilities of satellite religious programming that burden us with awesome new frontiers, or fix our eyes on novel promotional techniques. Creative planning is obviously not to be demeaned; the church needs more, not less. But the disciples assigned indispensable priority to waiting on the risen Lord. They did not simply hunger and thirst for His righteousness until by its absence they were more pained then condemned; they also valued waiting on the risen Lord's empowerment as being more important than talking and doing, lest they serve themselves and not Christ. Waiting on Him was most important even in those forty days immediately after Jesus' resurrection when the Sanhedrin circulated damaging reports that the disciples were somewhere hiding the corpse of a crucified criminal who had not really risen from the dead at all. It was most important also in the ten days between the ascension and Pentecost. It has not lost its priority today — even if the purpose for our waiting differs somewhat in the post-Pentecostal era. We are to recognize God's present sovereignty and providence in the closing as well as the opening of doors.

"Forbidden of the Holy Ghost to preach the word in Asia" (Acts 16:6), they turned elsewhere — not because the unreached Asians were uncondemned sinners, not because Christ did not taste death for them, not because the great commission blacklisted Asia, but only because the Holy Spirit charted the agenda. Even if Satan is ubiquitous, the apostles could be in only one place at a time. And God's immediate assignment was to Macedonia where already a harvest was ripe for reaping; meanwhile, by His Spirit, God was

Himself everywhere actively present in the cosmos and in history, confronting the minds and consciences of all mankind universally. In God's good time Paul returned to Troas, and spent two long years also nearby in Ephesus; Asian cities were high on the list when Peter later addressed his first epistle to believers scattered abroad. "Passing by Mysia," the early Christian witness met head-on the Macedonian summons for help which propelled the gospel from the port of Troas to Europe; thus the good news became even more multicontinental than through the African eunuch's conversion. In the aftermath of the many conversions at Pentecost, distant places received the good news from apostles who had been personal eyewitnesses of the risen Lord and could speak authoritatively of His nature and work. When Paul went to Philippi he scarcely dreamed the Spirit would soon lead on to Athens for a Mars Hill witness to the philosophers of Greece.

The early Christians knew well that God's activity is now oriented toward implementing Christ's lordship. They had existential fellowship with the risen Jesus and recognized as a spiritual reality His presence as Lord. They knew that in "the fellowship of the church of the Lord there is established," as Walter Künneth so rightly says, "the beginning of a new humanity."[6] For them the New Testament elaborated the altered meaning of life and death in view of Christ's resurrection power. But more than this, they recognized that on the Christ of the universe rested their total dependence as well as the fate of the nations. The risen Lord was for them the focal center of the movement and meaning of history. The stone quarried by "no human hands" would become a great mountain filling the whole earth (Dan. 2:31f., RSV). The triumphal entry was a dress rehearsal that unveiled the future King who would rule over the nations (Zech. 9:9f.). Christ would come to reign over the nations (Rom. 15:12), indeed, will rule them "with a rod of iron" (Rev. 2:26f.). In eschatological vision John foresees participants from every nation ranged about God's throne in triumphant praise (Rev. 5:9; 7:9). The church was to fulfill her worldwide mission in a context of expectant waiting.

TO THE JEW FIRST

Before the ascension Jesus outlined the mission of His followers — they were to be Spirit-empowered witnesses to Him "both in Jerusalem, and in all Judea and Samaria, and even to the remotest part of the earth'' (Acts 1:8, NASB). "The apostles and early Christians were led," writes John Rea, "to follow the order of this strategic plan by circumstances and the direction of the Holy Spirit, as the history of the spread of the Gospel is unfolded in the Book of Acts. The example of the apostle Paul is primary for the subsequent mission of the Church — 'to the Jew first and also to the Greek.' "[7] In His early days of public ministry Jesus enjoined the disciples not to go to the Gentiles (Matt. 10:5f.). The time comes, however, when in final words to the Jewish leaders at Rome the apostle Paul declares that God's salvation has now been sent to the responsive Gentiles (Acts 28:25ff.). Paul leaves no doubt, however, that even if in Christ there is "neither Jew nor Greek," the Jew has ongoing significance in the purpose of God; not only does salvation in Christ remain open to the Jew, but his salvation ought to be a matter of our fervent concern and prayer (Rom. 9-11).

Unfortunately Christians have weakened this principle — diluting it to mean to the Jew "no longer," or to the Jew "last," or to the Jew "also," or to the Jew only now and then in particular places or during special crusades, and usually with a view only of evangelizing individuals. As a result, evangelical theology in the twentieth century is often connected in the Jewish mind with the long and shameful record of anti-Semitism by baptized Christians — whether in ghettos, pogroms or Hitler's holocaust involving six million victims. The record of Christian attitudes toward the Jew might cause us to raise some provocative and perhaps embarrassing questions. Did those evangelicals who were interested in a regathered Jewry and a Jewish homeland either for the sake of fulfilled prophecy or in prospect of a novel evangelistic opportunity perhaps give insufficient attention to concerns of political justice and human rights? Should not wrestling with the question of God's historical purpose for the Jew — the meaning of Auschwitz, for example, and (by way of stark contrast) the emergence of the new state of Israel — have elicited more strenuous dialogue about the identity of the Messiah or the Suffering Servant? Further, we might note that the victory over evil forces won personally by the risen Jesus (who proclaimed the dawning kingdom of God and the imminent messianic era with its justice for the poor and healing of the afflicted) has seemingly been tabled for almost two thousand years of world history. Does this fact validate doubts about Jesus' messiahship, or signal some failure in the church's fulfilment of her mission in the world? Has the institutional church in disobedience and apostasy herself perchance passed into a postbiblical exile, a lostness in the world, which like the interbiblical period of the past may suddenly and unexpectedly climax in the Lord's coming? Could it be that, for all their evangelistic energies, even evangelical believers have neglected other important concerns and have thus needlessly etched a question mark over the finality and significance of the Easter victory and the messiahship of Jesus Christ? Could it possibly be that Christian teachers and church administrators and evangelists will be those who in the near future will hear one saying: "Woe to you, . . . hypocrites, because you shut off the kingdom of heaven from men . . . . You travel about on sea and land to make one proselyte . . . . For you tithe . . . and have neglected the weightier provisions of the law, justice and mercy and faithfulness; but these are things you should have done without neglecting the others" (Matt. 23:13, 15, 23, NASB)? The Pharisees obscured the kingdom from others by their tradition of external formalities; do we perhaps make the kingdom repulsive by completely internalizing pure religion (cf. James 1:27)? If the synoptic passages mean anything, they warn that the supposed people of God run the dread possibility of shutting up the kingdom of God to men by an improper fulfilment of vocation and mission. Making proselytes was not the point at which the Pharisees failed. Evangelical Christians likewise have done better here than in other respects. But for all their spectacular winning of proselytes the Pharisees made the kingdom of God repugnant. For them true religion was not something internal; for us the danger is that pure religion may mean nothing external beyond a godly personal life. Either omission is a serious sin, something that morally sensitive worldlings instinctively recognize as a threat to authentic religion. Moral duties like justice, mercy and faithfulness have become neglected concerns that ought instead to burden an uneasy conscience. The weightiest of all God's commandments, not excepting the great commission, concern love and justice. If we say with Paul that judgment will begin with the Jews (Rom. 2:6-10), and that their cup of wrath is fuller than that of others, what shall we say about ourselves? The law and the prophets are not summed up in evangelism exclusively. In proclaiming "to the Jew first," we must not confuse or confound him by reducing or minimizing the comprehensiveness of Christ's gospel.

THE PRESENT RULE OF CHRIST
IN CHURCH AND WORLD

Sure as the early Christians were of the coming final judgment of men and nations, they were equally sure that in relationship to civil government their stance was to be one not of rebelliousness or detachment, but rather one of responsible submission and moral relationship. What Paul affirms in Romans 13 must in the nature of the case have been frequently discussed in the churches both in the apostle's presence and also during his absence. Roman government influenced Christian fortunes in many ways — from Pilate's condemnation of Jesus, the safe and swift access the empire vouchsafed to Paul's missionary journeys, and the rights of citizenry which he so readily invoked, to the Neronian and other terrors to which believers were exposed. For good reason Paul included "persecution" on the manifest of hardships that, however severe, cannot undo the Christian's security in Christ (Rom. 8:35). In Revelation 13 Christians prepare for martyrdom as the alternative to anarchy. In the face of mounting Jewish hostility the idea that Christianity was not a new and therefore illicit religion but rather the fulfilment of the ancient Hebrew faith was polemically difficult to maintain, however theologically sound. To be sure the Jerusalem church of A.D. 56 or thereabouts was composed of "thousands . . . among the Jews . . . who have believed" (Acts 21:20, RSV). But Jewish rebellion against Rome which led in A.D. 70 to the destruction of Jerusalem and crushed nationalistic hopes so sealed the necessity for a decisive distinction between Christians and mainline Jewry that "to the Jew first," however imperative, became not only impractical but perhaps inadvisable if not inoperative.

Even after Roman persecution became frequent and severe, Christians maintained their characteristic attitude toward civil government. Established rulers, they maintained, are divinely ordained and hence should discharge their duties as God's servants and as His ministers of justice. They are to be conscientiously obeyed, even if one is unjustly treated on some particular occasion, since the appointed role of rulers is to serve God by rewarding good and punishing evil. Paul leaves no doubt that the Christian's public indebtedness is only to love, which completely fulfills the social commandments of the law (Rom. 13:8-10). The future age, the apostle adds, has already begun to dawn on us (Rom. 13:11f.); he declares this not to console Christians amid mere interim loyalties, but rather to reinforce their ethical commitments in fully manifesting — as C. H. Dodd so effectively puts it — "the life which is appropriate to the New Day."[8] Christ frees His subjects to live righteously (Rom. 14:17).

The Old Testament theocratic kings distinguished themselves from the supposedly superhuman kings of the ancient Near East by recognizing Yahweh as the only divine King and by expecting the coming messianic King. While the specific phrase, "the kingdom of the Lord," appears perhaps only once in the Old Testament (I Chron. 28:5), numerous variations of it occur. Deeply rooted in the Old Testament, the idea becomes the central theme of Jesus' teaching and is found frequently throughout the New Testament. The synoptic gospels announce that God's kingly rule has dawned messianically in Jesus' life and work. The kingdom is no longer only a transcendent reality rooted on earth in believing acceptance, nor simply a distant future, eschatological expectation.

Mark begins with a proclamation of the dawning kingdom (1:14f.). Matthew and Luke from the outset present Christ as King; the former introduces His royal lineage; the latter includes the angelic announcement that Christ will occupy David's throne (1:32f.). In the very first chapter of John, Jesus did not disown Nathaniel's identification of Him as "King of Israel" (1:49). Nor did Christ disavow kingship when questioned by Pilate (Luke 23:2f.; John 18:37), even though He did set His rule apart from the materialistic earth-oriented kingdoms marked by worldly pomp and brute power (John 18:36). Jesus' hardening foes, both Pharisees and Sadducees, saw in such claims the blasphemous pretenses of a false messiah (John 5:18; 19:12).

In contrast with Jewish nationalistic expectations, Jesus fulfills the prophetic messianic ideal of a universal kingdom (Ps. 2; 22; 72; Isa. 11:10; Dan. 7:13f.) in which Jews and Gentiles share alike. Only after crucifixion, with His claims to be the Son of Man vindicated, does He enjoin the great commission, and He does so by simultaneously claiming universal sovereignty — "all authority in heaven and on earth" (Matt. 28:19, RSV). Through the widening frontiers of the Book of Acts the church brings believers, Jew and Gentile alike, from many and distant nations into the orbit of His headship; His kingdom transcends all racial and geographical limits.

The imminent kingdom, in some respects already manifest in Jesus Christ, the sinless Son and risen Lord, encroaches ever and always upon the present world to which the exalted Christ will return in judgment and to reign (Matt. 16:28; Mark 13:26). The New Testament presents the kingdom as a phenomenon which is both present and still to be consummated. Central to both emphases is the New Testament affirmation of the risen Jesus as the manifested divine King. In its frequent application of this title to Jesus (John 1:49; 6:15; 12:13ff.; 18:33ff.; 19:12ff.; 19:19ff.), the fourth gospel implies that divine sovereignty already inheres in His messianic ministry. The conditional sovereignty of earthly rulers is limited; Christ invites and claims supreme and everlasting loyalty (Matt. 6:33; cf. Luke 1:33). The New Testament contrasts earthly kings, whether generically or specifically (Pharaoh, Herod the Great, etc.), with God and the messianic King. Divine rank is ascribed only to Yahweh or His Messiah. Earthly kings no less than all Jews and Gentiles must hear the gospel (Acts 9:15; cf. Rev. 10:11). Three times the apostle Paul quotes the formula "Jesus is Lord" (Rom. 10:9; I Cor. 12:3; Phil. 2:11, RSV), doubtless a part of every convert's confession at baptism. Christ is now both Head of the church and Head also of the universe (Eph. 1:22; Col. 1:18). While His universal kingship will not be openly manifest until His return "in power and glory," He is even now exalted to the place of universal dominion at the Father's right hand (Acts 2:33ff.; I Cor. 15:24f.; Eph. 1:20ff.; Phil. 2:9ff., etc.) and exercises His rule over all believers and over all things for their good (Eph. 1:22).

As mediator of God's new covenant the messianic King is supremely concerned for extending God's kingdom of justice and peace through the redemptive transformation everywhere of men and nations who are continually answerable to His daily and final judgment. What claimant to credentials that fulfill the Old Testament promise of Messiah could be indifferent to its overarching demand for personal regeneration and reconciliation to Yahweh on the one hand, and for social righteousness on the other? Modern ecclesiasticism gives priority to changing social and political structures apart from the moral and spiritual renewal of individuals — an approach predicated on the assumption that society consists of a corporate multitude of innocent victims of injustice, a vanguard of righteous activists, and a minority of privileged oppressors whose exploitative self-interest only a socialist order can defeat. To this approach the New Testament presents a strikingly transcendent alternative: "All have sinned and come short of the glory of God . . . . Repent, every one of you . . . . Except a man be born again he cannot see the kingdom of God . . . . I will write my law upon their hearts." The Bible proffers no hope for genuine eman-

cipation of the downtrodden and oppressed unless they seek divine
forgiveness and rescue from sin unto eternal life. Moreover, it
elevates these spiritual realities into personal priority. This does not
mean that Christians should condone injustice and oppression, nor
that they should ignore social betterment, the espousing of just
laws and the promoting of righteous causes. But Christians must
never consider such efforts per se as the implementation of the
kingdom. The kingdom of God is the risen Christ's rule, and no
man can see that kingdom apart from personal rebirth (John 3:3,
5). The new birth is not by any means the whole reality of the
kingdom, but it is nonetheless an indispensable beginning. The
kingdom is the righteous rule and reign of God manifested in
redemptive rescue of mankind amid the universal revolt against the
divine Creator and Lord.

The church by-passes enthusiastic visions of an instant millennium via social revolution because it recognizes that only "new
heavens and a new earth" will be "the *home* of justice" (II Peter
3:13, NEB, italics mine). Human unregeneracy and intransigency
limit what is attainable in ordinary history. Not only the privileged
but also the underprivileged and, in some respects, especially those
who promote preferred options, are answerable to God. The overthrow of one privileged preferred class has almost invariably led to
the entrenchment of another. Social ideals are soon manipulated by
semantic distortion or in any event reduced to beggarly fragments
of what the new covenant comprehensively stipulates. The
Christian knows that enduring justice requires the stamping of
God's law upon human hearts; hence the Christian is always and
everywhere Christ's ambassador who sounds a plea for spiritual
reconciliation with the King of Glory.

The risen Lord, having by His resurrection and in His own person already conquered the treacherous forces of evil, seeks daily to
extend that victory and anticipates the powerful consummation of
His kingdom. In that day men will lose their present option of
deciding for or against Him and His purposes. As reigning Head of
the church of the twice-born, Christ now daily widens His triumph
over satanic forces, containing sin's ferocious might by the
restraining and overcoming power of the Holy Spirit, and thrusting
believers into the life of the nations as empowered witnesses.
World-wide they proclaim the good news that Jesus Christ is Savior
and Lord, that no one need resign himself to the demonic powers,
that Jesus offers eternal life even here and now to all who come to

Him by faith, and that because of Him all the forces of oppression and exploitation become candidates for inescapable judgment. The Christ who wills justice and peace among the nations establishes the church as the new society in the midst of a perishing world, enables Christians to cope with a dark and putrefying social milieu, and empowers and expects them to live and labor as light and salt. This Christ will finally and irrevocably segregate the godly from the ungodly in a global judgment, the staggering demands of which are even now already fully met by Him for those whose lives are personally committed to Him, the coming King.

Even if society merely approximates the standards of Christ's eternal kingdom in a hesitant and very broken way, the Christian community should nonetheless commend every battle against injustice, should identify itself cautiously with the highest available public options, and should openly present, promote and demonstrate the divine ideal. By joyfully reflecting in its own individual and corporate existence the authority and power of the risen King, the Christian family will sensitize the public mind and conscience to the criteria by which the returning Lord will finally judge the world.

When rulers tried to suppress religious liberty, especially freedom to proclaim the gospel to the lost, the early Christians boldly declared the necessity of obeying God rather than man (Acts 5:29) — a wording that puts rulers in their place when they contravene divine imperatives. This principle applies not simply to the great commission but to all that Christ commanded (Matt. 28:19). The dichotomy sometimes made between freedom to "preach the gospel" and freedom to fulfill the social requirements of God's law reveals insensitivity to basic Christian rights and a constrictive view of the gospel.

It is clear, therefore, that the biblical gospel was not derived from, nor determined by, nor dependent upon changing political conditions. The God of holy love is the eternal Lord of the nations, and it is His eternal grace and judgment that determine their destiny. Without exception all great world powers have one by one become second-rate or worse. All nations are moving toward inevitable judgment by the invincible kingdom of God. In that judgment they can no longer plead ignorance concerning the crucified and risen Lord (cf. Acts 3:17; 17:31).

The Christian vanguard did not go first and foremost to the most hospitable areas. Instead it maintained a mobile witness wherever God's mandate made it "necessary" to go. Hence Paul both taught in Jewish synagogues and went to prestigious Gentile centers, including Rome. Changing political conditions influenced tactics but they never decided strategy. Not only the apostles but even lay workers like Stephen unwaveringly faced persecution, imprisonment and martyrdom.

On that bleak December day in 1941 when the Japanese returned from Pearl Harbor to their mobile flight station at sea, the commanding officer remarked: "I fear that we have awakened a sleeping giant and filled him with a terrible resolve." Little did he or his fellows envision the later counterassaults on Hiroshima and Nagasaki ultimately ventured in order to cut short the continuing loss of life and property. At Calvary it was not a sleeping giant but the Suffering Servant of Yahweh who was smitten by hostile foes. Little did they dream that He would awaken to resurrection life; little did they understand that the Messiah had voluntarily given His life to save the world. Today His followers stalk this fallen planet with a holy resolve to publish the awesome news of the soon-coming Judge of all the earth, and the beneficent tidings of new life still available for those who repent and believe.

Once the all-powerful risen Lord returns in glory the church need no longer be concerned about changing political conditions. When Joseph of Arimathea "besought Pilate" that he might remove the body of Jesus from the cross (John 19:38), that was the last time anyone had to beg a favor of an earthly ruler concerning Jesus. The day is soon coming when hostile rulers will be the beggars; at Jesus' throne they all shall bow to the King of kings and Lord of lords. After Pentecost — which in model anticipated the intelligible promulgation of the gospel in many tongues to many nations in mandated fulfilment of the great commission — the apostle Peter pictured Christ's present resurrection lordship over the nations much like a Damocles' sword poised to strike, a menacing judgment to be averted only by swift repentance: "Men of Israel . . . . You handed him over to be killed, and you disowned him before Pilate . . . . You disowned the Holy and Righteous One and asked that a murderer be released to you . . . . Repent, then, and turn to God, so that your sins may be wiped out, that times of· refreshing may come from the Lord, and that he may send the Christ, who has been appointed for you — even Jesus" (Acts 3:12ff., NIV).

THE JUDGMENT OF THE NATIONS

In a final glorious day all nations will be gathered before the throne of the King (Matt. 25:32) and the righteous sons of Abraham among the nations will inherit the kingdom of God! The Book of Revelation presents Almighty God as King of the nations (Rev. 15:3), identifies Messiah as King of kings and Lord of lords (Rev. 19:16; cf. 17:14), and elevates the sons of the kingdom of God or of Christ above all earthly rulers. At His coming Christ will take up His reign over the nations (Rom. 15:12) and will institute His millennial earthly reign together with His saints (Rev. 20:6). In the Revelation we see those who have conquered the beast singing praises to the King of the nations in an eschatological pilgrimage that anticipates the coming of all nations to worship Him (Rev. 15:1ff.; cf. 21:22ff.). Yahweh makes one nation from all peoples to serve as a kingdom of priests for the entire earth. The covenant blessing (Deut. 28:1-14) that was to reach all nations includes universal peace. It implies, therefore, that no nation shall any longer seek its own well-being at the expense of another (cf. Mic. 4:1ff.). Yahweh's establishment of the covenant will refashion all national life for blessing.

FOOTNOTES

N. B. Bible quotations are from the Authorized Version unless otherwise noted.

1. *Theological Dictionary of the New Testament*, ed. Gerhard Kittel (Grand Rapids: Eerdmans, 1964), s.v. "kosmos."

2. Ibid., p. 892.

3. Ibid., p. 893.

4. Walter Eichrodt, *Theology of the Old Testament* (London: S.C.M. Press, 1961), vol. 1, pp. 431-32.

5. *Theological Dictionary of the New Testament*, s.v. "ethnos."

6. Walter Künneth, *The Theology of the Resurrection* (St. Louis: Concordia Publishing House, 1965), p. 199.

7. *The Zondervan Pictorial Encyclopedia of the Bible*, ed. Merrill C. Tenney (Grand Rapids: Zondervan, 1975), s.v. "Nations."

8. Charles Harold Dodd, *Epistle of St. Paul to the Romans* (New York: R. Long and R. R. Smith, Inc., 1932), p. 210.

J. Herbert Kane

STRATEGY OF MISSION AND CHANGING POLITICAL SITUATIONS

INTRODUCTION

The Christian missionary carries with him two important documents, a Bible and a passport. The Bible identifies him as an ambassador for Christ. As such he is a citizen of the world. He is a true internationalist. He represents a universal king, Jesus Christ. He belongs to a universal institution, the church. He carries a universal message, the gospel. In this capacity he would like to think of himself as being above politics, national and international.

The passport links him irrevocably with an earthly kingdom. For better or worse his fortune is bound up with that of his own country. When it performs well, he is happy and proud. When it fails to perform well, he is distressed — sometimes ashamed. Never for a moment can he forget that he is an American, a Canadian, or a Norwegian, as the case may be.

The apostle Paul had no such problem. He was a Roman citizen and ministered within the borders of the Roman Empire. When he got into trouble he had only to appeal to the local authorities for justice and protection.[1] Modern missionaries have not had it quite so easy. Many of them have been caught in the cross fire of the Sino-Japanese War, the Arab-Israeli War, the Indian-Pakistani War, and in civil wars in Nigeria, Zaire, Vietnam and Burundi, to say nothing of the Cold War that has a way of heating up from time to time.

Very seldom did Jesus refer to politics. His clearest statement was: "Render therefore to Caesar the things that are Caesar's, and to God the things that are God's" (Matt. 22:21). That kind of dichotomy is difficult to achieve even in a democracy. It is much more difficult in a totalitarian state, where the government demands full and ultimate allegiance, leaving little or nothing for God. In all such countries the Christian, especially the missionary, requires the wisdom of Solomon to avoid giving offense.

GENERAL OBSERVATIONS REGARDING THE PAST

It might help us in our discussion if we place the problem in perspective by making certain observations.

(1) In the past the modern missionary movement was closely linked with Western imperialism. This was especially true of Roman Catholic missions, which were actively aided and abetted by the kings of Portugal and Spain in the sixteenth and seventeenth centuries when they were building their empires in the East Indies and the New World. While the link between missions and colonialism was not nearly so strong in Protestant countries such as Great Britain and the Netherlands, still it was there; and it was underscored when some missionaries left religious work to join the diplomatic corps.[2]

Actually there were three forms of colonialism — political, economic, and cultural. The diplomats represented the first, the merchants the second, and the missionaries the third. At least this is the way it appeared to the nationalists on the receiving end.[3]

Apart from a few remaining pockets colonialism is dead.[4] The memory continues to fester in the minds of many nationalists, however, and doubtless it will be several decades before we can live down the ugly image we have acquired.

(2) The missionaries as a body did not regard the colonial system as inherently evil. From time to time they inveighed against exploitation and repression and other excesses, but few of them ever questioned the legality or the morality of the system itself. For the most part they regarded colonialism as God's way of opening up Asia and Africa to the gospel of Christ.[5] Almost to a man they considered Western civilization superior to any other and came to regard themselves as engaging in a "civilizing" as well as "Christianizing" mission to the "heathen." Indeed, the two were virtually synonymous in their thinking.

(3) On the other hand, it was the missionary who sowed the seeds of nationalism. Wherever he went he established schools in which were taught the ideas and ideals of democracy, including the dignity of man, the worth of the individual, freedom of thought and speech, and so forth.[6] In Africa he was for many decades the sole purveyor of education. This gave him a unique opportunity to mold the minds of a whole generation of Africans. It is safe to say that had it not been for the missionary and his schools, not a single country in black Africa would be independent today. With few exceptions today's leaders in black Africa were educated in mission

schools, and many of them when independence was achieved publicly acknowledged their indebtedness to the missionaries.

(4) Traditionally, missionaries as a body did not engage in the politics of the host country. They left politics to the colonial administrators. Nor did they identify themselves with the independence movements in the various colonies. They did not even encourage their converts to join the struggle for independence. They preferred to remain aloof from politics, regarding it at best as worldly, at worst as corrupt.

(5) Like other human beings the missionaries were the product of their time, no better and no worse than their compatriots. They had blind spots like everyone else. Left to themselves they tended to support the *status quo* until it became unbearable. Consequently they were content to make the best of a situation they themselves would not necessarily have chosen. They were willing to support any government capable of maintaining law and order and of upholding some elementary principles of social justice.

(6) Missionaries have always supported the government of the host country in time of war. During the Sino-Japanese War (1937-1945) the missionaries in China supported Chiang Kai-shek and the Nationalists against the Japanese. It was they who exposed the atrocities committed by the Japanese army.[7] Conversely, the few missionaries left in Japan sided with Japan and sent cablegrams to the State Department urging the United States not to stop the flow of scrap iron to Japan. At the present time the missionaries in Israel wholeheartedly support the Jews in their struggle for survival in the Middle East, whereas missionaries in the surrounding Arab countries are equally persuaded that justice lies with the Arabs.

(7) Of all political issues, the one that has been of deepest concern to the missionaries is the matter of religious freedom. Rightly or wrongly they have regarded religious freedom as the greatest of all forms of freedom.[8] It is because of this that missionaries the world over have taken a strong stand against Communism. In many cases they have supported oppressive and corrupt regimes because the only alternative was totally unacceptable. They knew that if the Communists ever came to power all forms of freedom would be curtailed if not abolished, and both church and mission would suffer irreparable damage. Man has two basic needs: food for his body and freedom for his spirit. The Communists provide the first; they deny the second. The missionary, believing that man does not live by bread alone, is not prepared to sell his religious

birthright for a mess of economic pottage. No institution, religious or secular, can be expected to acquiesce in its own destruction.

POLITICAL REALITIES OF THE NEW ERA

There is no doubt about it; we are living in a new day. The last thirty years have seen more changes in the political configuration of the world than any previous period. Since the demise of the colonial system following World War II, the missionary now finds himself in a political milieu vastly different from that of any previous generation, and he needs to understand the temper of the times. Certain basic facts, however unpleasant, should be recognized.

(1) The collapse of the vast colonial system was a good thing even though it brought many problems in its wake. This is not to say that colonialism was an unmitigated evil, as some militant nationalists would have us believe. It had both its good side and its bad side. It is probably too early to make an ultimate judgment on the fringe benefits of the colonial system. It must be clearly stated, however, that the system was morally wrong and every right-thinking person must applaud its demise. The right of self-determination is one of the inalienable rights of mankind. Every nation wants to be sovereign in the conduct of its own affairs. Good rule is no substitute for home rule. The unholy alliance between the gospel and the gunboat was a millstone around the necks of the missionaries. They can be devoutly thankful that the burden has been lifted. Now they are free to be what they are — ministers of Jesus Christ, not the running dogs of Western imperialism.

(2) The collapse of the colonial system has resulted in major changes vis-à-vis the missionary movement.

It has changed the role of the missionary. In the past he was the leader; today he is the servant. In most places he is still needed and wanted, but only on condition that he understands his new role. If he is able and willing to fill the servant role, he will find a warm welcome and a fruitful ministry. If not, he might as well remain at home.

The status of the church has likewise changed. It is no longer under the control of the mission, nor is it part of the "mother" church in the West. It enjoys full autonomy with its own constitution, organization, and membership. It is in no way subservient to the Western mission that brought it into existence. It has reached maturity; it has declared its independence. Today's missionary must be prepared to work not only *with* the church, but *under* it as well.[9]

One other thing has changed — the image of Christianity. From the beginning of the modern missionary movement Christianity was identified with colonialism, and that fact greatly hindered its acceptance. But no longer. The foreign flags have come down and the gunboats have been withdrawn. Christianity is now free to chart its own course, develop its own structures, and project its own image without reference to Western missions. Church leaders can now hold their heads high. No longer are they regarded as second-class citizens whose first allegiance is to London, Geneva or New York.

(3) Every sovereign state has the right to exclude or expel any person deemed to be undesirable. For years the United States government kept Orientals out. When the government of Burma in 1966 nationalized all banks, businesses, schools, and hospitals, thousands of Indians, Pakistanis, and Chinese were obliged to leave the country. In 1973 some forty thousand Asians were summarily expelled from Uganda, leaving behind all their goods and assets. Protests in and outside of the United Nations were of no avail. President Amin carried out his order. All Communist countries are closed to Christian missionaries; so are half a dozen Muslim countries. There are still some countries that welcome non-professional missionaries but only on the understanding that they not engage in religious propaganda. Still other countries limit the stay or restrict the movements of missionaries within their borders. Some countries, like Burma, have expelled all missionaries; others, like South Korea, India and Taiwan, have expelled certain individual missionaries whose political views or activities were suspect. This is both frustrating and frightening, but it is a fact of international life. The day is gone when Uncle Sam or John Bull could do whatever he pleased.

(4) Today's missionary is a guest in the host country; as such he has no rights, only privileges. In colonial days the white man enjoyed enormous prestige and was afforded rights and privileges denied to the nationals. In many instances he took advantage of his exalted status and exploited the natives in a shameful fashion. The missionary was never as arrogant as the other expatriates, but he enjoyed the deference paid to him as a member of the ruling race.

Now all that is gone. The missionary, instead of being at the head of the immigration line, may find himself at the end. It may take him three days and ten visits to various offices to get his personal possessions through customs. One missionary in Bolivia waited two years to get his driver's license. Another had to pay three thousand dollars duty on his secondhand car. This is hard on the missionary's time and pocketbook but it is good for his sanctification.

(5) Very few countries in the Third World are genuine democracies. Civil rights, taken for granted in the West, simply do not exist. Third World nations started out well; democracy was tried but found wanting. One by one, duly elected governments were overthrown, political parties were banned, constitutions were scrapped, and dictatorships were established. Independence, which was supposed to solve all their problems, turned out to be a mirage and the long-suffering people were worse off than before. The white sahibs were replaced by black and brown sahibs.[10] Worse still, economic stagnation and political instability continue to plague the dictatorships. In some parts of the world, governments rise and fall almost with the barometer. The American missionary, with his tradition of an open society with multiparty politics, freedom of speech, press and assembly, will find life in a dictatorship very irksome.

(6) The *American* missionary is particularly vulnerable. Time was when an American passport was an asset. In some parts of the world today it is more of a liability. The American missionary has several strikes against him.

The United States, the most powerful country in the world, has enormous influence. A nod from our president has been known to topple a government overseas.[11] A provocative statement by a United States senator will be carried by satellite to the ends of the earth in a matter of hours. The immense clout of our multinational corporations has aroused the ire of the smaller countries that have no way of competing with what they call "neo-colonialism." The international editions of *Time* and *Newsweek* often carry articles critical of other governments and their leaders. Such articles have been known to lead to anti-American demonstrations in the capitals of the Third World.[12] In the postwar period almost a hundred American buildings overseas have been burned to the ground, and only the Lord knows how many times our flag has been desecrated by rampaging mobs venting their anti-American feelings.

The vicissitudes of the Cold War have taken their toll. The

world is divided into three camps — the Free World headed by the United States, the Communist World led by Russia, and the neutral countries of the Third World that do not want to be drawn into the conflict between Moscow and Washington. The American involvement in the Vietnam War, which lasted ten years and ended in a humiliating defeat, did nothing to enhance the image of the American missionary in the Third World. International tensions have eased somewhat in recent years; but the Cold War is by no means over, as the situation in Angola attests. When the United States sided with Pakistan in 1971 it alienated India, and immediately the American missionaries in that part of the world felt the chill. If the United States finally decides to abandon Taiwan in favor of Red China, the American missionaries there will be in a very unenviable position.[13]

The subversive activities of the Central Intelligence Agency have done irreparable damage to the integrity of American foreign policy. For years the Communists have been accusing the Central Intelligence Agency of subversive activities in all parts of the world, but few of us believed them. We held both the Federal Bureau of Investigation and the Central Intelligence Agency in high esteem and were not likely to turn our backs on them at the suggestion of the Kremlin. But in recent months we have been appalled at the revelations coming out of Washington. Now the whole world knows the sordid details of this incredible story. It is a safe bet that the image of the "Ugly American" is now uglier than ever. To make matters worse both the Central Intelligence Agency and the White House have insisted that they will continue to use American missionaries on a voluntary basis in the intelligence-gathering operation.[14] All this has had an adverse effect on the image of the American missionary abroad, and when one remembers that two-thirds of all the Protestant missionaries in the world are from North America, it can easily be seen what devastating effects this whole business will have on the church and missions around the world.

SUGGESTED STRATEGY FOR THE FUTURE

It is always easier to assess the past than to predict the future. Of one thing we can be sure: the future will be very different from the past. "One age has died; another is striving to be born. We stand in the time of birth-pangs, in which the future still remains obscure."[15] However, certain guidelines may help us as we try to chart our course in the years ahead.

(1) The missionary must always remember that he is an ambassador for Jesus Christ, not for Uncle Sam. Consequently his allegiance is to a higher power, and one day he will stand before the Judge of all the earth to give an account of his stewardship. He is not particularly interested in exporting the American way of life, the capitalist system, or parliamentary democracy, though he may be persuaded that all three are highly desirable. His lodestar is not Robert's *Rules of Order*, or *The Wall Street Journal*, or the *Congressional Record*, but the Holy Scriptures.

He is a world citizen and his chief task is to build the kingdom of God on earth. This being so, he is under no obligation to support, much less defend, all the foreign policy pronouncements of the United States. Certainly he will abhor the approach which says, "My country, right or wrong." When his country is right, he will in all sincerity try to explain and defend it. When it is wrong, he will have the courage and candor to say so. When his enemies, including the Communists, speak the truth — which they do now and again — he will side with them. Truth does not cease to be truth when it falls from the lips of a Communist.

(2) The missionary must not equate the kingdom of God with any particular political, economic, or social system. All human systems, including his own, are under the judgment of God and should be evaluated in the light of Holy Scripture. Indeed, the church itself must acknowledge the lordship of Christ. In today's pluralistic world the missionary must be prepared to live and labor under alien systems of various kinds without trying to undermine or overthrow them. He must resist the temptation to jump on every passing bandwagon that promises to solve the problems of the day.

The nineteenth-century missionaries have been criticized for their failure to distinguish between Christianity and Western civilization and for the naive manner in which they imposed their cultural mores on their converts, making them "little Americans" in the process. Today's missionaries are in danger of doing in the political realm what the early missionaries did in the cultural realm. One gets the impression that there are some who would advocate a return to the concept of Manifest Destiny so prevalent at the turn of the century; but instead of the American flag and American commerce, they are advocating the American legal and political systems with their checks and balances, including all the freedoms that have characterized our open society.

(3) The missionary must not assume that Western democracy is

for everyone. Democracy to be effective must be supported by other institutions — a free press, a multiparty system, a universal franchise, a secret ballot. But what is the use of these things if the majority of the population is illiterate? Moreover, it must be remembered that in many parts of the world the common man has no burning desire to be part of the decision-making process. For centuries he has lived a communal life, with others, usually the tribal chief, making his decisions for him. The same is true of the peasant in his paddy field. He could not care less about free elections and a secret ballot. All he wants is to be left alone with his family and his fields. If his rice bowl is filled twice a day, that is all he asks. That is one reason why the American forces in South Vietnam did not get more support from the peasantry. They were fighting for something that was not really meaningful to the Vietnamese.

In some countries the social and economic problems are so massive that it is doubtful they can be solved by democratic means. Maybe the best we can hope for in the immediate future is a "benign dictatorship." Dictatorship is a dirty word in the North Atlantic community, but not so in other parts of the world. It is simply a matter of fact that many of the developing countries are not ready for democracy. That may come in the future, and when it does we hope it will be an improvement on our own variety. Certainly American democracy, honeycombed with corruption and plagued with inefficiency and bureaucracy, has little to commend it to the rest of the world. The missionary, then, need not be too greatly disappointed that Western democracy is not sweeping the world.

(4) The missionary must be prepared to work and witness under political and social conditions that are not to his liking. It was assumed that the demise of the colonial system would bring a full measure of freedom to the oppressed peoples of the Third World, but it has not worked out that way. Of the 158 nations in the world only 40 enjoy complete freedom, 53 are partially free, and 65 have few if any civil rights.[16] To make matters worse, the vast majority of missionaries are living in the countries listed in the last two categories.

In Latin America only five countries are democracies,[17] in Asia only two,[18] and in the Middle East only one — Israel. India, once the largest democracy in the world, last year outlawed all opposition parties and jailed many of their leaders. In some countries, such as Greece and Turkey, there is political freedom but little religious freedom. In other countries, such as South Korea, Taiwan, the Philippines, and Chile, there is religious freedom but little political freedom. In many countries there is neither. Most Muslim countries and all Communist countries fall into this last category.

(5) The missionary in the present situation must be content with whatever freedom is permitted. He is not likely to be afforded more liberty, religious or civil, than is granted to the nationals. It is both foolish and futile for him to demand what the government is not prepared to grant.

Under a repressive regime what is he to do? He has two options: mind his own business and continue his work, or speak out against the regime and be expelled. Each missionary must make up his own mind what to do in a given situation. If his conscience will not allow him to remain silent, he will have to speak out. In that case he is almost sure to be expelled.[19]

POLITICAL COMPLEXITY OF TODAY'S WORLD

Today's missionary finds himself in a highly complex world as different from the nineteenth century as day is from night. Democracy has been tried and abandoned. Dictatorships of both the right and the left are endemic. By their very nature they give rise to coups, and coups lead to countercoups. Of the forty-six nations in the Organization of African Unity only half a dozen have not experienced at least one coup, successful or abortive, in the past fifteen years.[20] The situation differs from continent to continent and even from country to country. For the purposes of this discussion it might be well to divide the countries into five categories.

(1) In the first category I would include Rhodesia and South Africa, where the problems have moral as well as political overtones and where the issues are rather clearly defined. The sympathy of the missionary will definitely be on the side of the Africans struggling for dignity, liberty, and equality. For a white missionary to declare himself in favor of the white racist regime of Ian Smith would be the kiss of death. How and to what extent he should actively aid and abet the cause of nationalism is another matter. Before deciding to fight the government, he should carefully weigh the consequences of his action. What *in the long run* is in the best interest of the kingdom? If he is expelled, what will happen to the work? Will the church and the community be better off or worse

off without him? If he is the only doctor in a one hundred-bed hospital, what will happen to the patients when he is gone? It may require more wisdom and courage to remain at his post under very trying circumstances than to sound off and be expelled from the country.

(2) The developing countries of Africa and Asia present a different picture. Their experiment with democracy ended in fiasco and today they are ruled by dictators who came to power by way of the bullet rather than the ballot. In these countries the missionary had better keep his nose out of politics. The politicians are in and out of office with all the commotion of musical chairs. Governments rise and fall almost overnight, and the traffic moves back and forth between parliament and prison. For the missionary to inject himself into the kaleidoscope of African politics would be an exercise in futility. He has neither the experience nor the expertise to make a solid contribution. Moreover, it is doubtful if Africa is ready for democracy. In the meantime, a benign dictatorship is the best he can hope for.

(3) Another distinct group comprises the Muslim countries of the world. Even here the picture is by no means uniform. On the one hand there is Indonesia, where freedom of religion is guaranteed by the constitution and honored in practice. On the other hand there is Afghanistan, where freedom of religion is unknown. Iraq, Syria, Libya and Somalia, which once had missionaries, are now closed lands. Saudi Arabia and Mauritania are so anti-Christian that missionaries have never been permitted to enter.

In most Muslim countries the missionary is tolerated for the benefit that can be derived from his medical and educational institutions. Those who engage in evangelistic work must walk the tightrope; one false step and down they go. Missionaries in all such countries must be content with the modicum of freedom they have. To demand more would be to close the door altogether.

(4) The countries of Latin America gained their independence 150 years ago but are still in the throes of economic, social, and political upheaval. Many Latin American theologians are calling for the overthrow of the unjust power structures and the creation of a new social order. They equate the kingdom of God with socialism; at the same time they denounce capitalism as anti-Christian.[21] They are suggesting that if North American missionaries do not identify with the revolutionary struggles of the oppressed, their days in Latin America are numbered.

The kind of revolution advocated in Latin America is definitely Marxist. If it succeeds it will lead to the kind of totalitarian regimes found in China and Russia. In China the institutional church has been completely destroyed and in Russia it has been under severe attack for over fifty years. For the North American missionary to join the revolutionary forces in Latin America would be a form of hara-kiri. If the people of Latin America, including the Christian theologians, feel that their only hope is a Marxist revolution, that is their decision and we wish them well; but we have grave fears that the end result will be disastrous for the Christian church. This is not to deny that Latin America has gargantuan problems that may be insoluble by democratic means, but those of us who have lived under a Communist regime can be forgiven if we hesitate to throw in our lot with the Marxists of Latin America.

(5) Several countries of Asia have had a fairly successful history of democracy but in recent years have settled for a modified form of totalitarianism — South Korea, the Philippines, and India. It is a great pity that these three countries, which started off with such promise and progress, have found it necessary to resort to dictatorships. In these countries, especially South Korea and the Philippines, there is a large number of American missionaries. Most of them have accepted the *status quo* with a certain degree of equanimity. A few have spoken out against oppression and have been expelled.

FREEDOM: CIVIL AND RELIGIOUS

It should be borne in mind that it is the first responsibility of any government to protect its citizens from enemies without and within. When national security is threatened a government will frequently declare a state of emergency. It may go further and impose martial law, in which case civil rights will be suspended for the duration.

If the threat comes from without, the people usually rally to the support of their government, especially if the situation leads to war. But what if the threat comes from subversion within? In that case the populace may be divided, some supporting the government and others opposing it. Much will depend on the character and conduct of the regime under siege.

It is fair to ask: Is martial law always detrimental to the welfare of the people? Nationals and missionaries coming out of India and the Philippines all testify to the fact that conditions have greatly improved since the government clamped down on "subversive elements." The streets are safer, business is better, politics is cleaner. To be sure, certain persons, usually described as "dangerous" or "subversive," are in jail merely for political reasons. Opposition parties have been banned and some newspapers forcibly discontinued.

On the other hand, most law-abiding citizens are going about their business with no interference. In the case of the Philippines the threat of an imminent Communist takeover has been averted. Most Filipinos think that is a good thing. Interestingly enough, in all three countries there has been no curtailment of *religious* liberty. Some Korean pastors are in jail, but not for carrying out their religious duties. They were jailed because they agitated against the "oppressive measures" of the government.

In this respect it is curious to note that some Christian leaders regard *civil* liberty as more important than *religious* liberty. The World Council of Churches has been rightly concerned about the denial of civil rights in Chile, the Philippines, South Korea and Taiwan;[22] but its leaders have not shown the same concern for the blatant denial of religious liberty in Muslim and Communist countries. If missionaries in the past have been content to live and work in the Middle East which had little or no religious freedom, why should today's missionary find the lack of civil rights so intolerable that he must speak out at the expense of being expelled?

The cry for freedom is heard all over the world, and God knows how much it is needed in some areas. The missionary, however, must be on his guard lest he be tempted to join the chorus, shout the slogans, and wave the banners with all the "freedom fighters" of the world. When it comes to the highly complex and often doubtful issues of politics, the missionary does well to recognize the limitations of his own calling, knowledge, and expertise; he should hesitate to rush in where angels fear to tread. He need not assume that his allegiance to Jesus Christ requires him to join the picket line every time an opposition newspaper is banned or a local politician goes to jail. The jails of the Third World are filled with political prisoners, some of the right and some of the left. There is little that the well-meaning missionary can do about it. To identify with one group is to alienate the members of the other groups. The missionary's aim is to become all things to all men that by all means he might win some (I Cor. 9:22).

Stephen Neill sounds a word of caution: "Nothing would be

gained if the Church were to identify itself uncritically with 'the forces of revolution.' For revolution nearly always incorporates itself in one political party, and a Church which has become the Church of one political party has ceased to be the Church of all other political parties."[23] Malcolm Muggeridge said virtually the same thing at the Lausanne Congress in July 1974.[24] No one has expressed it better than Gonzalo Castillo Cardenas: "The Church has no right to deny her own nature, her own message, by identifying herself with any human program of social transformation."[25]

The missionary's chief task is to preach the gospel to every creature and to make disciples of all nations. He should think twice before allowing any cause, however worthy, to jeopardize his high calling as an ambassador for Jesus Christ.

FOOTNOTES

1. Acts 16:37-39; 18:12-16; 22:25, 26; 25:10-12.

2. Peter Parker in 1855 became America's first commissioner to Peking and Leighton Stuart became America's last ambassador to the Nationalist government in Nanking just before the Communist takeover.

3. Dr. Wu Yao-tsung, Chairman of the Three-Self Patriotic Movement, called Christianity "the opiate of the people, the runningdog of imperialism, the forerunner of cultural aggression." *Documents of the Three-Self Movement* (New York: National Council of Churches, 1963), p. 4.

4. Remaining pockets include Hong Kong, Macao, Timor, and the Panama Canal Zone.

5. Paul A. Varg, *Missionaries, Chinese and Diplomats* (Princeton, NJ: Princeton University Press, 1958), p. 5.

6. Joseph L. Grabill, *Protestant Diplomacy and the Near East* (Minneapolis: University of Minnesota Press, 1971), p. 54.

7. Varg, *Missionaries,* pp. 258-59.

8. In this they took their cue from the early church. Cf. Acts 4:19, 20; 5:28, 29.

9. Today's call for "moratorium" is an attempt to achieve authentic selfhood for the national churches.

10. This statement was made at the Bandung Conference in 1954 by the Foreign Secretary of the Philippines.

11. Ngo Dinh Diem, President of South Vietnam, was assassinated in 1963 a few days after President Kennedy suggested that a change of policy vis-à-vis South Vietnam might be necessary!

12. An uncomplimentary article in *Time* about Bolivia led to an attack on the United States embassy in that country.

13. More than 90 percent of the 800 missionaries in Taiwan are Americans.

14. Senator Mark O. Hatfield appealed recently to President Ford and former CIA

Director Colby to place all American missionaries out of bounds to the CIA, as is the case with the Peace Corps. Both leaders rejected the appeal on the grounds that missionaries "play a significant role and can be of assistance to the United States through CIA with no reflection upon their integrity nor their mission." *Congressional Record* 121, No. 185 (Dec. 15, 1975).

15. Stephen Neill, *Colonialism and Christian Missions* (New York: McGraw-Hill, 1966), p. 422.

16. *U.S. News and World Report*, January 19, 1976, pp. 24-25.

17. Venezuela, Surinam, Colombia, Costa Rica and El Salvador.

18. Japan and Thailand.

19. The White Fathers pulled out of Mozambique and the United Church (USA) evacuated Angola when in their view it became apparent that their continued presence would have compromised the gospel.

20. The more stable states include Egypt, Tunisia, Tanzania, Zambia, and Kenya.

21. Gustavo Gutierrez, *A Theology of Liberation* (Maryknoll, NY: Orbis Books, 1973), pp. 111-12.

22. A four-man team representing the World Council of Churches, the National Council of Churches (USA), and the Asia Christian Conference visited South Korea and the Philippines in the summer of 1974 to investigate issues relating to human rights (*Ecumenical Press Service*, Oct. 3, 1974, pp. 5-6).

23. Neill, *Colonialism*, p. 424.

24. *Let the Earth Hear His Voice*, ed. J. D. Douglas (Minneapolis: World Wide Publications, 1975), p. 452.

25. C. Peter Wagner, *Latin American Theology: Radical or Evangelical* (Grand Rapids: Eerdmans, 1970), p. 26.

RESPONSE / Richard M. Winchell

INTRODUCTION

In responding to these two excellent papers, may I comment that to move from theology to strategy is the correct order. Dr. Henry starts with Christ's reign over the twice-born, empowering them to cope and to sensitize the public conscience, and rises to the observation that there is a future of peace and harmony for the nations. Theologically, our hope is in our eschatology. One day "Jesus shall reign . . . ."

EXPECT CHANGE

Until then we are to expect the ongoing particularity of nations and we must expect them to be diverse and changing.

It is true that Israel in Old Testament times had only vague indications that salvation was promised to all peoples, but early Christians had no doubt about their world mandate. It is strange that some evangelicals today are joining the call for moratorium which began in the liberal camp. Where is the nation that is fully evangelized? In most of the world the church is still a tiny minority. South Korea is called the most Christian nation in Asia, but even optimistic estimates put the figure of nominal Christians at 10 percent.

THE REAL BATTLE IS SPIRITUAL

Dr. Henry reminds us to wait to be empowered. Spirit-filled men and women will be guided as to time, place and method. The hand-wringers and breast-beaters will bemoan closed and closing doors, but God is sovereign still.

Two years ago we saw the doors closing in Chad. Some missionaries were expelled, others were advised to leave. The church asked that they stay — a key factor in their decision to do so. A *coup d'état* has now rendered the door more widely open than ever. Only days ago I was there and learned that the name of the mission is a virtual "open sesame" with the government. This friendliness has its dangers, too, for the political fortunes could change again.

It is only a matter of weeks since I traveled in Rhodesia, including the areas of current guerrilla activity. What will happen? Who knows? An unsatisfactory system could be replaced by a far more oppressive one. What is significant to me is that I found African Christian leaders and missionaries alike more concerned with church and mission relationships than with the impending political dangers. African leaders are eager and optimistic about the whitening fields around them, while the storm clouds gather above them. They are challenging the missionary to change his role. We admit to being slow to do this, but are heartened by a church leadership that has gracefully accepted this challenge and is eager to join with us in a renewed and balanced effort to achieve a brotherly relationship rather than the old parent-child relationship.

UNDER THE CHURCH OR WITH IT?

Dr. Kane suggests the need to fill the role of servant to the church. I agree, but ask, "What of the vast unreached areas where the church is nonexistent, or is so small that it desperately needs help?" There is need for dedicated servants, be they from North America, Europe, Asia, Africa, or Latin America, to press forward in pioneer evangelism. I agree with Dr. Kane that today's missionary must be prepared to work under the church, but it must be a church that won't stifle evangelism and planting new churches. The mere existence of a fellowship of churches does not render the foreign missionary forever absolved of responsibility to obey the great commission in that particular world area.

CONDITIONS ARE SELDOM IDEAL

I also share Dr. Kane's observations regarding strategy for the future, especially that of being prepared to work under a political system which one may not like or with which he cannot agree. Many years of missionary service in southern Africa have taught me that. We shall need wisdom to cope with a variety of political situations from the newly totalitarian to the ancient citadels of religious or political bigotry. There will be the ongoing particularity of nations, but of one thing we can be sure . . . there will be change. This should not deter us. In recent years we've seen visas granted for some most unlikely areas, Nepal, Sri Lanka, India, among others. Changing political conditions are not always adverse to the gospel. ''He that observeth the wind shall not sow; and he that regardeth the clouds shall not reap'' (Eccles. 11:4).

RESPONSE / Horace L. Fenton, Jr.

There is much reason to be thankful for and to be stimulated by these papers. Both suffer inevitably from the limitations of space and time imposed on them; each of the subjects treated demands something of book length. But within these limitations there is more than enough here to challenge our thought and to move us to constructive action.

Dr. Henry begins by reminding us that we do not have systematic or detailed guidance in the Scriptures on dealing with changing political situations. Nevertheless, he finds in both the Old and the New Testaments sufficient teaching to enable us to see clearly the world mandate which has characterized God's purpose from the beginning and which was given explicit expression by our risen Lord.

In developing the significance of this, he insists that we face certain forgotten or overlooked truths. He reminds us that, for the early church, "Wait" was just as much a command of God as "Go." And he wisely sees a danger of our engaging in a missionary activism in the name of urgency — an activism which may be more humanistic than biblical.

He insists that we face anew the challenge to "to the Jew first," and states that this will mean more than the evangelization of individual Jews; it calls also for grappling with the problems which have perplexed world Jewry (Auschwitz, the identity of the Suffering Servant, etc.).

He rightly points out that the only hope for social improvement lies in the new birth of individuals, at the same time reminding us that the law and the prophets are not summed up in evangelism alone, and that "the weightiest of all God's commandments, not excepting the great commission, concern love and justice." Moreover, his statement about our making a wrong dichotomy between the freedom to preach and the freedom to fulfill social requirements has implications that ought to be pondered by all of us.

Dr. Kane is refreshingly frank in describing our past failures in the realm of colonialism and our consistent defense of the *status quo*. He perceptively recognizes and delineates the change that has taken place in recent years in the status of the missionary, the church, and the image of Christianity. He might well have added a section on the change in the status of the missionary organization.

His suggested strategy is thought-provoking. He calls for revolutionary changes in our attitudes, and the call ought to be taken seriously.

Some of his statements are perhaps too sweeping. His unqualified declaration that a nod from our president will topple a government in Africa or Asia would be a surprise to the leaders of North Vietnam, where a nod and hundreds of thousands of troops were not enough. It is strange to hear him say that it is too early to make a judgment on the colonial system, and then immediately admit that the system was immoral and that its death is to be applauded. His application of "being all things to all men" as justifying political neutrality seems a bit forced.

Dr. Kane has helped us immeasurably in facing our new situation, and we shall be wise to give careful consideration to his suggested new strategy.

RESPONSE / Gleason L. Archer, Jr.

I found Dr. Henry's discussion remarkable for its single-minded concern for the teaching of both the Old Testament and the New concerning the witness of God's people to a lost and disordered world. It centers its attention on the various ways in which *kosmos* is used in the Greek Scriptures, both as the organizing principle of fallen mankind in revolt against God, and as the inhabited world which is the sphere of the church's missionary challenge. Most commendable, it seems to me, is the depth of perspective displayed in tracing the evangelistic imperative all the way back to Genesis 12 with its promise that Abraham's seed would be a blessing to all the nations of the earth, and to Isaiah 9:6 with its promise of a God-man Redeemer intended for the entire human race. There is a constant emphasis upon the inherent obligation of even the Israel of the Old Testament to make known to the pagan world the holiness and redemptive grace of the God of the Hebrews, rather than to remain smugly content with their privileged status under the covenant with Abraham.

Another motif that stands out in this paper is the leadership role of the Holy Spirit Himself in directing the people of God in their missionary task. Pointing to the restraint put upon Paul and Silas in pushing into the province of Asia, Dr. Henry reminds us that God is the One who plans the best strategy of all. In this case, of course, it was best that the missionary pioneers turn westward and evangelize Macedonia instead. Along with all the vital information supplied from the developing study of church growth, valuable as it is, we need to remember that God knows best when we are to stop and wait — which may also be important for obedience to the great commission — and when we are to move into an entirely new area or one to which human logic might not direct us. The final section of the paper dwells upon the glorious assurance of the ultimate victory of Christ over all the world forces that now oppose Him, and the establishment of a righteous and law-abiding world order under

His personal sovereignty. It is this certainty of final triumph which makes every sacrifice and bitter trial altogether worthwhile for the church militant during this age of fierce and determined attack against the gospel of Christ. It is also emphasized that implicit in the missionary imperative is a consistent concern for justice and mercy and the total welfare, both physical and spiritual, of all those to whom the gospel is proclaimed. "Moral duties like justice, mercy and faithfulness have become neglected concerns that ought instead to burden an uneasy conscience." Nor should it be forgotten that the good news is to be shared with the Jew as well as the Gentile, and that too with a proper concern for the preservation of the Jewish state in Palestine, not simply as a fulfilment of prophecy, but also as a refuge to which that persecuted race is entitled, even before or apart from their ultimate conversion to faith in Jesus their Messiah.

As might be expected from a missions analyst as well informed as Dr. Kane, his paper presents a clear and comprehensive survey of the cultural, ideological and political challenges confronting today's evangelical missionary in South America, Africa and Asia. The cautions against involvement with political ideologies and against maintaining inward attitudes of nationalism or pride in American cultural outlooks are very well set forth, and deserve earnest study by any candidate for foreign missionary service in today's world. The warning against active alignment with Marxist-leaning movements resorting to violence in order to advance what they call "the rights of the people" is a very needful reminder that whenever such movements have succeeded, they have resulted in a more tragic and complete loss of the rights of citizens than was the case under the previous regime. Those missionaries who espouse such movements today betray the Christian cause and contribute to the complete suppression of the Christian message under brutal Communist dictatorship.

Here and there, however, I find what seems to be a bit of overstatement, or even an occasional error of detail. As one who regularly attended an evangelical church in Athens, conducted by Greeks for the Greeks, I am a little surprised to learn that Greece has no religious freedom. Since the military dictatorship was peacefully voted out of power in 1974, there seems to be a completely relaxed attitude there in regard to religion, except that public or aggressive proselytism is still discouraged. But almost any brand of Protestantism that cares to start a work there seems to receive at least grudging toleration — Presbyterians, charismatics, Jehovah's Witnesses, Anglicans, and all the rest. The chief problem in Greece is public apathy, and the close association between patriotism and the Greek Orthodox Church which exists in the minds of the great majority of the population — except, of course, for the university students who are being bombarded with Marxist propaganda and who are embracing an attitude of complete skepticism towards even the Bible itself.

The deprecatory estimate of nineteenth-century colonialism seems a bit overdrawn, even in the light of other admissions that come later in the paper. It was well stated that "the unholy alliance between the gospel and the gunboat was a millstone around the necks of the missionaries" and that "they can be devoutly thankful that the burden has been lifted." But on the other hand, the comment that those earlier missionaries "almost to a man . . . considered Western civilization superior to any other and came to regard themselves as engaged in a 'civilizing' as well as 'Christianizing' mission to the 'heathen' " appears to me to require evidence to show that this attitude was altogether unjustified. Perhaps I betray my provincialism when I say this, but I find that Western and American civilization in particular furnishes a way of life and a framework of freedom and opportunity far surpassing that found in the pagan world. I am also impressed with the cordial reception accorded those blatant manifestations of Western civilization such as modern medicine, works of engineering, sanitation, the development of natural resources, the erection of steel mills and factories, the construction of skyscrapers, the paving of broad, smooth highways used largely by Western-invented trucks and automobiles — all of these welcomed and appreciated by the populations of the decolonialized nations of Africa and Asia. It certainly looks as if in these respects, at least, those countries themselves acknowledge and appreciate the superiority of Western civilization. Add to that the inestimable social and political benefits that accrued to them under colonial regimes, such as the suppression of bloody intertribal warfare and the practice of slavery, the control of epidemics and the introduction of concepts of sanitation, the restraint of brigandage and grossly cruel forms of native superstition — all of these are part of history, and should not be misrepresented or forgotten. The recent outbreaks of bloody, genocidal tribal warfare in some of the African states is a forceful reminder that in some ways the populations concerned were better off while they were protected by a colonial regime. On the other hand, we cannot forget that the arrogant functionaries of the colonial power all too often withheld from the natives the gentlemanly regard and respect they deserved as human beings. For the removal of this blight we certainly should be thankful to God. From the standpoint of the progress of the gospel it is most strategic that missionaries can now be seen only as true servants of Jesus Christ, not secret or open agents of their national government. In this framework it is most difficult for a candidate to go to the field with an attitude of racial superiority or patronage; he must go with a total commitment of love and devotion to the people to whom the Lord sends him to serve.

REPLY / Carl F. H. Henry

Competent dialogue is always profitable, and the observations by Professor Archer, Horace Fenton and Richard Winchell are most helpful.

Dr. Archer is a lion among linguists and I have learned that unless one is a Daniel in this particular cage of confinement he had better leave well enough alone. I incorporated into the final draft of my essay incidental changes that cover the points he made in dialogue on the topic under discussion. We are at one, of course, in the overall emphasis of the paper, and I appreciate the vigor with which he supports the missionary imperative as a mandate that inheres in both testaments, the indispensable role of the Holy Spirit in the missions enterprise, and the sure outcome in the final victory of God of the deep conflicts that now vex human history.

Dr. Fenton captures the spirit of my paper well, and specially notes that the good news includes the risen Lord's assured victory over all the powers of Satan, sin, death, oppression and injustice.

Mr. Winchell speaks out of the practicalities of missionary engagement to remind us how imperative it is — even as the Spirit opens and closes doors among the nations in the external world — that we as God's witnesses be ourselves Spirit-filled for the evangelistic thrust to the world. He points up the fact that in virtually every country the problems of penetration take different contours, but the one message of God's unfathomable grace carries a content and power to achieve everywhere its intended goals.

REPLY / J. Herbert Kane

Dr. Archer's statement about religious freedom in Greece is basically true, but one must bear in mind the essential difference between freedom and toleration. A draft version of the new Greek constitution, drawn up in 1975, guarantees freedom of conscience but prohibits proselytism. The Greek Orthodox Church is declared to be the state religion in Greece and any attempt to make "converts" of its members will not be tolerated. Evangelical pastors have been sent to jail for distributing gospel tracts and portions of Scripture among Orthodox believers. The Greater Europe Mission has a Bible school in Athens, but it was deemed advisable to call it the Society for Biblical Studies for fear of reprisals. The section on religion in the draft constitution is basically the same as that in the constitution of 1952.

Dr. Archer's remarks about the "superiority" of Western civilization is precisely the attitude adopted in the nineteenth century by most missionaries. Kenneth Scott Latourette, speaking of the missionaries in China, said: "Bigoted and narrow they frequently were, occasionally superstitious, and sometimes domineering and serenely convinced of the superiority of Western culture and of their own particular brand of Christianity."[1]

Referring to the Chinese nation, Henry Fowler, a Methodist bishop, said:

> This moral mummy is embalmed and wrapped in superstitions four thousand years old and more than ten thousand layers deep. These superstitions touch every act of life, and every word and every secret thought. They are victims of luck, fortune-tellers, and necromancy. They live in a world packed to the very stars with powerful spirits, which must not be offended. All ranks and classes, from the emperor down to the poorest coolies, are steeped and boiled and parboiled in superstition. By these superstitions the university men and the priests govern and rob and torment all classes.[2]

If the bishop had been talking about some primitive or barbaric society, he might have had a point; but to speak in such pejorative terms of Chinese civilization is an unpardonable sin. One Chinese writer complained that all missionaries were guilty of a superiority complex: "Their experience of China may be lifelong; their information accurate. But their viewpoint is never that of the people they describe. Underlying everything that is written or spoken about China is the foregone conclusion that the Chinese are 'inferior' and their ways of doing things wrong."[3]

Dr. Fenton objects to my statement that a nod from our president will topple a government overseas. He cites our enormous, costly, and unsuccessful attempt to bring Hanoi to its knees. My statement was simply a dramatic way of describing the enormous power of an American president. It is a matter of record that the Central Intelligence Agency has been successful in overthrowing "undesirable" governments and propping up "desirable" governments. Even today the experts are saying that if the United States doesn't do more to support Sadat of Egypt his government may fall. Certainly if we were to withdraw our support from Israel its government would topple in no time at all. The recent revelations regarding the Central Intelligence Agency show only too plainly the extent to which the United States has been involved in the rise and fall of regimes in various parts of the world.

Dr. Fenton finds it strange that I should condemn the colonial system and at the same time admit that it is too early to make a final judgment on it. There is no real contradiction here. The colonial system per se was morally wrong, but there were many fringe benefits derived from it. Few systems are so completely immoral that they afford no benefits whatever. Nigeria was occupied by the British for more than half a century. Ethiopia was never reduced to colonial status except for a few years under the Italians during World War II. Today Nigeria is far more advanced and progressive than Ethiopia — thanks to British colonialism. That does not, however, make British colonialism right. It is still too early to make a *final* judgment regarding the colonial system.

FOOTNOTES

1. Kenneth Scott Latourette, *A History of Christian Missions in China* (New York: The Macmillan Company, 1929), p. 824.

2. Paul Varg, *Missionaries, Chinese, and Diplomats* (Princeton, NJ: Princeton University Press, 1958), pp. 113-14.

3. Lowe Chuan Hwa, "The Christian Peril in China," *The Nation* (Feb. 7, 1923).

PART
SEVEN

Summaries
of the
Reports

PREAMBLE

Entering the last quarter century of this millennium we face two perils — a theology without evangelism and an evangelism without theology. Biblical theology based on an inerrant, authoritative Scripture produces biblical evangelism whose goal is not only decisions but disciples and whose outcome is growing churches. As in the inspiration of the Scriptures, the Holy Spirit is the essential dynamic in evangelism.

But this sequence is not automatic or unchallenged. In recent years world congresses and councils have focused attention on theological issues which bear on the mandate, motivation and methodology of the church and its mission.

In at least a partial fulfilment of Toffler's prediction of future shock we live in a period of "compressed history" — trends developing in variety and intensity at a rate faster than we can cope with them.

How does the church relate to the powerful factors operative in the world which she is commanded to evangelize? How can new movements and methods within the church be evaluated? How can a contemporary "school of the prophets" produce Elijahs for America's third century — Elijahs who will evangelize with a prophetic voice? How can present and future missionaries be prepared to communicate an eternal message in a kaleidoscope of cultures and concerns?

Bound together by a total commitment to the inerrant Scriptures and deeply conscious of the responsibility entrusted to the church as God's agency for achieving His purpose for this age, the participants in this consultation have sought to identify some basic issues, relate them to biblical principles and consider practical implications in areas which involve thoughtful evangelicals. The resultant materials do not necessarily represent the official position of Trinity Evangelical Divinity School or any other group, but do reflect the research and experience of the theologians, missiolo-

gists, mission administrators, pastors, and professors who participated. Their criterion was biblical theology and their concern was
effective evangelism. Of necessity only selected subjects could be
considered, but these include a high proportion of contemporary
evangelical concerns and questions, if not confusions.

In seeking to apply biblical principles, a serious attempt was
made to avoid both detailed debate and simplistic solutions. The
consultants sought to relate the issues to biblical principles and to
face their implications for the church at the end of the twentieth
century.

The Emerging Attitude Toward
Charismatic Theology
and the New Pentecostalism

The consultation acknowledged the phenomenal expansion of the charismatic emphasis and also the divergent views of evangelicals toward this phenomenon. The discussions brought out majority and minority views.

The Majority Expression

(1) There was a manifestation of tongues in the apostolic age.
(2) There is a difference of viewpoint as to whether this manifestation is valid for the present age.
(3) Speaking in tongues is sought by charismatics more often than are other gifts.
(4) The emphasis is experience-oriented but "Scripture always judges experience, not experience Scripture."
(5) This is a divisive issue in noncharismatic groups.
(6) Evangelicals must adhere to a biblical doctrine of the Holy Spirit, and in practice manifest total dependence on Him for purity of life and power in service.
(7) Our sovereign God is the giver of all good gifts to the church and to individuals in the church for the edification of the body of Christ.
(8) Love must control our attitude toward and relationship with brethren who differ with us.

Minority Expressions

(1) There is an increasing balance in the theology of "old line Pentecostals" with greater emphasis on the fruit of the Spirit along with gifts of the Spirit.
(2) We must keep in mind the biblical injunction, "forbid not to speak with tongues."
(3) The charismatic emphasis on doctrine and practice is a vital factor in the outstanding growth of charismatic groups.

Implications

(1) There must be a continuous, strong Bible exposition to enrich the lives of the believers in local churches and to ground them in the truth.

(2) There must be recognition of the preeminent role of the Spirit of God in the missionary enterprise.

(3) There must be proper discipling and encouragement for each individual believer to discern his spiritual gifts for employment in the local body.

(4) There must exist mutual respect and love among brethren in Christ who hold differing views on this subject.

(5) There must be a willingness to learn from the growth of some charismatic groups, particularly in relation to the emphasis on a lay ministry to the entire body through the exercise of gifts, on warm supportive fellowship, and on the disposition to identify with receptive culture groups. It was also noted that many noncharismatic churches have enjoyed the same measure of growth.

The Contextualization of Theology

Since contextualization is a new term which may be variously interpreted, it must itself be qualified by the setting in which it is used.

Within an evangelical framework, cultural contextualization of Christian truth involves a dynamic process of sympathetic understanding leading to empathetic identification with the culture so that Christianity may be "inculturated" within the indigenous forms of the recipient peoples. Nothing of the supracultural is to be lost or distorted.

Certain assumptions must be made. First, there is a divine revelation which is supracultural and both understandable and applicable to every culture. Second, theological formulations are culture-based, speaking to man's needs. Third, the nature of the church is to be a ministering body performing essential functions within each culture. Fourth, the message is understood by responsible adult Christians under the guidance of the Holy Spirit in each culture.

Biblical Principles

The gospel itself cannot exist apart from culture. It is inherently cultural. Whereas the message of the gospel is of divine origin, it must be understood by man within his own life pattern. The recipient in his own environment must interpret the message under the illumination of the Holy Spirit.

(1) The incarnation of Christ is the supreme example of contextualization (John 1:14; Heb. 2:16-18).

(2) The gospel is a universal message given by God to all peoples in all cultures and is equally applicable to all (Acts 17:24-31; Rom. 1:16).

(3) The gospel must not simply root itself in the soil of each culture, it must also judge the culture. The principle of careful judgment of a culture must precede the adaptation to that culture (Eph. 4:17-32).

(4) Examples of contextualization with regard to practice and communication:

    (a) The Jerusalem conference (Acts 15:1-29).
    (b) The exhortation of Paul on a related topic (I Cor. 8:1—10:22; Gal. 2).
    (c) The reference to pagan moral standards (I Cor. 5:1-8).
    (d) Household relationships (Col. 3:18 — 4:1).

Implications

(1) Because the gospel is the "genuine article" and contextualization is the packaging, the missionary must thoroughly know the content and not be overly committed to a particular style or design of "wrapping" learned from his own culture. His question must be: What is content — the scriptural revelation of the gospel — and what is "packaging"? To present that content in packaging that will be understood by the hearer is absolutely essential and requires a knowledge of his culture.

(2) There must be confidence that the gospel, empowered by the Holy Spirit, will do its work of enlightening and awakening men in their various cultures to their need and God's provision of redemption. This assumes, of course, that care has been taken that the message is not obscured by foreign accretions.

(3) As the gospel is applied to the life and practice of the convert, it must be applied within his culture, speak to the problems he faces, and deal with issues he encounters. Foreign systematic theologies may not have spoken to issues confronting the national believer, such as the question of syncretism or spirit worship. The biblical truths which are pertinent to this situation need to be brought forth clearly. In this sense a contextualization of theology may well occur — not a modification of the revealed gospel but an application of biblical truth to a given situation. Biblical hermeneutics must determine the expression of theology within each culture.

(4) The theology resulting from each such expression, though emerging from within the culture, will be universally recognized and accepted because it is validated by the absolutes and the normative nature of the gospel.

Contemporary Evangelism and Catholicism

It is increasingly apparent that Vatican II introduced new dynamics into the Roman Catholic Church which have both internal and external ramifications. Because this body is a multifaceted institution it is impossible to describe a universal experience for post-Vatican II Roman Catholics.

One obvious by-product of the apparent changes in the Roman Catholic Church is the openness to dialogue and to cooperation with nonbelievers as well as non-Catholic Christians. This openness affords opportunity, challenge and risk for evangelicals the world over.

Questions of Concern

The following questions that must concern evangelicals emerged from the discussion groups:

(1) Is it possible to describe with accuracy the true nature of the Roman Catholic Church in today's world? What cautions and guidelines should be followed in seeking an understanding of the nature of a local or national expression of the Roman Catholic Church?

(2) What kinds of objectives for dialogue and cooperation with Roman Catholics are legitimate? On what basis? To what extent? What should be the outcome?

(3) To what extent are evangelicals knowledgeable and articulate in areas of theological tension with Roman Catholic thought such as authority, justification, and mediators?

(4) What biblical principles provide guidance for dialogue with Roman Catholics? Must all dialogue have conversion as its objective?

(5) What principles or counsel do Scripture and practice offer concerning the church membership of Roman Catholics won to Jesus Christ?

(6) Do missionaries raised in pluralistic North American society have the right or freedom to pursue dialogue and cooperation with Roman Catholics without prior consultation with, and the approval of, the national church?

(7) Since the church of Rome has at least temporarily adapted to the trends of the day, what are the long-term implications for evangelicals who overidentify with Catholicism today?

(8) What creative alternatives exist to official cooperation or identification with local institutional Roman Catholicism?

Serious concern was expressed about the emphasis on universalism within contemporary Roman Catholic theology.

Evangelicals were reminded to offer thanksgiving to God for any and all signs of the moving of the sovereign Spirit of God within the Roman Catholic Church. Moreover, it should be the hope and prayer of evangelicals that the spiritual renewal taking place may continue to the point where the Roman Catholic Church might recover the biblical doctrine of justification by faith alone.

Implications

(1) While being thankful to God for a new openness among Roman Catholics, evangelicals ought to exercise Spirit-led caution in pursuing dialogue and cooperation.

(2) Theological curricula must give more emphasis to teaching and demonstrating the significance of the evangelical heritage and the distinctive doctrines of historic Protestantism.

(3) Evangelicals engaging in dialogue with Roman Catholics need to exercise caution lest they assume that the Roman Catholic usage of traditional theological terms is the same as that of historic Protestantism.

(4) While the new mood in Catholicism which views non-Catholic Christians as brothers affords opportunity to share the biblical gospel of Christ, evangelicals engaging in formal or institutional dialogue must seriously consider both positive and negative long-term implications of such activity.

(5) Ministry to Roman Catholics must have as its objective not merely conversion to Christ but discipleship which results in responsible membership in a New Testament church.

(6) Evangelicals must trust the sovereign Spirit of God to give wisdom and guidance to converts won to Christ from among Roman Catholics as they make decisions about their church affiliation and continue to mature in the faith.

The Theology
of Church Growth

As the participants in the consultation discussed the position papers and expressed their personal reactions and concerns, attention concentrated in three main areas: the theological basis of the church growth movement, questions about its premises and principles, and expressions of appreciation for its evident contribution to world-wide evangelization.

Its Nature

A few participants tended to conceive of the movement and its principles as a method — a contemporary, success-oriented program of human origin and of doubtful biblical validity. Most, however, understood it to be an attitude and a series of insights which draw upon successful experiences and the behavioral sciences but, nevertheless, direct activity toward biblical goals.

Its Validity

Some considered the lack of a well-defined theological base prior to the development of church growth principles a cause for questioning whether such a rationale can indeed be established. However, most concluded that although not articulated, a biblical basis had been assumed and that later biblical tests have validated most church growth concepts.

Areas Consistent with a Biblical Theology

(1) The definition of evangelism.

(2) The essential work of the sovereign Holy Spirit in evangelism.

(3) The centrality of the church as God's agent in evangelizing and discipling.

(4) The nature of the church and the spiritual gifts given to each member of the body.

(5) The importance of Spirit-empowered individual believers in the discipling, growing process of the local church.

Areas of Expressed Concern

(1) The concept of the homogeneous group was questioned. Most understood that the formerly used designation *people movement* (suggesting group conversion) had been clarified and modified by the current term *multi-individual conversions*. However, the concept of a homogeneous group after salvation, that is, an exclusive racial, economic or social group comprising a local church, was seriously questioned by many. A divergence of

opinion remained as to whether Christ is best revealed through a mixed type of local church membership or through a homogeneous group.

(2) The terms *winnable peoples* and *resistant peoples* were questioned, especially as they were viewed as involving absolute states. They seem to imply that some are "nonwinnable." "More easily winnable," and "more (or less) receptive" were considered more accurate. A continued probing and communication were urged for groups now considered resistant. As it cannot be assumed that groups which are presently receptive will always be receptive, so it was pointed out that experience has shown that resistant groups may not always be resistant. Further, the life in the seed may take longer to germinate in some soils than in others.

(3) The concept of the sovereignty of God was considered by some to be compromised by the extraordinary activity of those involved in implementing church growth principles. Most considered the danger of human underinvolvement in evangelism to be a greater danger than overinvolvement, especially in the light of the emphasis on increasing fruitfulness in John 15 and abundant sowing in I Corinthians 9.

Its Contribution

(1) The church growth movement has brought missions back on the track of evangelism which leads to church planting and growth.

(2) It has provided insights, tools for measurement, and practical helps for more productive work.

(3) It has encouraged an optimism in evangelism.

(4) It has focused attention on the centrality of the church.

(5) It has clarified the continuous nature of the process of pre-evangelism, conversion, and discipling with emphasis on the goal of responsible, reproducing believers related to each other in a local church.

Conclusion

Some theologies may not have issued in evangelism and some church growth principles may not initially have been derived from theology. However, the consensus of the participants was that, as the church growth movement subjects itself to the scrutiny of inerrant Scripture and as theologians face evangelism as the inevitable conclusion of biblical theology, both have much to gain and much to accomplish together.

Dialogue with the Non-Christian Religions

In a world of religious pluralism and competing claims to truth, Christians must be prepared to witness to their faith in any context and to give an answer to everyone who asks a reason for the Christian hope (I Peter 3:15).

Person-to-person sharing of the message lies at the heart of our incarnational faith in which "the Word became flesh and dwelt among us," thereby pointing the way for our involvement with others by entering into their loneliness and longings, their questionings and quests. As such the incarnation is a model for dialogue understood as personal sharing of the good news.

Dialogue, in English usage, implies conversation and an exchange of ideas. Jesus used conversational dialogue as a teaching method. So did the apostle Paul. But dialogue in the Socratic or classical Greek sense of "discussion with a view to the discovery of truth" is not to be found in the New Testament.

In a day of resurgent ethnic religions, an ecumenical call to dialogue with men of other faiths has become fashionable. This dialogue, partaking more of the Socratic than of the biblical model, frequently has tended to minimize the uniqueness and finality of Christ in a common search for religious truth and spirituality.

Evangelicals are called to participate in dialogue with adherents of other world views, but without compromising their commitment to biblical truth and to Jesus Christ as unique Son of God, Savior and Lord.

For evangelicals dialogue is a method of mutual listening, as well as speaking, in order to understand the beliefs and needs of others. Its aim is to build bridges and to understand men of other faiths so as to communicate the gospel compassionately, persuasively, and effectively in any context.

Those engaging in dialogue should not shirk the discipline of careful study and preparation. In the process of dialogue the Christian communicator should also recognize his dependence upon the Holy Spirit who brings conviction of sin and guides men in comprehending divine truth.

Evangelical Christians should not hesitate to involve themselves in interreligious dialogue provided that:

(1) It is motivated by biblical concern.

(2) It is true to biblical revelation.

(3) It aims at mutual understanding.

(4) It has conversion as its ultimate objective.

(5) It depends throughout on prayer and the ministry of the Holy Spirit.

It has been said of first-century Christianity that "dialogue was a method; proclamation was its nature; and conversion was its goal." So should it be today.

Theology of Missions and Changing Political Situations

Jesus decreed the permanence of the church when He said, "Upon this rock I will build my church; and the gates of hell shall not prevail against it" (Matt. 16:18). Thus He assured the survival of His church despite the rise and fall of governments and political systems in the world. "The biblical gospel was not derived from, nor determined by, nor dependent upon changing political conditions" (Carl F. H. Henry).

While early Christians boldly declared the necessity of obeying God rather than man, they were likewise insistent that they were responsible to civil government and that "their stance was to be not one of rebelliousness or detachment, but rather one of responsible submission and moral relationship" (Carl F. H. Henry).

Questions at Issue

(1) What should be the response of a Christian citizen to a hostile government?

(2) What should be the attitude and response of the missionary guest to the host government under which he works, whether friendly or hostile?

(3) What does it mean to exercise "responsible submission and moral relationship" in some nations today?

Biblical Principles

(1) Jesus, by example and word, taught obedience to government — "render therefore unto Caesar the things which are Caesar's" (Matt. 22:21) — even while foretelling opposition, persecution, and hatred from those in authority. The early apostles, faced with determined efforts to stifle the gospel witness, appealed to a higher law — "obey God rather than men" (Acts 5:29).

(2) Paul taught submission to government and intercession for those in authority (Rom. 13; I Tim. 2). As a Roman citizen he took full advantage of the rights and privileges of his citizenship.

Implications for the National Believer Today

(1) The national as a citizen of his country should support government in principle and be subject to authority but should also avail himself of all the rights accorded him under the law.

(2) The churches should include in their teaching ministry the clear principles of Scripture on what constitutes obedience to God in situations that threaten to compromise the Christian testimony. A familiarity with the experience of Christians who live under

hostile governments in other parts of the world will be helpful in this regard.

(3) National believers who find themselves in difficult political situations must be able to distinguish those issues which are moral, biblical, and theological (and therefore call for obedience to God at any cost) from those which are merely political (and therefore allow for more individualized discretion in the mode of response).

(4) The regenerate church is the new society called to proclaim and exemplify to the world the standards of the coming King. This new society is, from generation to generation, the nearest approximation to the kingdom of God to be found in the history of fallen mankind.

(5) National church leaders faced with hostile governments in the future should be prepared for alternate patterns of church functions and ministries — house meetings, lay ministry, Scripture memorization.

Implications for the Foreign Missionary Today

(1) The missionary is not a representative nor an advocate of the political system of his home country. Though he is inescapably identified as a citizen of his own nation, there is a sense in which his orientation must be supranational.

(2) The missionary's responsibility is to "call out a people for His name" (Acts 15:14) and to have a prophetic witness by words and a life-style which reflect purity, justice and other characteristics of full Christian commitment.

(3) Though there may be mutual consultation between missionaries and national church leaders resulting in agreement on theological and biblical issues, at times there will be room for different political responses. The long-range well-being of the church should be the paramount consideration. This calls for responsible submission and moral leadership and suggests the importance of a prophetic role. The attempt of a missionary to be neutral in a given situation of tension may actually result in support for the *status quo* rather than for the status to come — the kingdom of God at the return of Christ. Therefore, he must consider whether or not he can exercise a prophetic role without becoming a political activist.

(4) God in His sovereignty works above, beyond, and even through political change to further His purposes. On occasion, He has used hostile political environments to purify the church and to scatter and multiply the Christian witness. A biblical philosophy of history can eliminate unwarranted utopianism on one hand, and unscriptural despair on the other.